CATHOLIC
CATHOLIC REFLECTION 1538-1850
COLLECTING

Objects as a measure of reflection on a Catholic past and the construction
of Recusant identity in England and America

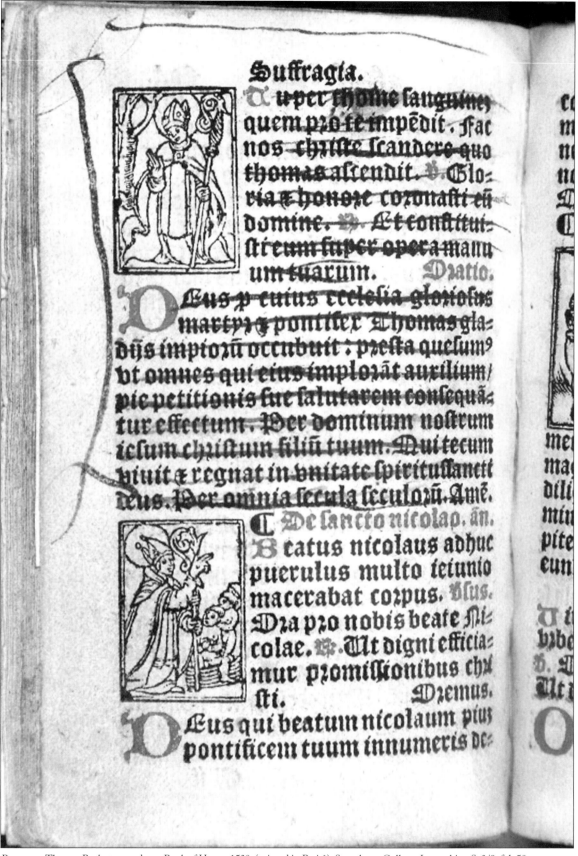

Suffragia.

~~uper thome sanguine~~
~~quem pro te impedit . fac~~
~~nos christe scandere quo~~
~~thomas ascendit. Glo~~
~~ria et honore coronasti eu~~
~~domine. Et constitui~~
~~sti eum super opera manu~~
~~um tuarum.~~ Oratio.

Eus p cuius ecclesia gloriosus
martyr q pontifex Thomas gla
diis impioru occubuit: presta quesum9
vt omnes qui eius implorat auxilium/
pie petitionis sue salutarem consequa-
tur effectum. Per dominum nostrum
iesum christum filiu tuum. Qui tecum
viuit t regnat in vnitate spiritussancti
deus. Per omnia secula seculoru. Ame.

De sancto nicolao. an.

Beatus nicolaus adhuc
puerulus multo ieiunio
macerabat corpus. Vlus.
Ora pro nobis beate Ni
colae. Ut digni efficia-
mur promissionibus chri
sti. Oremus.

Eus qui beatum nicolaum piu9
pontificem tuum innumeris de-

Prayers to Thomas Becket crossed out, Book of Hours, 1530, (printed in Paris?), Stonyhurst College, Lancashire, S. 3/8, fol. 50v

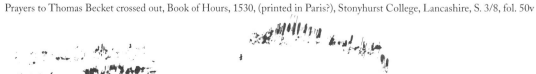

CATHOLIC
CATHOLIC REFLECTION 1538-1850
COLLECTING

Objects as a measure of reflection on a Catholic past and the construction
of Recusant identity in England and America

curated by

Virginia Chieffo Raguin

with contributions from

A. I. Doyle, Durham University

Janet Graffius, Stonyhurst College

Seth Hindin, Harvard University

Amanda Luyster, College of the Holy Cross

Roderick O'Donnell, English Heritage

Simon Roffey, King Alfred's College

Robert Scully, S.J., LeMoyne College

editorial assistance by Christine Coch

for John H. Wilson
1936 - 2006

Organized by the College of the Holy Cross

February 22 - April 13, 2006

Iris and B. Gerald Cantor Art Gallery

College of the Holy Cross, Worcester MA

Support for the catalogue was provided by the

Deitchman Family Foundation

ISBN-13: 978-0-9616183-0-8
ISBN-10: 0-9616183-0-2

catalogue distributed by The Catholic University of America Press

Front cover illustration: **Petre Chalice**, London, 1640-1660, associated with Silversmith Albert Moore, Georgetown University Collections and **Shrine with Instruments of the Passion**, England, 1623, Stonyhurst College, Lancashire

Back cover illustration: **Shireburn Chapel**, Mitton, from Thomas Dunham Whitaker. *An History of the Original Parish of Whalley and Honor of Clitheroe in the Counties of Lancaster and York*, Second edition, London 1806.

646 2240

CONTENTS

Acknowledgements

I first want to express my thanks to the following without whom this exhibition could not have taken place: Roger Hankins, Director of the Iris and B.Gerald Cantor Art Gallery; Mark Savolis, Director, Archives Division of Dinand Library; William Shea, Director of the Center for Religion, Ethics, and Culture; Paul E. Sheff, Vice President of Development; Rev. Michael C. McFarland, S.J., President of the College of the Holy Cross; and the committee on Fellowships, Research and Publication of Holy Cross. In particular, I want to express my personal gratitude for the generous support from John V. Deitchman and Cornelius B. Prior.

We are all in debt to the representatives of the lenders: Rev. Philip Endean, S. J., Campion Hall, Oxford; Sr. Christina Kenworthy-Browe, The Bar Convent, York; Marty Barringer and LuLen Walker, Georgetown University; Sally Metzler, formerly The Loyola University Museum of Medieval, Renaissance, and Baroque Art; and James Welu, Worcester Art Museum. I am also grateful to David J. McGonagle, Director of The Catholic University of American Press. It has been a privilege to work with the contributors to the catalogue: A. I. Doyle, University of Durham; Seth Hinden, Harvard University; Naomi Kline, Plymouth State College; Christine Koch, College of the Holy Cross, Amanda Luyster, College of the Holy Cross; Roderick O'Donnell, English Heritage; Simon Roffey, King Alfred's College, Winchester; and Robert E. Scully, S. J., Le Moyne College.

Advice and material support came from many sources: I want to thank Penny Hebgin-Barnes, my colleague in the English Corpus Vitrearum, who first introduced me to Stonyhurst College, and Eamon Duffy, Cambridge University, for his essential work and encouragement. Support also came from: Marilyn Beaven, Sudbury; Aidan Bellenger, Downside Abbey, Bath; Brenda Bolton, St. Albans; Susan Bourne, Curator, Towneley Hall, Burley; Sarah Brown, English Heritage; Peter Davidson, University of Aberdeen; Anne Dillon, Lucy Cavendish College, Cambridge; Martha Driver, Pace University; Gail Gibson, Davidson College; Roberta Gilchrist, The University of Reading; Sr. Gregory Kirkus, I.B.V.M, The Bar Convent; David Knight, Stonyhurst College; Richard Marks, York University; Andrew Nicoll, Columba House, Edinburgh; Virginia Reinburg, Boston College; Joseph Spooner, London; Jane Stevenson, University of Aberdeen; Dennis Taylor, Boston College; R. W. Taylor, Catholic Records Society; and Paul Williamson, Victoria and Albert Museum.

Several of my Holy Cross colleagues made contributions to the catalogue: John Hamilton, Anthony Kuzniewski, S.J., Edward Vodoklys, S.J., Thomas Worcester, S.J., James Kee, and John Cull. I also thank for their support: Nancy Andrews, Lorraine Attreed, Michel Beatty, James Bidwell, William Clark, S.J., Alison Fleming, Alan Karass, Alice Laffey, Todd Lewis, Rick Murphy, David O'Brien, Joanne Pierce, John Reboli, S.J., William Reiser, S.J., Susan Schmidt, Sarah Stanbury, Matthew Schmalz, Helen Whall, and Joanna Ziegler. From deep resources were the contributions of John H. Wilson and Thomas M. C. Lawler with whom I first explored this world in the Interdisciplinary Humanities Sequence, "England, Genesis of a Culture." Students were also vital: for the catalogue Mallory Zeising and Lisa Litterio, and for the exhibition, Mary Cirbus, Kate Curran, Jennifer Geiger, Eliana Hidalgo, Karin Jorgensen, JanetRose Kolodziej, Emily LaClair, and Samantha Morr.

For technical help I am deeply indebted to: Timothy Johnson; Sharon Matys and Thomas Parsons, Graphic Arts; Jesse Anderson and John Buckingham, Audio-Visual Services; Margaret Nelson and Mary Morrisard-Larkin, Educational Technology; Lois Hamill, Archives; Faye Caouette, Visual Arts; and Linda Honan, University of Massachusetts, and to institutions: The Blairs Museum, Aberdeen Scotland; The Library at the College of the Holy Cross; Harvard Libraries: Widener, Fine Arts, and Houghton; and Tufts University Libraries.

LENDERS TO THE EXHIBITION

The Bar Convent, York, Congregation of Jesus and the Institute of the Blessed Virgin Mary

College of the Holy Cross, Worcester, Massachusetts

Georgetown University, Georgetown, Maryland

The Loyola University Museum of Medieval, Renaissance, and Baroque Art, Chicago

Society of Jesus, Campion Hall, Oxford

Stonyhurst College, Lancashire

Worcester Art Museum, Worcester, Massachusetts

The Trinity as the "Shield of Faith," *Hours of the Virgin* printed by François Regnault, 1526, Stonyhurst College, Lancashire, S. 3/6, fol. 14v

PREFACE

English and American recusant art, the subject of this exhibit curated by Holy Cross art history professor Virginia Raguin, is an apt subject for examination at Holy Cross' Iris and B. Gerald Cantor Art Gallery and in this catalogue. From an academic standpoint, the exhibit invites the kind of interdisciplinary consideration that is fundamental to a liberal arts education. The items assembled here can be studied from a variety of approaches: historical, religious, political, sociological, and artistic, among others.

Moreover, *Catholic Collecting, Catholic Reflection 1538-1830* presents a unique opportunity to celebrate the courage of a community that managed to remain united, even in the face of severe persecution. The chalices, vestments, books, and other objects represented here served to express and honor the faith of their creators and owners, but also to inspire and maintain devotion in a hidden community where physical unity was not often possible. For more than three centuries, Catholic men and women guarded these treasures and so protected the vitality of their beliefs and traditions. This exhibit and catalogue serve as a remarkable testament to their fortitude and, more importantly, to their deep faith.

Of course, the prominence of many Jesuit priests in the recusant resistance has special meaning for us at Holy Cross, where our Jesuit identity animates and guides our educational mission. Jesuit presence in England in the 16th – 19h centuries played a pivotal role in keeping alive the recusant church, for which many extraordinary Jesuits were rewarded with martyrdom. Among them was Edmund Campion, S.J., after whom one of Holy Cross' oldest buildings Campion House, is named. On display in this exhibit is an *Agnus Dei* that Fr. Campion carried with him until just before his capture and execution. Artifacts like this, which were such important sources of strength for our community in the past, retain their power to inspire us as we look to the future. They also remind us of the scandal and destruction caused by religious conflicts and move us to pray and work for greater unity among the Christian churches and greater understanding among all religions.

I would like to express my deep gratitude to John V. Deitchman and Cornelius B. Prior, without whose generosity this catalogue and exhibition would not have been possible. Our community also extends its thanks to the Jesuit institutions of Stonyhurst College and Campion Hall, Oxford, to whose impressive collections and knowledgeable scholars we are indebted. Finally, I am truly grateful to curator Virginia Raguin, whose vision, passion and hard work brought these significant pieces together.

Rev. Michael C. McFarland, S.J., *President*
College of the Holy Cross

Deposition, mid 17th century, Low Countries, Antwerp? In Shireburn Chapel, Stonyhurst by 1713, Stonyhurst College. Photo: Virginia Raguin

X

INTRODUCTION

This exhibition focuses on early modern Catholic culture in England and the English colonies that have become American states. Many of the treasures that are now in museums and rare book libraries have come down to us because of individuals who were dedicated to preserving pious texts and images, even in the face of opposition. When England became a Protestant state in the sixteenth century, religious imagery was largely banned in the visual arts, and Catholics were forbidden to erect buildings. They came to identify their faith with the illicit statues, paintings, chalices, processional crosses and other objects of ritual, prayer books, and works of devotional literature that they were able to acquire. Many Catholics became known as recusants – recusing themselves from oaths of loyalty and participation in the state-sanctioned religion. The objects they collected embodied their bonds with God, church tradition, and each other.

Attention to the motivation for collecting forces us to address equally vehement motives for disuse and even annihilation of beautiful religious objects. Religious works of art that have survived from the Middle Ages in England have done so in the face of aggressive campaigns of destruction by rulers and Reformers. Today we may think of the Taliban's prohibition of art and the destruction by dynamite of what was then the largest Buddhist image in the world. The deadly struggle over possession of Jerusalem's Temple Mount, known to the Islamic world as the Haram al-Sharif, testifies to the mesmerizing function of the place and the tangible object to cultural identity. We see the history of possession in the importance of the restoration of objects pilfered from Jewish citizens by the National Socialists in the German pogrom - sold on the art market and ending up in collections of American museums. The itinerary of the work of art - here sacred objects - has become a major contemporary interest.

Such destructive moments are invariably recalled through verbal and visual testimonies of pubic approval. Orderly ranks of spectators witness the events; happiness abounds. The destruction of the market cross at Cheapside, London, provides an example. Long a place of contention during the English Reformation, it was variously interpreted as a civic construction and thus entitled to remain, or a religious symbol and subject to destruction. A monument mingling rulership and religion

Destruction of Cheapside Cross in London, May 2, 1643, etching by Wenceslaus Hollar. British Library (G 4099); Permission of the British Library

Christ saying Goodbye to his Mother, mid 17th century, Low Countries, Antwerp? In Shireburn Chapel, Stonyhurst by 1713, Stonyhurst College. Photo: Virginia Raguin

through juxtaposed images of monarchs and bishops as well as Christ and the Virgin Mary, it was periodically defaced and repaired during the time of Elizabeth only to be ultimately pulled down during the Commonwealth. Many pamphlets were issued against it during 1642-43 and its final destruction orchestrated May 2, 1643. Careful safety measures were in place with a troop of horsemen and two companies of foot soldiers to guard the cross during its demotion. "Dromes beat, tru(m)pets blew & multitudes of Capes warre throwne in ye Ayre and a great Shoute of People with ioy," was recorded by the inscription in a print published the same year (Wenceslaus Hollar, engraver: Aston 1989, 76-80, fig. 10). Commentators were quick to observe that May 2 is day before the feast of the Invention of the Holy Cross, the commemoration of the discovery of the Cross of Christ by St. Helena in the fourth century, as celebrated in the Catholic calendar. In retrospect, such recorded joy was not shared by all at the time, and possibly fewer in the present.

The suppression of Catholics in England lasted for close to three centuries. Catholicism was not the only non-conformist religion to be marginalized: Quakers, Unitarians, even at some moments Puritans, were among the religious expressions routinely labeled as dangerous to the public realm. Aggression, in addition, invariably occupies a two-way street. Under Protestant rulers like Elizabeth I the penalties for recusancy were primarily monetary yet could extend to imprisonment and loss of life (Morey, 133-55). Though Elizabeth was loath to employ extreme measures in matters of religious reform, her long reign saw 123 Catholic priests put to death. Jesuit missionaries from the continent were particularly feared for their powers of persuasion over English subjects. On the other side, during the rule of her Catholic sister, Mary I, 273 Protestants were burned, among them bishops Nicholas Ridley and William Latimer, as well as Thomas Cranmer (1489-1556), the archbishop of Canterbury. Cranmer's case poignantly demonstrates the severe psychological distress undergone by individuals in this age. Cranmer had actually renounced the Protestant faith, embracing the doctrine of Transubstantiation, the seven sacraments, purgatory, even participating in Catholic liturgy and asking for sacramental absolution during Lent. If canon law had been applied justly, Cranmer, as fully reconciled to the Church, should have been spared. Governmental expediency ruled otherwise. At the very last minute, in the pulpit at the University Church (St. Mary the Virgin in Oxford), where he was to have asked for forgiveness, he repudiated his former confessions, affirming his Protestant writings. Pulled from the pulpit, he perished in the flames, first incinerating his "unworthy right hand" that had signed the abjuration (MacCulloch 1996, 593-605).

The issue of martyrdom looms large in this history. For both Catholic and Protestant sides, the experience of persecution, and the numerous instances of capital offences designated for what later societies would deem private and essentially inoffensive practices, animated responses from the average person. Miri Rubin has recognized "a strong impulse towards the recognition of merit and its application to the common good [that] moved people to recognize the victims of unmerited violence as martyrs, and to elaborate cultic practices in their honour" (Rubin 1993, 169). She considers the "fundamental structure of martyrdom cult: once recognized as a martyr's death, that death is made into a significant marker: of one group as opposed to another, we and they" (ibid., 163). Perhaps this can be most vividly profiled in the case of Thomas Becket, killed in 1170 by armed knights while at prayer (see in this catalogue "Relics and the Two Thomases"). The Proclamation of Nov. 16, 1538 abolishing his cult explained that "it appereth now clerely" that the bishop was known "stubburnely to withstand the holsome lawes establyshed agaynste the enormities of the clergie, by the kynges highnes mooste noble progenitour, kynge HENRY the seconde for the common wealthe, reste, and tranquilitie of this realme." The brief maintains that Becket's death is "vntrueley called martyrdome" for Thomas provoked the "gentle men" with vile slanders and actually attacked one of them, necessitating his rescue and Thomas's own death (in Borenius, 109-110). Thus Becket becomes not only a troublemaker, disrupting the tranquility of England, but a violent individual, actually causing his own death. Such reworking of history and the hardening of positions as "either with us or against us" seems to emerge whenever societies feel compelled to justify a received past. The contemporary illustrations I leave to the reader to supply.

Yet despite this massive shift in the political landscape, there remained Catholics in the mainstream of English life. William Byrd (1543?-1623) joined the Chapel Royal in the 1570s. With Thomas Tallis, his teacher, he was the most prominent composer of church music of his day; he and Tallis held the printing monopoly for music in England until 1585. Alexander Pope's (1688-1744) brilliance was honed outside of the public school or university for which his religion rendered him ineligible. Charles Towneley (1737-1805), collector of classical antiquities like the *Discus Thrower* and one of the principle founders of the British Museum, was of the recusant Towneley family of Yorkshire. Catholic gentry survived especially in the north, but in isolated areas elsewhere. As Edward Norman observed, "In a deferential society Catholics of property and station were usually accorded the respect due them, whatever the peculiarity of their religious profession" (Norman, 51). Public worship was facilitated by the chapels maintained by embassies in London, deliberately large and frequently sumptuous. They were able to accommodate considerable numbers of Catholics residing in the capital or visiting on business. The Portuguese chapel, for example, constructed in a Continental Baroque mode of triumphalist Catholicism, had eight Masses on Sunday (O'Donnell; Norman, 50).

Important Catholic families of England who preserved religious works of art include the Arundels and Jerninghams, both of whom are represented by collections in the United States. These families are noted since the time of Henry VIII and continued to exercise their influence despite restrictions on Catholics, fined and barred from public office. Thomas Howard, Earl of Arundel (1585-1646), has been the subject of scholarly interest for his collecting. A century later, his descendant continued the tradition. Henry, 8th Baron Arundel, patronized John Thorpe, an English Jesuit living in Rome in the latter half of the eighteenth century (English Jesuit Archives: folio 51). Fr. Thorpe acquired art for Baron Arundel, in particular the 1660 ebony and silver Flagellation now in the Martin D'Arcy Gallery of Art (Rowe, No. 78). The Jerninghams were a Norfolk family whose country seat was Costessy Hall just south of Norwich (Jerningham). They were particularly important in Anglo-Catholic affairs between the Catholic Relief Act of 1778 that removed restrictions on leasing and inheriting land and the Act of Emancipation of 1829. Around 1800 Sir William built a new family chapel for his own use and to serve as the parish church for a substantial portion of the population of the village of Costessy (Shepherd). Sir William imported authentic medieval glass to set in its windows, works of art that brought a strong identification of Catholicism (see in this catalogue "Stained Glass: Medieval Context and Modern Catholic Retrieval, pp. 201-204"). Costessy Hall was dismantled in 1918 and the Jerningham panels are represented in the collections of the Harvard University Art Museums and the Worcester Art Museum. The survival of these works of art testify to Catholicism as a minority religion, even a severely marginalized one, where the tangible object functioned as a testimony to the vitality of past faith and promise of its future.

The Butler-Bowdens were a Catholic family that kept the single extant copy of *The Book of Margery Kempe*, most probably copied about 1450, and kept in the Carthusian monastery of Mount Grace in Yorkshire until the Dissolution under Henry VIII. The Butler-Bowdens also possessed one of the prize objects of the fourteenth century, an extraordinary cope embroidered by the world-famous English textile workers of *opus anglicanum* with sacred scenes, apostles, and saints. The same saints observed in stained glass and rood screens of England are featured in the cope: Lawrence, Mary Magdalene, Helena, Stephen, Edward the Confessor, Nicholas, Margaret, John the Evangelist, John the Baptist, Katherine, Thomas of Canterbury, Edmund, and the Apostles. The cope was acquired by the Victoria and Albert Museum, London in 1955 (T.36-1955: King, 38-39, No. 77, cover pl.).

The importance of the objects in the present exhibition includes not only their production in a Christian (or in a post-Reformation era, Catholic) context but also their present Catholic ownership. Most of them are owned by Jesuit institutions. Stonyhurst College, Lancashire, was the home of the Shireburn family and the site of the first known school to transfer from the continent to England following the first Catholic Relief Acts. Other lenders include Campion Hall, Oxford; Georgetown University; Loyola University, Chicago; and the College of the Holy Cross. The Bar Convent, York, influenced by Jesuit principles, is represented by two objects. A number of works have a particular resonance since they were Mass vessels produced in England when such products for Catholic use were in principle, at least, a death sentence for the clergy using them. A silver chalice made during English prohibition is dated 1684. The chalice is inscribed so that it is possible to know that it was made as a gift of Elizabeth Rookwood, whose residence was Coldham Hall in West Suffolk. The maker, however, preserved anonymity by not marking the vessel. The inscription designates its use for the Jesuit administrative division called the College of the Holy Apostles, comprising the counties of Norfolk, Suffolk, Essex and Cambridge. Another dates from 1724 and is attributed to a silversmith from Galway, Ireland. The later chalice was made for the Dominican convent of Burisoule (Burrishoole) founded in 1669 in County Mayo in the West Country of Ireland.

The early years of many American colonies also entailed proscriptions against Catholic worship. A history of the beginnings of this worship reveals the extraordinary importance that a single painted image or chalice could have. A series of liturgical vessels brought with the Jesuit missions to Maryland include a chalice secretly produced in Elizabethan times and used in Charles County in the early eighteenth century. For expedience, base metals rather than the traditional silver and silver gilt were sometimes pressed into service. A pewter chalice and paten of presumed Maryland manufacture long associated with the missions date to about 1650-1700. Links with the mother country remained important for subsequent immigrants, as recorded for St. Louis, founded as a Catholic city, which imported paintings from France in 1818 to embellish its first cathedral. The foreign donations from Catholic countries were specifically noted in the founding of churches, for example the first Catholic parish in the city of Worcester, Massachusetts, St. John's (originally Christ's Church), a predominantly Irish congregation with its French communion vessels.

The College of the Holy Cross itself owes its existence to the tradition of English recusancy. The pioneer priest of the Worcester region, James Fitton, descended from hardy Catholic souls in Lancashire, his father having immigrated to Boston from Preston. Lancashire even in the 1720s had more than twenty percent of its land held by Catholics. Born in Boston in 1805, Fitton was baptized in the church, later cathedral, of the Holy Cross on Franklin Street. Bishop Benedict Fenwick ordained him on December 23, 1827. His early ministries took him to Maine, where he preached to the local Passamaquoddy Indians and in 1834 he was assigned to Western Massachusetts and scheduled to say Mass in Worcester once a month.

Indeed, for the contemporary researcher, the survival of the objects in this exhibition gives pause. The first reaction is a sense of their ephemeral nature. For a building, book, vestment, or picture, no matter its immense significance for its time, no matter its deeply venerated function, and no matter its often significant investment of economic resources, survival depends on multiple factors. Some, certainly, are chance events such as natural disasters or transformation of locale. Other factors are decisions, often costly, made by individuals. The second reaction, then, is one of empathy. What gave these people, those many named and unnamed, distinguished and ordinary, the courage to resist? A central government had seized the high road, enforcing conformity not only by edict, but by successfully characterizing as ignorant, superstitious, and traitorous the beliefs held by Catholics and the material culture associated with those beliefs. Yet the resistance was deep and sustained: "the common experience of suffering for the preservation of the faith, the more exacting tests, and greater consequent clarity, which they experience who hold to allegiances *contra mundum*" (Norman, 2), allowed the recusant a significant role in the preservation of vastly significant ideals and of culture. And thus the researcher reflects on the role of minorities in resisting the political elite, certainly experiences that include numerous social issues as well as the control of religion. What are the roles of the academic and the liberally educated person in preserving any aspect of the past, in championing the voiceless, contested now far more by fast changing economies and popular trends than by government edict?

How might the many issues in this exhibition have relevance today?

Piety as a cultural artifact: In viewing the display of ritual objects such as chalices, vestments, altar furnishings, and prayer books, it is inevitable that one reflects on the importance of religion to daily life in early modern times. These practices defined the rhythm of life. Wealthy individuals were expected to provide support to religion and community religious activities cemented social bonds.

Culture/Politics/Religion and Freedom of Conscience: The objects represented are part of a clandestinely-practiced religion. In early modern times in Europe, as in many countries today, the religion of the ruler was the religion of the people. After Henry VIII's break with Rome and under the reign of Elizabeth I, the practice of Catholicism was a treasonous act, and many (including Edmund Campion, after whom one of Holy Cross College's earliest buildings is named) lost their lives defying the ban on administration of the sacraments or preaching. What indeed is freedom of religion, and how do we see it in a contemporary world?

Art and its Patrons: Major types of art ceased to be produced in England with the Reformation: religious imagery was condemned, and carvings, stained glass, and paintings not only ceased to be commissioned but were mostly destroyed. Prayer books used by Catholics were required to have the images of God and the saints defaced. Later, imagery for chapels in private homes was acquired primarily from the Low Countries (Belgium and the Netherlands), especially in the late seventeenth and eighteenth centuries. What reliance does a culture have on visual depiction? Do we demand images – newspaper, film, photographs – in our lives or worship? How is artistic expression shaped by culture? One might reflect, for example, on why Mel Gibson's 2004 film *The Passion of the Christ* had such an impact on viewers.

Literature, Art, and Religion: The exhibition displays books from Reformation debates. Books from both Catholics and Protestants carried abundant imagery of martyrs and other polemical images. Poetry of the time, for example of John Donne and Richard Crashaw, contains some of the most visually compelling imagery in the English language. How do societies use the "beauty" or aesthetic appeal – some may say the sensuality – of verbal or visual expression to further political or doctrinal ends?

Erasure and also Reconstruction of a Past: The development of museums as public institutions in the nineteenth century restructured attitudes towards the past. What the English government had seen as seditious and/or blasphemous could now become objects of aesthetic beauty, models and inspiration for contemporary craftsmanship, or testimonies to a patron's social position. The past of England became "our past," with little reference to bloody dispute or the role of the government in the destruction and suppression of art. This is not uncommon. In twentieth-century China, during the Cultural Revolution, art treasures were at first destroyed as decadent examples of the feudal past. They were eventually rehabilitated as the superb products of the exploited working classes under an oppressive regime. How do cultures, especially in times of transition, reconstruct their histories, and the meaning of the artifacts of those histories?

Communication, Meaning, and Display: The exhibition provides a moment to reflect on the broader issues of the inevitable loss of meaning in the display of one culture by another – both for current cultures geographically separate and also cultures separated by time. How do we display African, Native American, or Islamic art as well as that associated with Catholic practice? Objects in stained glass, sculpture, paintings and metalwork now exhibited in "art museums" such as the Metropolitan Museum were not created for museums. They were originally part of a vital, living culture. Thus their presentation dislocates ritual objects from their cultural and religious contexts and represents them to an audience for many of whom they are alien. We are now in an era when religion does matter, with fractious debates and wars of aggression, when we may make a difference discussing iconoclasm and antipathy and also variety and tolerance as normal aspects of discourse in life and in art. It is hoped that this experience will focus thought on many examples of the intersection of culture, religion, and art in the contemporary world.

Timeline from Henry VIII to Victoria with Sovereigns, Their Consorts and Specific Events of Importance to Catholic Recusancy

House of Tudor, 1485-1603

HENRY VII 1485-1509 (grandson of Henry V)

> **Elizabeth of York** 1486-1503

HENRY VIII 1509-1547 (Henry VII's second son)

> **Catherine of Aragon** 1509-1533. Divorced
> **Anne Boleyn** 1533-1536. Executed
> **Jane Seymour** 1536-1537. Died
> **Anne of Cleves** 1540 Jan.-July. Divorced
> **Kathryn Howard** 1540-1542. Executed
> **Katherine Parr** 1543-1547. Widowed

Henry VIII broke with the spiritual authority of Rome in 1534. He had married his brother's widow, Catherine of Aragon, who bore him no male heirs. When the pope refused to grant an annulment he pressured Parliament to declare him head of both state and church so that he would be free to marry sacramentally. Inroads into church power continued; in 1538 came the dissolution of the monasteries and confiscation of their goods by the state. The same year saw the condemnation of Thomas Becket and removal of his image from churches and his commemoration from church calendars and books of prayers.

EDWARD VI 1547-1553 (Henry VIII's son by Jane Seymour) During Edward's reign, Protestant Reformers made considerable changes, with injunctions against Catholic sacraments, liturgy, and imagery. The English language *Book of Common Prayer* was the only tolerated form of worship. Imagery was ordered to be removed or defaced.

MARY 1553-1558 (Henry VIII's daughter by Catherine of Aragon) married to **Philip I of Spain** 1554-1558. Mary reinstituted Catholicism as the state religion and 273 Protestants were burned, among them bishops Nicholas Ridley and William Latimer, as well as Thomas Cranmer (1489-1556), the archbishop of Canterbury.

ELIZABETH I 1558-1603 (Henry VIII's daughter by Anne Boleyn) Elizabeth reinstituted Protestantism as the state religion, continuing most of the policies operative during the reign of Edward VI. The profession of Catholicism was seen as an act of treason, and during Elizabeth's reign 123 Catholic priests as well as members of the laity were put to death. Cautious about alignment with a Catholic consort, she remained unmarried.

Mary Queen of Scots (1542-1587)
Known for her tragic life, the daughter of James V took the Scottish throne 8 days after her birth. In 1558 she married Francis II, who became King of France. She returned to Scotland after Francis's death in 1560, where the Reformation had since made great progress. In 1565 she married her cousin, Henry Stuart, Lord Darnley. Their son would later become James I, King of England. In 1567 Darnley was assassinated. Mary wedded the suspected murderer, Earl Bothwell, later that year. The Earl became a fugitive, with Mary being held captive. Upon her escape she attempted to resume power, and when that failed, she fled to England for Queen Elizabeth's help. Instead Elizabeth detained her as a state prisoner

for 18 years, during which time Mary became regarded by many as the head of the Popish party. She was tried for conspiracy to murder Elizabeth, was convicted, and suffered decapitation in 1587.

The **Spanish Armada** of 1588 diminished any tendency for Catholic tolerance. During Elizabeth's reign, invasion by Spain remained a constant threat. In 1588, Philip II authorized the launch of the Armada. The attack was crushed decisively, a success for both English naval strategy and propitious weather. The event enhanced the queen's popularity with her people and confirmed suspicion of Catholics as potential conspirators with foreign powers again the sovereignty of the nation.

House of Stuart, 1603-1714

JAMES I 1603-1625 (great-great-grandson of Henry VII; son of Mary Queen of Scots)
     Anne of Denmark (1574-1619 married 1589) daughter of Frederick II of Denmark

The **Gunpowder Plot** of 1605 encouraged national distrust of Catholics. English Catholics had expected James I to be tolerant towards their religion, but he did not reverse Elizabeth's policies. Several Catholics formed a plot to kill James and members of his Parliament in hopes that James' daughter Elizabeth would take the throne as a Catholic. One night, conspirator Guy Fawkes and his associates managed to fill the cellar of the House of Lords with 36 barrels of gunpowder. As he went to light the fuse, Fawkes was caught by guards and tortured until he gave up the names of his co-conspirators. The criminals suffered the penalty of death. In celebration of his triumph, James began a yearly tradition of a great bonfire on Nov. 5th, in which an effigy of the Pope is burned at the top. The tradition continues in some places today, with Fawkes' effigy burning alongside that of the Pope.

Henry Garnet S. J. (b. 1553-4; d. 1606) Garnet was presumably a conformist until the age of 20, but then embraced the "old faith" becoming a Jesuit in Rome on Sept. 11, 1575. There he met with many influential recusants, such as Persons, Weston, and Southwell. Garnet was sent to England on May 8, 1587; after the arrest of the Jesuit Superior of the English Province the following year, Garnet assumed that office, holding it for the rest of his lifetime. Under his guidance the English Jesuit mission prospered, growing in membership from one to forty. In 1605, Garnet came to learn the details of the Gunpowder Plot from his fellow priests. When the plot was discovered, Garnet was arrested as a possible conspirator. Garnet confessed all his knowledge of the plot, and resultantly he was tried and executed at Old St. Paul's on May 3. 1606.

CHARLES I 1625-1649 (born 1600, second son of James)
     Henrietta Maria (1609-1669; married 1625) daughter of Henry IV and Marie de Medici of France. In 1625 she married Charles who was then the Prince of Wales. In 1626 Charles had the Queens House Greenwich built for her. She was the first Catholic princess to marry a Protestant prince, and as such she required special permission of the Pope. Despite her religion, the English originally accepted Henrietta Maria, prizing her beauty and vivacious personality. However, she grew unpopular as she was believed to support the papacy over English interests. In 1642 Charles I clashed with Parliament; Parliament revolted, plunging the country into civil war against a Puritan army headed by Cromwell from 1642 to 46. Henrietta Maria fled the country before the war began in order to avoid persecution. She traveled to the Netherlands, where she amassed funding and ammunition. In 1643 she returned to England with the hopes that these supplies would help her and Charles regain power. However, the attempt failed, and Henrietta Maria was forced to make a permanent escape to France in 1644. Henrietta Maria briefly visited England again for the 1660 restoration of her son, Charles II. She died in 1669 at the convent of Chaillot, near Paris.

COMMONWEALTH 1649-1660 Under the leadership of **Oliver Cromwell**, the parliamentarians defeated the royalists in 1646. The victors abolished the monarchy and eventually put Charles I on trial, beheading him in 1649. Cromwell had let Parliament rule in the 1640's, but instituted the Protectorate in 1653 with himself as head. Cromwell died in 1658 and his son Richard took over as Lord Protector. However, Richard was an ineffective ruler. Fearing that anarchy might ensue, the newly elected Parliament of 1660 took action and invited Charles II, son of the executed Charles I, to become king.

CHARLES II 1660-1685 (born 1630, oldest son of Charles I). Charles II came to power in Britain by means of the English Restoration. Charles had already been King of Scotland and parts of Ireland and England since 1651. He accepted rule over Great Britain and the monarchy was restored. Throughout his reign, Charles II was known for seeking absolute power and learning towards Catholicism. On his deathbed in 1685, Charles II declared himself a Roman Catholic.

      Catherine of Braganza (1638-1705; married 1662) daughter of John IV of Portugal. Apparently a pious woman, she supported the establishment of a house of Mary Ward's Institute in 1667. She was accused of complicity in the **Popish Plot** of 1678. This alleged plot was the invention of Titus Oates. Oates was a failed Anglican clergyman who was rejected from his endeavor to convert to the Catholic priesthood. He retaliated by becoming an anti-Catholic informer. In an effort to further England's anti-Catholic sentiments, Oates fabricated a rumor of a Jesuit-guided plan to assassinate Charles II, which would hasten the succession of the Catholic James II. Oates' alleged Popish Plot developed into national hysteria and the worst persecution of Catholics since Elizabeth's reign. Not until after the arrest of about a hundred clergy, the execution of seventeen, and the deaths of twenty-three in prison did Charles II regain the initiative in favor of the succession of his Catholic brother James (1685-1688).

JAMES II 1685-1688 (brother of Charles II) died in France at St. Germain, 1701
      Anne Hyde (1637-1671; married 1660) daughter of First Lord Clarendon
      Mary Beatrice of Modena (1658-1718; married 1673) daughter of Alfonso IV, duke of Modena. The marriage, heavily promoted by the French crown, occurred when James II was still the Duke of York. James II became a Catholic convert (public declaration in 1672). He acceded to the throne after the death of his brother Charles. The birth of a son in 1688 caused further concerns that England would revert to Catholicism as a state religion. Deposed by Parliament in the Glorious Revolution, James fled to France to gain support from Louis XVI, then to Ireland where he was defeated by William of Orange at the battle of the Boyne, July 1, 1690. In the wake of these conflicts there then ensued a distrust of Catholicism as a threat dominated by foreign influence and vehement anti-Catholic legislation. In exile on the continent, Mary lent support to Mary Ward's Institute.

Glorious Revolution 1689
WILLIAM OF ORANGE (grandson of Charles I) and **MARY** (born 1662, daughter of James II married in 1677 to William)
[**WILLIAM AND MARY** 1689-1694; William as **WILLIAM III** to 1702]
The English nobles offer the crown to William of Orange, Stattholder of the United Provinces of Holland from 1672 .
ANNE 1702-1714 (daughter of James II and sister of Mary)

HOUSE OF HANOVER, 1714-1834

GEORGE I 1714-1727 (great-grandson of James I)
GEORGE II 1727-1760 (son of George I)
GEORGE III 1760-1820 (grandson of George II)

The Jesuit Suppression of 1773. The powers of each Catholic state had grown wary of the Jesuits' support of the papacy, their missionary fervor, and their international way of proceeding, a way that gave relatively short shrift to national interests and authorities. France's anti-papal Gallicans were especially opposed to the Jesuits. The Jesuits found more problems when their papal loyalty drew them into the struggle between the papacy and the Bourbon monarchies. As a result of pressures from several monarchs, Pope Clement XIV signed a 1773 decree that aimed to suppress the Jesuits everywhere. The order was upheld in Portugal, France, the Spanish empire, Parma, and the two Sicilies, but ignored in some other countries such as Russia, whose Orthodox Tsar did not recognize papal authority. The scholarly Jesuit Society of Bollandists was able to survive in the 1770's and 1780's by moving from Antwerp to Brussels, but in 1788, the Austrian government also turned to suppress the Bollandist Society. The ideas that spurred the Suppression may also have helped to prepare the way for the French Revolution of 1788-1799. However, in the early nineteenth century, Europeans grew tired of the excesses that resulted from the Revolution. This change in attitude included a gradual re-acceptance of Catholic authority in European government. In 1814 Pope Pius issued the bull *Sollicitudo Omnium Ecclesiarum* restoring the Society of Jesus throughout the world.

Catholic Relief Act of 1791 The act repealed the laws against Catholic worship and education. It was now legal to hear Mass and to conduct a Catholic school. Catholics were still forbidden to employ external trappings of religion that might intrude on the image of public uniformity. The act also removed many of the oaths of office that had made it impossible for a Catholic to enter public service.

GEORGE IV 1820-1830 (son of George III)

Catholic Emancipation Act of 1829 This act removed restrictions on Catholic worship and guaranteed free exercise of religion. Catholics could now attend English Universities. The Catholic hierarchy, restored only in 1850, was forbidden from reclaiming any old territorial ecclesiastical titles in use by the Church of England.

WILLIAM IV 1830-1837 (brother of George IV)

House of Saxe-Coburg

VICTORIA 1837-1901 (niece of William IV)

THE DAILY EXPERIENCE OF DEVOTION

Virginia C. Raguin

For Henry VIII, the primary impetus for separating the English church from Rome was political, not doctrinal. Henry was faced with a need to set aside his first marriage to his brother's widow, Catherine of Aragon, in order to marry Anne Boleyn in the hope that she would produce a male heir where Catherine had failed. This required church approval, which the Pope would not grant, so Henry arranged for the English church to be declared independent with himself as Supreme Head. Henry was a ruthless centralist who believed royal power was absolute. He saw himself as mediating between the citizen and God, rejecting European reform movements like Lutheranism and Calvinism that taught that individuals could relate to God directly. Although his church renounced papal supremacy, it at first retained most other Catholic practices. Influential advisors to the king then advocated bringing in more reformed doctrine. The *Articles to Establish Christian Quietness* for 1536 with the *Injunctions* of 1536 and 1538, repudiated along with "the Bishop of Rome's usurped power and jurisdiction," purgatory, the cult of the saints and images, relics, and pilgrimages. "To the intent that all superstition and hypocrisy . . . may vanish away, they shall not set forth or extol any images, relics, or miracles for any superstition or lucre, nor allure the people by enticements to the pilgrimage of any saint" (Gee and Hardy, 257-81, quote 271). Reformers struggled with traditionalists at court and in the Council. By 1539, Henry felt

Detail from Calendar for April, "folk. . . goon on pilgrimages", Book of Hours printed in Paris by Simon Vostre, 1512, Stonyhurst College, S. 3/3, fol. 3

that reforms were going too far, and encouraged Parliament to enact *The Six Articles* that defined late Henrician orthodoxy (31 Henry VIII, Cap. 14: Gee and Hardy, 303-319). Under penalty of death by burning, subjects could not deny the validity of transubstantiation (that the Eucharist was actually the "body and blood of our Saviour Jesus Christ"), the binding laws of chastity for those in the religious life, the value of privately said Masses, or the efficacy of the Sacrament of Penance (Confession).

Despite the reign's quasi-conservatism, the practices of the common worshipper were considerably altered. Average parishioners were not involved in scholarly debate over the hypostatic union or Thomistic logic. They were accustomed to a pattern of devotion that cemented community relations at the same time that it satisfied religious injunctions. Relics, sacred images, and the existence of a purgatory where souls awaited release to heaven provided the underlying reasons for routine practices like pilgrimages (Marks and

Williamson, 424-35). As Chaucer presented so vividly in the *Canterbury Tales*, when April comes with its good weather, its "showres soote" that prick the bud to bloom, it simply follows:

> Thanne longen folk to goon on pilgrimages
> And palmeres for to seken straunge strondes
> To ferne halwes, kowthe in sondry londes
> And specially, from every shires ende
> Of Engelond to Caunturbury they wende,
> The hooly blisful martir for to seke
> That hem hath holpen, whan that they were seeke. (Prologue: lines 12-18)

It was the rhythm of life, a rhythm deeply imbedded into landscape, architecture, paths, buildings, statues, and images. The cult of the saints and the tradition of relics, attacked by Henry and subsequent reformers, were part of the Church since the very earliest years of the Christian religion (Brown 1985; Binsky, 11-21). Places of worship grew up over the sites of significant graves. In the fourth century, the Emperor Constantine built the basilica of St. Peter over a cemetery believed to contain the grave of the first pope. The demand to be close to the tangible remains of heroic Christians, great confessors and martyrs, especially in the founding of new churches, encouraged the partition of bodies to allow the sacred "aura" that facilitated God's grace to be shared among a growing community. Churches were founded with relics as their essential "talisman" and stone altars with cavities inscribed with their list of relics date from 320, a practice that was later routine. For the founding of Canterbury in the fifth century, according to Bede (673-735), the pope provided Augustine with "all the things needful for the worship and service of the church, namely, sacred vessels, altar linen, church ornaments, priestly and clerical vestments, relics of the holy Apostles and martyrs and also many books" (Hist. Eccl., I, xxix).

Throughout the entire Middle Ages, and in Catholic Europe through the Renaissance and Baroque eras, the possession of relics of important saints made sites popular. Veneration even included significant displacement to visit these relics. The well-known autobiography of Margery Kempe (ca. 1373-1440s), who journeyed to numerous shrines, invariably associates them with relics, even locally, as at the tomb of St. William of York (Windeatt, 234-35). They encouraged her wide-ranging travels to the Holy Land and the Holy Sepulchre, Santiago of Compostela and the tomb of St. James the Great, or Aachen, among many others (Ibid., 159-228). The pre-Reformation English worshipper did not believe that the souls of the saints remained in such relics (bones, clothes worn, or elements of their martyrdom, such as the stones used to kill Stephen), but that these things would act as conduits to grace. They would link the revered intercessor, the saint favored in the eyes of God, to his or her faithful supplicants on earth (Finucane).

Saints were also commemorated on their feast days throughout the year, and by parishes and organizations that placed themselves under a particular saint's protection (Duffy 1992, 155-205; Van Os, 28-39). Within individual churches, such as the small urban parish of St. Michael's Spurriergate in York, parishioners honored saints at special altars. In this parish of 350 adult communicants, besides the high altar, there were at least eight other altars dedicated to the Name of Jesus, the Trinity, Mary, and saints John the Baptist, Mary Magdalene, Thomas, Nicholas, and Margaret, with a shrine to St. Anne in the church yard and additional saints honored by statues including Michael, patron of the parish, Crux, Agnes, and Sith (Barnwell, Cross and Rycraft, 91-93). Civic/religious associations such as guilds also invoked specific aspects of devotion and the saints (Platt, 112-20; Westlake). The Corpus Christi guild, for example, formed one of the most influential associations of a town, organizing complex activities associated with the procession of the Eucharist held annually (Rubin 1991; Westlake, 49-65). In the Norfolk town of Swaffam, guilds honoring the Trinity, the Ascension, St. Peter, St. Helen, St. John the Baptist, St. Nicholas and St. Thomas Becket had activities linked to commemorative feasts (Duffy 1992, 48). Invariably, the guilds listed their duties as maintaining a candle (many candles if the guilds were wealthy) before the patronal image on festivals as well as attendance at services, repairing church fabric, vestments, books, and other ornaments, aiding the poor and sick, and attending funerary masses for deceased members. Through interpersonal actions and festive meals, as well as such devotions, these associations also served to knit communities beyond kinship ties (Brown 1995, 132-58).

The function of a saintly patron is exemplified by Morebath, a small village of some 150 souls in the county of Devon, where the parish priest, Sir Christopher Trychay (pronounced Tricky) kept a meticulous register of parish activities from 1520 to 1574. Sir was the title for a priest, the equivalent of "Father." Sir Christopher took as one of his first parish projects the augmentation of devotion of St. Sidwell in order to give his parish a distinctly personal protector. St. Sidwell was a Saxon virgin from Exeter in Devon, reputed to have been decapitated by a

Recusant women wearing rosary beads, led off by soldiers, detail, Robert Persons, *De Persecutione Anglicana Libellus,* 1582, Stonyhurst College

jealous stepmother. Legend described the saint carrying her head to the place where she desired a shrine, and miracles occurred. This shrine/church was located outside the east gate of the city of Exeter. Sir Christopher's project involved placing a statue of St. Sidwell next to the statue of Christ over the altar where Masses commemorating the dead were held. Such a statue was acquired through the priest's own contribution but also those of parishioners. In 1520, two gifts associated with the devotion are noted: a banner depicting St. George (patron saint of the parish) on one side and St. Sidwell on the other and a hive of bees for the production of candle wax "to maintain a lamp burning before the figure of Jesus and before St. Sidwell every principle feast in the year, to burn from the first evensong [i.e. first vespers of the feast] until high Mass be done the next day" (Duffy 2001, 75). Later gifts include a silver cross to the statue of Jesus and a wedding ring to St. Sidwell which was melted down to make a silver shoe for the statue. Rosary beads were also given, a distinctive and personal gift since Tudor women wore such beads hanging from their waists and they clearly mark the Catholic recusants being arrested in the *De Persecutione Anglicana Libellus* of 1582. They were often the most expensive pieces of devotion/adornment possessed by an ordinary woman. Their placement on the statue during festive times would serve as a reminder of the donor and augment her status in the community.

Wills consistently record donations for veneration of the saints and participatory activities, especially the maintenance of candles before statues and altars, and Masses for the dead, practices particularly excoriated by the Reformers (Barnwell, Cross and Rycraft, 57-107). A record of the will made in 1519 by Joan Ingrame, a widow who had resided near Lincoln, corroborates the routine:

> I give and bequeath to the mother church of Lincoln [cathedral], 4*d.* Also to the high altar for my tithes forgotten, a cloth of diaper [damasque]. Also to St. Sunday's altar in that church, a sheet with a seam of black silk. Also to the rood light [the light before the crucifix on top of the chancel screen] half a pound of wax. Also to St. Katherine's light, as much. Also to St. Christopher's light a quarter of a pound of wax. Also to St. Thomas' light, as much. Also to St. Margaret's light, as much. Also to St. Anne's light, as much. Also to Master John Schorne's light [Schorn was a sainted vicar of North Marston: Marks

and Williamson, 434-35, No. 325] a pound of wax. Also for burial in the church [of North Marston, Ingrame's local parish], 3 pounds 6 shillings, 8 pennies. . . . Also I give to a priest to sing for my soul in the parish of North Marston, five marks (Goldberg, 282).

With the death of Henry and the ascension of the nine-year-old Edward VI, Protestant reformers increased their vigor (Duffy 1995, 448-77). The council of Regency was favorable to the new ideas and there was a considerable influx of individuals committed to the new European creeds settling in England. The first Parliament removed almost all the restrictions on reformed practices established in the past two centuries, eliminating Henry's decrees against heresy and allowing the Sacred Scriptures to be translated into English and read both publicly and privately by laypeople. Soon, clear changes were mandated: Latin service books were forbidden and replaced by books in English, and a *Book of Common Prayer and Administration of the Sacraments and other Rites and Ceremonies of the Church, after the use of the Church of England* was established in 1549 in the first Edwardian Act of Uniformity (2 & 3 Edward VI, Cap. 1: Gee and Hardy, 358-66). In 1552 it was followed by a second Act of Uniformity with a revised *Book of Common Prayer* which endeavored more clearly to distinguish between the old and forbidden "Mass" and the reformed Holy Communion and Lord's Supper. The word "altar" was replaced with "table." In the same year the old Catholic church vestments and liturgical objects such as chalices were required to be turned over to the Crown. Some parishes were clearly enthusiastic about the Reform, suggestive in the record of the East Anglian parish of Cratfield selling in 1544 "a peyre of Chalys a peyre of censers and a cross" (Nichols, 168). During the restoration of Catholicism under Queen Mary, Cratfield is recorded as having very few Catholic objects left, three altar cloths, two corporals, two chasubles and a cope, and one burse in contrast to a rich assortment inventoried in 1528 (Ibid., 167). Morebath appears to have been more reticent, yet recorded its compliance with the injunctions against ancient vestments in 1552.

At Edward's death, however, Mary, daughter of Henry and the Spanish Catherine of Aragon, assumed the throne to reign for five years, 1553-1558. Mary was avowedly Catholic and reinstituted the old religion, reviving heresy laws under which a large number of Protestant leaders were imprisoned and burned. During these five years, the Morebath parish took out its old objects, which, as in most parishes, had been set aside rather than destroyed.

Under Elizabeth the Reform returned (Morey). The Act of Uniformity of 1559, issued the year after she assumed the throne, was the local expression of the prevailing principle of *cuius regio, eius religio*, the religion of the ruler is the religion of the state and its citizens (1 Elizabeth Cap. 2: Gee and Hardy, 458-75). By the Act, the *Book of Common Prayer* was imposed as the only legitimate act of worship and all citizens were required under penalty of fine to attend Sunday services. The publication of the *Thirty Nine Articles* in 1563 defined the new Protestant doctrines that would have lasting impact on the cultural landscape: the Scriptures as the sole rule of faith (Art. VI), the denial of papal authority (Art. XXXVII), definition of church art and repudiation of superstitious images (Art. XIX), justification by faith and repudiation of indulgences, good works, and other actions as having merit (Art. XI), and the repudiation of the Mass as a sacrifice (Arts. XXVIII and XXXI).

Such abrupt swings of government allegiance understandably had the clergy and their parishioners in an awkward situation. Many in the early years of Elizabeth's reign wondered if the pendulum would again swing and outlawed practices once again become obligatory. The length of Elizabeth's reign and the support for Reform among her counselors insured that henceforth the state religion would be the institution of the Church of England, distinct from Roman Catholicism. In Morebath, Sir Christopher's accounts make it clear that the parish acquired a mandated register of baptisms, weddings, and burials, and a book of the poor to be kept in a church chest. Thus compliance of all members of the community could be verified. Worship service demanded the *Book of Common Prayer*, a pulpit for preaching and a "decent table standing on a frame for the Communion Table [which they] shall decently cover with carpet, silk, or other decent covering, and with a fair linen cloth (at the time of ministration) the

Communion Table." At Morebath the table was covered with a silk cloth made from a set of High Mass vestments. Sir Christopher, as "minister" was required to wear "a comely surplice with sleeves" for services and use a chalice of recognizably Protestant form (The Advertisements of 1566: Gee and Hardy, 471).

What a modern world might label as "externals" or simple "form" was for both Catholic and Protestant sides essential elements of religious and personal identity. As Eamon Duffy, recent historian of the Morebath parish, phrases it, "ultimately the Reformation came to be, quite literally, part of the furniture" (Duffy 2001, 177). The record of Morebath reveals that these accouterments were not left to chance, their conformity and use verified by numerous visitations, appearances before the archdeacon and bishop, and even fines for non-compliance. The local priest was obligated to school his flock in the Psalms and "usual prayers" and also, through periodic government directives, to pray for fellow Protestants such as the persecuted Huguenots of France (Duffy 2001, 179). The "Ten Commandments upon the east wall over the said table" took the place of imagery behind what had been called the altar in the Catholic worship (Gee and Hardy, 471; for Elizabethan Commandment Boards, see Aston 1988, fig. 16 and Marks 2005, fig. 173). For Devon the 1566 "Advertisement" was strengthened by a regional directive in 1568. In the early 1570s the area which included Morebath was the subject of an Episcopal campaign to gather up all chalices that had been in use in Catholic times and melt them down for the refashioning of Protestant communion cups. In 1571 Morebath, for example, was required to turn over its chalice to Royal Commissioners, for which it received payment for the purchase of a communion cup (see, in this catalogue, "Liturgical Vessels"). England is rich in communion cups of this era, for example, one dated 1570 from Cirencester, a tall, plain cup, almost an urn shape with a cover (Cripps, 237, no, 14; Oman, 198-99, pl. 62a), is visibly distinctive from the wide brimmed medieval type with stem and knop. Of large size, the communion cups were designed to be used by the entire congregation (I Edward VI, Cap. 1: Gee and Hardy, 322-28; also 446, I Elizabeth Cap 1). Despite the 1571 surrender of its chalice, the parish used a second, smaller chalice at least for the following three years until Sir Christopher's death in 1574 (Duffy 2001, 178).

These new practices, and the denial of many of the old, impacted much more than Sunday services. The parish had been organized around community operation, as attested to by the Morebath records. Gender and marital status marked primary divisions. The batchelors, the maidens, the men, and the women were distinguished and assigned particular roles, a practice well documented through earlier times. In the late thirteenth century, Jacobus de Voragine, author of the *Golden Legend*, a collection of saints' lives ordered according to the liturgical calendar, recorded information about several major processions during "Rogations" or times of petition. He describes the Greater Litany organized into seven ranks of participants: "first came the clergy, then the monks and religious, then the nuns, then the children, then the laymen, then the widows and virgins, and lastly the married women (Voragine, 278; Vauchez 1993, 129-37). Duffy's reading, however, expands our understanding of such systems; as much as they represent segregation they also guaranteed inclusion since participation from all the groups was carefully orchestrated as part of service to the church. There were standard and expected responsibilities for each group, among which there was a rotation of duties. With the curtailment of the practices of veneration of the saints and devotional activities such as processions, embroidering banners, and caring for devotional objects, many of these responsibilities disappeared to the extent that parish life became far more restricted, with a small group of elite dominating all church activities.

Just as Protestant worship was enforced through external compliance in dress, language, and furniture, so too, recusant Catholics identified validity of religion with external comportment. In these times, the wearing of the proper priestly vestments was a necessary and essential part of the performance of the Sacrament. Thus we can have some perspective on the context of the set of vestments (CATALOGUE) worn by Edmund Arrowsmith, S.J. and hidden in a horse skin covered chest. Vesting for the Mass required the priest to wear first an alb, a long white garment with long sleeves completely covering the body and held at the waist by a cord called a cincture. Over this came a stole, a long narrow section of

Trunk, showing partial contents owned by Edmund Arrowsmith S.J., England, early 17th century, Stonyhurst College. Photo: Virginia Raguin

fabric, indicative of preaching authority, hung around the neck, then a long tabard-shaped robe called a chasuble, and a maniple, a large folded piece of fabric that derived from the ancient napkin over the arm used by deacons during the ritual handwashing. The vestments were designed in the liturgical colors codified since the time of Innocent III (1198-1216), in a widely followed, but not rigid system. Green, the dominant color of Arrowsmith's cache, was used for the feasts of confessors and "ordinary time" (Sundays from the feast of the Holy Trinity until Advent), thus being one of the most frequent colors. White was for liturgies honoring the Virgin Mary, other important virgin saints, and major feasts such as Easter, Corpus Christi, and Christmas; purple was used for times of penance in Advent and Lent; and red was reserved for Pentecost and feasts of the Holy Cross, apostles, and martyrs. Black vestments, when a community was wealthy enough to afford a set, were for funerals, masses for the dead, and All Souls Day. Colors, however, had wide variety in local practice. Some scholars maintain that the codification was primarily post Reform (Barnwell, Cross and Rycraft, 39-40). What is clearly evident is that particular vestments were often preferred for certain feasts because they were the most elaborate, costly, and in the best condition (Platt, 107-108; Johnstone, 21-25).

Arrowsmith also carried a rosary (CATALOGUE), a small single-decade style that was unobtrusive. The English Jesuits were active supporters of the Confraternity of the Rosary, an institution closely associated with the Dominicans (Winston-Allen). In 1593 Henry Garnet, the Superior of the Jesuits in England since 1586, wrote a handbook called the *Societie of the Rosary* that served also as a catechism, following the Ignatian technique of composition of place (Morey, 150). As the faithful recited a series of prayers such as the ten Hail Marys while fingering ten beads in a row, they were instructed to meditate on one of the subjects called either the Joyful, Sorrowful, or Glorious Mysteries taken from the Life of Christ and the Virgin Mary. The Joyful Mysteries are the Annunciation of the Angel Gabriel to Mary, the Visitation of Mary and Elizabeth (mother of John the Baptist), the Nativity, the Presentation of the

Infant Jesus in the Temple, and the Finding of the Boy Jesus in the Temple. The Sorrowful Mysteries are the Agony in the Garden, Christ Scourged, Christ Crowned with Thorns, Christ Carrying the Cross, and the Crucifixion and death of Christ. The Glorious Mysteries are the Resurrection, Christ's Ascension into Heaven, the Descent of the Holy Spirit, the Assumption of Mary into Heaven, and the Coronation of the Virgin as Queen of Heaven.

In the absence of a priest for Mass and regular instruction, the rosary served as an admirable substitute and was promoted as such by Fr. Garnet. First, the devotion could be led by a layperson, making it ideal for family or community practice on a daily basis. In previous times, daily Mass in family chapels was characteristic of the upper classes. The saying of the rosary with its mediations on the essential elements of the Life of Christ and his mother assured that proper instruction would be continued, even in the absence of those trained in catechesis. Above all, the Confraternity offered solidarity, assuring the recusant Catholic that no matter how beleaguered and sequestered, he or she was part of a universal faith with numerous believers in all parts of Europe, strong in allegiance to Catholicism and offering up their prayers for aid of their embattled brethren. The

Virgin on a crescent surrounded by the rosary, Book of Hours, 1530 (Paris?), Stonyhurst College, Lancashire, S.3/8, fol. 197

adherent participated throughout life, and especially at the hour of death, in the prayers, penances and good works of all of the members of the confraternity. The Confraternity of the Rosary also carried with it a rich tradition of indulgences applicable to the souls in purgatory, in the tradition of piety practiced in England before the Reformation. Representations of the Rosary appear in Books of Hours, such as the two Parisian examples of 1526 and 1530 in this exhibition. An early pre-Reformation example of enrollment in the Confraternity is found in the Plumpton Correspondence. In 1486 the priest Thomas Betanson, who signed himself "your servant and bedman" (beadman, meaning priest) wrote to Sir Robert Plumpton from London: "I send . . . a pauper of the Rosary of our Ladye of Coleyn and I have registered your name with both my Ladis names, as the pauper expresses, and ye be acopled as brether and sisters" (Stapleton, 50).

In the American Colonies the rosary continued to be advocated among Catholics. John Bolton, a Jesuit priest, is recorded to have given a sermon on the rosary on the feast of the Assumption in Newport, Maryland in 1780. He presents the devotion as "serviceable to piety, if, and according to the direction of those books which prescribe the method; by leading the mind thro all the misteries of man's Redemption and giving it a frequent opportunity of a grateful acknowledgement of all that God had done for us. This may be particularly helpful to such as cannot read" (Kupke, 188). Bolton is at pains to explain that confidence in the good of a confraternity "being a voluntary engagement of pious persons in frequenting the sacraments, in prayer and fasting and the material assistance of one another can deserve no censure." He condemns, however, those "pretending to be assured of salvation upon the ceremony of what they wear or the formality of some prayers" (Kupke, 191-92), an understandable injunction at any time, but particularly important for a minority religion challenged on the value of such practices by the Protestant majority.

CATALOGUE

Green Vestments owned by Edmund Arrowsmith

Alb, Cincture, Chasuble, Stole, Maniple, Chalice Veil, Burse (into which the priest places the corporal)

England, early 17th century

Silk, linen, with silk embroidery

Stonyhurst College, Lancashire, gift of the Myerscough family

These vestments were found in a seventeenth-century box, now known as The Pedlar's Box. The box was discovered at Samlesbury Hall which was at that time in the possession of the Southworth family. As was typical of Catholic practice in the early seventeenth century, the recusant family used the house to shelter missionary priests. Edmund Arrowsmith was associated with the mission at Samlesbury Hall as was Edmund Campion some forty years earlier. Arrowsmith was captured, imprisoned in Lancashire Castle, and finally hanged on August 28, 1628.

The box (13 ¼ in. height x 14 ½ in. width x 33 in. length) is made of wood covered with horse skin on the exterior and wallpaper on the interior. When found, the box opened to reveal a bonnet (30 in. long by 19 in. wide) of brown linen with a pink silk lining dating to the 1620s on top of folded lengths of cloth. The pieces of cloth, however, were actually the components of altar coverings which covered a final layer of priestly vestments. The contents were extensive: in addition to those listed above, the case contained: an altar hanging (frontal) with a cross in silver outline and matching maniple and stole; a brown silk chalice veil with a red cross, a green chasuble with brocade orphreys, and a green chasuble with rose color orphreys with matching stole and maniple. Smaller objects include: a plain linen altar cloth and a length of linen for making more; a badly burned linen cloth with a cross; a neck cloth; a linen pillow case (18 ¾ x 30 ¾ in.) with Catholic symbols embroidered front & back. There were three corporals: a linen corporal embroidered with a small cross; a linen corporal embroidered with a large cross; and a corporal embroidered with the Jesuit emblem (the IHS within a glory, with a cross resting on the crossbar of the H and a heart below. This is precisely the form displayed on the recusant Petre paten that traveled with the Jesuits to Maryland (see in this catalogue "The Founding of Maryland and Catholics under British Colonial Policy," pp. 174, 177). The heart, however, differs in its being overlaid with two crossed arrows, instead of the three nails at the top.

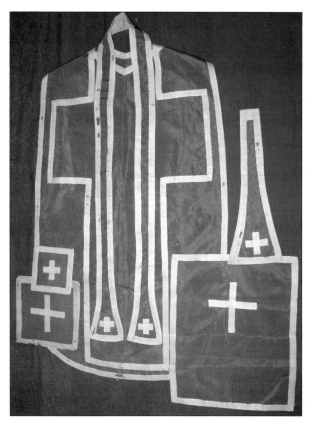

Green vestments owned by Edmund Arrowsmith S.J.: Chasuble, Stole, Maniple, Chalice Veil, and Burse, England, early 17th century, Stonyhurst College. Photo: Virginia Raguin

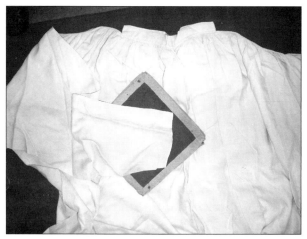

Alb with burse, owned by Edmund Arrowsmith S.J., England, early 17th century, Stonyhurst College. Photo: Virginia Raguin

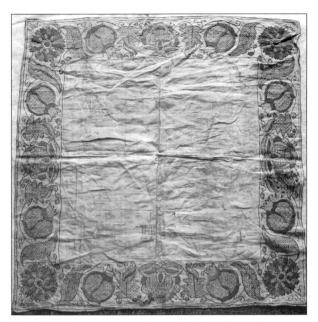

Corporal with pomegranates and roses, England, 1590-1600, Stonyhurst College. Photo: Virginia Raguin

Corporal with pomegranates and roses, detail, showing repair, Stonyhurst College. Photo: Virginia Raguin

Corporal with IHS Image found in Arrowsmith's trunk
England, 1620s
Linen, with silk embroidery, 19 ¼ x 21 in. (48.9 x 53.3 cm.)
Stonyhurst College, Lancashire

Corporal with Pomegranates and Roses
England, 1590-1600
Linen, with silk embroidery, 19 in. (48.3 cm.) square
Stonyhurst College, Lancashire

The corporal is a linen cloth over which the priest consecrates and consumes the host during Mass. Thus the cloth actually touches the sacramental Body of Christ believed as an article of faith by Catholics. Medieval piety maintained rituals to emphasize the sacredness of the host for the worshippers. Only the consecrated hands of the priest were allowed to touch the host and believers received the host as a priest laid it on their tongues. In addition, gloves were employed by those caring for these cloths, as testified in the records of Morebath, Devon by a payment for "glovys to wasse the corporis" (Duffy 2001, 67). During the Reformation, these objects could assume immense significance. For Catholics deprived of the Sacrament by the absence of a priest, the corporal itself could serve as a powerful evocation of the sacred in its ability to evoke that

longed-for moment of consecration. The cloth has been delicately - reverently - mended, attesting to the significance accorded to the object. Its symbolism is enhanced by the roses, symbol of Christ's gift of his blood, and the pomegranates, symbols of resurrection, a long-standing tradition since antiquity. The IHS is the familiar symbol of the monogram of the name of Jesus; below it is the Sacred Heart.

Corporal with IHS Image found in Arrowsmith's trunk, England, 1620s, Stonyhurst College, Lancashire. Photo: Virginia Raguin

Rosary Bracelet
England, ca. 1600
Mother of pearl, agate, steel chain, length 4 in.
(10.2 cm.)
Stonyhurst College, Lancashire

The rosary is associated with St. Edmund Arrowsmith (Camm, 183-201). Rosary beads were a part of devotional practice since the thirteenth century and were expressly condemned in 1547, during the first year of Edward VI's reign. Rosary beads have also remained associated with Nicholas Postgate who died at the age of 82 in 1679 in the violence occasioned by the "Popish Plot."

His rosary made of bone, is a standard fifty-bead version, and is preserved at St. Hilda's, Whitby (Camm, 299, ill. opp. p. 300). Postgate served a series of manorial families; the Hungate, Saltmarsh, Meynell families, but mainly lived in a thatched cottage at Ugthorpe, on the moors, five miles from Whitby. A rosary from about 1500, with twenty-seven turned wooden beads (provided with a modern string) was excavated in London in 1890. It is large, 1.15 cm. in length, and is now in the Museum of London (No. 5079; Marks and Williamson, 342, No. 222).

Rosary bracelet, associated with Edmund Arrowsmith S.J., England, ca. 1600, Stonyhurst College. Photo: Virginia Raguin

Devotional Objects and Cultural Context: The Medieval Parish Church

Simon Roffey

Today, one may walk into most medieval churches and fail to believe that once such buildings were testaments to contemporary artistic achievement and cultural sensibility of the highest order. Filled with sacred objects, these repositories were often framed with breath-taking art and architecture, their sacred spaces were suffused with lights; the vaulted fabric, vibrating with the sound of sacred liturgy and the whole space infused with the otherworldly smell of incense. An overly romantic vision of a lost legacy, perhaps? Or, a reality hinted at by surviving fragments and records? Despite some tinges of nostalgia, recent studies unearthing evidence such as churchwardens' accounts and archaeological remains reveal that the medieval parish church was indeed structured to offer this veritable vision of heaven; here reflected and reconstructed within the earthly medium of art, architecture, and a myriad of devotional objects and pious gifts.

Churchwardens' accounts may be a particularly fruitful source of information in that "they address lay priorities and (the) community concerns" (French 2001, 11). Surviving churchwardens' accounts for England are detailed both by Ronald Hutton and Beat Kumin (Hutton; Kumin). However their survival is sporadic. For example, the survival rate, in the medieval and Reformation period, is for the diocese of Winchester, 9%; for Bath and Wells, 11%; and for Salisbury, 15% (Foster, 78). The documents that relate to the dissolution of the chantries in the mid-sixteenth century (the so-called chantry certificates) are also a valuable source of information about individual chantry foundations that were in existence at the dissolution; their goods, services and location within the church. Coupled with the analysis of relevant documents, the archaeological examination of the surviving physical structure and topography of medieval parish churches can provide an insight into the form and fabric of religious belief that, in many cases, remains largely 'invisible' from primarily historical sources.

For over a thousand years, the parish church has been a symbol of collective spiritual and social aspiration. The origins of the "parish" church are obscure but certainly by the ninth century at least, the local church permeated medieval society. Particularly in rural settlements, the church was a focal point for communal relationships. Here, the major passages of one's life in baptisms and marriages would be formally acknowledged and family and friends interred within the burial grounds. Archaeological evidence suggests that many churches were originally timber-built but by the mid-twelfth century most were replaced with masonry structures. Although relatively simple, English parish churches were now built for endurance, and would, through their material longevity, attest to the continual life–cycle of a community.

By the eve of the Reformation, some four hundred years later, the local parish church would be scarcely recognizable from its twelfth-century precursor. Aisles, spacious naves and chancels, light-filled clerestories, ornate side chapels and the burgeoning of chantries, guilds and fraternities greatly expanded church space and fabric, exemplified by Holy Trinity Church of Long Melford (Suffolk) (fig. 1). Such progressions reflected a desire for more opportunities to express individual piety in the communal context. They also attest to the importance of the arts of sculpture, painting, stained glass, metalwork, and textiles. The Reformation, however, was to bring about a series of dramatic changes, sweeping away a whole tradition of devotional practice and instigating the "dismantling and destruction" of this highly "symbolic world" (Duffy 1992, 1). In the "necessity of destroying, of cutting, hammering, scraping, or melting into a deserved oblivion the monuments of popery" much has been lost (Ibid., 480). Movable or temporary decorations, especially textiles such as altar cloths and vestments and items such as candles, bells, patens

1. Internal view of Long Melford church, Suffolk, ca. 1480. Photo: Virginia Raguin

and chalices were most vulnerable. Although Catholic practices were now forced underground, and many churches drastically altered, many devotional objects and works of art remained vital to religious practice in recusant circles, as this important collection here testifies.

To place such objects in their context one must examine the setting in which they were used. Whether for medieval parish church or chantry or post-Reformation private chapel, *context* can provide greater insight into the meaning of devotional artifacts. They were not made to stand alone, but were part of a wider framework. It is the purpose of this paper to examine this material setting so that we can better understand the wider social relationships behind such objects. The role of the Mass, the central and common ritual around which all else revolved is our starting point.

The Medieval Mass

The Mass was the most important ritual in the medieval church. In Reformation England, however, its celebration was proscribed and, in some instances, punishable by death. Despite such injunctions, it was still celebrated fervently in recusant circles. At the moment of the elevation, the viewer gazed upon the Eucharistic host presented as the transubstantiated, living flesh of Christ. Through this ritual the believer was made to understand that souls could be saved by Christ's sacrifice. Thus the Mass was associated with intercession and the safeguarding of the soul after death. A common strategy for intercession was the chantry - the establishment of Masses to be sung for a specified number of days, or in some instances, in perpetuity for an individual or, in the case of guilds and fraternities, for a group of individuals.

Intercessory Masses were known from early times. St. Gregory (540-604) established what has been termed the "trental," a series of thirty intercessory Masses that was well received in England. The "trental" appears as part of the memorial liturgy in the *Regularis Concordia* composed at Winchester by the reforming bishop Aethelwold in the mid tenth century (Symons). The practice continued throughout the Middle Ages as exemplified by the will of Edward Curteys of 1413, requesting a "Gregrestrental" to be celebrated after his death in the church of St. Cuthbert, Wells (Weaver 1901, 65). The numbers could be multiplied; in 1417 Richard Weyvyle requested 3,000 Masses to be said for his soul in the three days immediately following his death (Weaver 1903, 80). Founders undoubtedly influenced the form and location of their respective chapels and chantries and also the liturgy performed within them. For example, Thomas Lord Burgh of Gainsborough, Lincolnshire, was able to specify which Masses he wished to be performed at his chantry altar; namely to the Holy Trinity (Sunday); Holy Spirit (Monday); Mary Magdalene (Tuesday); Requiem (Wednesday); All Saints (Thursday); Jesus (Friday) and the Blessed Virgin on Sunday (Richmond 1994, 198-9). In contrast, the will of John Maudeley of Wells on the eve of the Reformation in 1540 specified "a virtuous priest" to perform for a specific period a "Masse of Requiem and Masse of (the) fyve Wounds with this psalme 'miserere mei Deus' and 'De Profundis'," as well as every Friday to sing psalms of the Passion, and David's psalm once in Advent and once at Lent (Weaver 1903, 59).

Devotional objects were vital to the setting of the Mass and documentary evidence provides some information about the nature of these objects. Most tellingly, there were not just service objects for the liturgy, but decorative ones as well (though one may argue that most fulfilled both functions). See in this catalogue the entries on Liturgical Vessels and Liturgical Textiles. For example, at Bridgwater, Somerset, such decorative textiles included vestments of black, blue and white damask, a cope of red silk, a chasuble of green silk and various embroidered altar and wall hangings (Jones, 102). At Mere, Wiltshire, items included black vestments with ostrich feathers (Jackson, 326).

During the Mass, particularly chantry Masses, the prayers of the community were valued; the more prayers the more efficacious the ritual. The public, in turn, benefited from increasingly elaborate and plentiful ceremonies and what they felt were the powers of the Eucharistic ritual. The *Lay-Folks Mass Book* written by John Myrc in the fifteenth century mentions, among other benefits of the Mass, protection from sudden death, from ageing, and lack of food (Peacock, 10). Masses could also be said for

2. Decoration on outside of Bromham parish church, Wiltshire, detailing angels with Instruments of the Passion juxtaposed with heraldic devices. Photo: Simon Roffey

3. East end at Old Basing church, Hampshire, showing chancel and flanking chapels. The addition of such chapels in the late medieval period greatly expanded public space whilst introducing new and varied liturgies. Photo: Simon Roffey

protection against storms, trouble of the heart and temptations of the flesh (Warren 1913). Such expected benefits indicate a belief in the ability to influence both natural and personal predicaments through prayer. The rituals united all levels of worshippers; "the mystic and the irretrievably mundane, the devout individualist and the communal fanatic" (Bossy 1991, 148). Transubstantiation itself offered not only the potential of salvation, but also the very act itself of the bread turning to flesh offered a very real message of transformation. One could aspire to change. The Mass therefore embodied a message both inspirational and relevant to all.

Lay Devotion and Communality

The late-medieval era was a period of demographic change and parish churches were expanding. Outstanding examples of parish churches of this era, such as at Southwold and Lavenham, Suffolk, and the smaller-scale Bromham in Wiltshire, attest to both the wealth and growing social aspirations of the laity, and also to communal pride expressed in the desire to use architecture, light and space to provide a fitting aesthetic context for divine worship (fig. 2). There was a concerted attempt to provide more church space for augmented services.

Some have argued that such space was created and decorated by a clerical and lay elite primarily for their own

4. The squint. This architectural feature facilitates visual access between various parts of the church. This example from Holy Trinity, Long Melford, a double squint provides a view to Clopton chapel and the High Altar. Photo: Virginia Raguin

CULTURAL CONTEXT

social and spiritual benefit. The presence of personal gifts, often embellished with patronal signatures, and the foundation of chantries and so-called private chapels do much to support this over-simplification. Indeed, some well-known studies have tended to emphasize that religious practice in medieval parish churches was an increasingly privatized affair, the general laity providing a largely passive supporting role (e.g. Cross 1976; Richmond 1984). Such studies often neglect links between elite and common religious practice or ignore religion at a common level (Thomas; Cross 1976). Recent historians, however, have attempted to re-address this imbalance (Scarisbrick; Burgess 1985, 1991, and 1996; Duffy 1992; Kumin 1996). In particular, Eamon Duffy has argued for the widespread appeal of late medieval popular Catholicism, maintaining that "no substantial gulf existed between the religion of the clergy and the educated elite on the one hand, and that of the people at large on the other" (Duffy 1992, 2). Topographical arrangements in churches, recent research has shown, included strategic location of tombs and altars, devotional architecture, and squints providing visual access (Roffey 2004b; Roffey, *in prep*). Rather than imagine a reductive hegemony, we now consider a complex network of interactions and visual relationships within the parish church, bonding the community in its religious practices as sacred areas of the church were linked into a common and universal structure.

5. Once highly embellished, this defaced pier at Lacock, Wiltshire, replete with painted creatures attests to the intricacy of artistic detail in the medieval period. Photo: Simon Roffey

Earlier scholarship such as Kathleen Wood-Legh and Christopher Brooke saw these chapels as monuments to individualism claiming that they were "off-limits" to the general laity. Others continued to see them as primarily status symbols demonstrating the power and prestige of local families (French 2001, 155, 171). Chapel and chantry foundations, however, operated in a much wider social and religious context. They embodied, in a sense, both individual *and* communal motives typical of society in the medieval period (Kumin 1996, 160). It is more reasonable to see chantry foundation, particularly multiple chantry foundation, as fostering a "communal self-regard producing a parish which in its own estimation mattered" (Burgess 1996, 252).

Many medieval churches reserved significant space for chapels and chantries. At St. Thomas's, Salisbury, there were fourteen chantry priests attached to the church by 1394 (Tatton-Brown, 104). This implies a potentially crowded and busy church in which lay access and participation could hardly have been restricted in practice. In a smaller town like Old Basing, Hampshire, the north and south Paulet chapels are over two-thirds the size of the nave (fig. 3). Furthermore, the space and size of some chapels indicate that they were built to accommodate more than a single priest and a few exclusive individuals. In the majority of cases, it was the custom to make chapels visible from public areas of the church, through location or by positioning squints to allow views of the respective altars (fig. 4). Such evidence argues that intercessory rituals enacted in such chapels were tied into the general "network" of rituals within the parish church itself, such as those celebrated within other chapels and especially at the high altar (Roffey 2004a, Roffey *in prep).*

Chapel foundation could have additional benefits. The placement of some chapels provided for the construction of a porch, thereby creating an extra-liturgical area for important public rites such as marriages and funerals. In certain instances, chapel construction also led to the embellishment or rebuilding of the parish church and the addition of vestries serving the parish church may have been an integral component of chapel foundation. At Devizes, Wiltshire, the provision for an anchorite cell appears to have been integral with the construction of the Lamb chapel.

Far from being vain ostentation, the decoration of many churches collaborated in a "sophisticated intellectual construction containing a vision of heaven, and a celebration of the history of salvation" (Goodall, 165). Decoration defined sacred space, providing a metaphysical setting for the ritual and a colorful and emotive context for both private and public piety. One need only enter a modern Eastern Orthodox church or a Tibetan Buddhist temple, for example, to see the effects that light, color, display and symbolism can have on ritual and on the way that ritual and devotional objects are perceived by those observing or performing. The structure of medieval churches was partly devised to induce a mood of reverence, to refine or sharpen the senses, to engage the emotions with the spiritual practices enacted, and to provide a ritual backdrop to liturgical practice. In the parish church of Lacock, Wiltshire, the inside of the Sharrington chapel is decorated with sculpted and painted images of plants and flowers and small animals that hang and crawl around its arches, piers and shafts (fig. 5). Such an effect suggests an attempt to evoke a natural forest glade within the chapel, targeting a particular aesthetic response. Many other chapels contain varied embellishments in the form of canopied niches (no doubt once containing devotional images), sculptures and wall paintings. They enhanced the complex rituals within, subtly lit by lights and scented with incense, such as the frankincense used at Bramley, in Hampshire, and the "pepper" at Stoke Charity, in the same county, referred to in churchwardens' accounts. Liturgical and devotional objects were undeniably a part of these settings to witness cupboards (aumbries) in and around churches and evidence for hangings, such as the iron riddles found at Boldre and Stoke Charity, Hampshire. Significantly, the Lady Chapel at Corsham, Wiltshire contains a large table tomb, whose very size suggests its dual use as both a tomb and a table for the display and use of devotional objects.

Sound was also another important element of late medieval religious practice. It is likely that most Masses would have been sung (instead of recited), providing a "compound mnemonic effect" to church ritual that would act as the verbal element to the highly visual setting. "Unadorned plainsong" has been characterized as "the backbone of the liturgy and was customary on all parish churches" (Kumin 2001, 70). Instrumental music, however, was also practiced; some chantry priests, in particular, were able to sing and play, particularly organs. At Bodminch, Cornwall, a pair of organs was installed in 1472. At the parish church of St. Neots, Cambridgeshire, a will of 1531 provides a bequest to the church organ for liturgical texts of a gradual and a breviary. In the south of England, we find documentary evidence for organs for Andover, Hampshire, although archaeological evidence is unsurprisingly scant. A particularly early Post-Reformation example survives at Brympton, Somerset, and may arguably (and admittedly tenuously) represent an early musical emphasis in this area.

Visual Arts

Within medieval religious practice all the senses were often called into play – the hearing of bells and litanies, the smell of incense, the aural murmuring of supplications, and the feeling of sensuous discomfort at kneeling during the performance of Mass. However, the primary means of communication was through sight; a particular emphasis in lay devotion rested upon seeing (Roffey 2004 a; Roffey *in prep*). Visual communion with the host at the elevation at Mass was crucial, but more indirect visual contact with the architectural elements of the church itself, images, paintings and memorials, was also important. The use of sculpture and painting in chapel elaboration may have also helped illustrate the wonder and mystery of medieval Christian theology to a largely illiterate laity. The imagery provided a highly colorful and symbolic visual context for the transmission of traditional devotional allegories. At Ashton, Devon, for

6. Leigh chapel, Godshill, Isle of Wight, showing Christ on the Lily Cross. Photo: Simon Roffey

screen to north Chudleigh chantry is adorned with images of the Annunciation, Visitation and, unusually, the Transfiguration. Similarly, the decorated recess canopy with images of the Adoration of the Magi and Annunciation, found in the north chapel at Brympton as well as on the elaborate though defaced "Jesse" reredos in the south "Tanner" chapel at St. Cuthbert's, Wells, may have had a similar effect.

Colin Richmond has claimed that the "physical and psychological and material and spiritual" aspects of such representations "should not be distinguished" (Richmond 1994, 188). In this sense the images were viewed as very real and, more importantly, very responsive figures - objects of prayer, hope, and wonder. They were essentially archetypes, containing levels of meaning within their histories and emblems that reified their powers of healing and salvation. The Virgin Mary, for example represented one who had "experienced to a preternatural degree the sorrows of a mother, yet had not been broken by them" (Richmond 1994, 188). Her humanity combined with the perceived sensitivity of her femininity to make her particularly accessible for intercessional prayers. The power of these archetypes extended beyond intercession and security to function as paradigms for ways of living a good life.

The survival of image corbels and niches, such as the elaborate canopied niche arrangement on the reredos of the chapel of St. Katherine, at St. Cuthbert's Wells, is rare. At Yatton, Somerset, the churchwardens' accounts for 1503 mention payment for a "carved corbel" in the north transept that "Katherine now stands on." It is possible that this is one of the surviving "carved" or canopied niches on the east wall of the north chapel. Other survivals are the images of St. Stephen, St. Elmo, St. John the Baptist and St. Augustine in the chapel of St. Nectan at Cheddar, Somerset. The presence of these saints is of particular interest with regard to communal piety. The head of St. John has been associated with Eucharistic practice, whilst St. Elmo, as well as being a safeguard against the perils of sea travel, is also traditionally associated with protection from sudden death. Similarly, some fifteenth-century sources associate the *Deus Propicius Esto* prayer with St. Augustine, a prayer whose recitation will protect from fire, water and sudden death. Such images and their various implications may have been particular relevant to the laity, offering security and protection from very real fears. The position of these images also suggests that they are consciously placed to be in full view (and therefore accessibility) of the laity in the nave. The sculpted image of St. Gregory celebrating Mass in the Hampton chapel at Stoke Charity is crudely executed in cheap and brittle local chalk. It is interesting to surmise that this may have been made by a local artisan, perhaps as a physical act of personal piety. Like the examples from Cheddar above, this was also placed in a highly publicly visible area in the north-east corner of the chapel.

Image niches in many chapels were consciously positioned to make them visible to the laity in aisle and naves. For example, the niche in the Darrell chapel at Ramsbury, Wiltshire, and the image of the "Mass

7. Window from West Lavington church, Wiltshire, showing gothic D's of Dauncey family juxtaposed with chalice and Eucharist. Photo: Simon Roffey

of St. Gregory" in the angle of the north and east walls in the Hampton north chapel at Stoke Charity enable them to be seen primarily by the laity in the nave. As mentioned earlier, St. Gregory was instrumental in the development of early intercessory rituals. He was also the subject of a popular story of a vision of the suffering Christ. As Gregory celebrated Mass, Christ actually appeared above the altar to convince an unbelieving bystander of the reality of the transubstantiation. Images of the miracle were widely disseminated, accompanied by a powerful indulgence granting remission of many years of suffering in Purgatory. St. Gregory would thus have been particularly relevant in the context of chantry practice with its focus on intercessory Masses.

In all of these cases, the relationship is reciprocal. Devotional features consciously or unconsciously involved the viewer in intercessory rituals or prayers, provoking the conscious observer to become a subconscious participant in the act of intercession. This is attested by rare surviving images in painted form. The north wall of the chancel south aisle at St. Thomas's, Salisbury, Wiltshire, depicts scenes from the life of the Virgin, while that at Great Chalfield, in the same county, depicts St. Katherine. Scenes of the life of St. Gregory appear on the east wall of the Hampton chapel at Stoke Charity. On the east wall of the Leigh chapel at Godshill is an unusual and elaborate painting of Christ on the lily cross, an image that may be a form of rebus. Is the "lily" a play on words for the name Leigh, such as Leigh, Leigh' or "le Leigh?" If so, then this depiction becomes more obvious, in that it identifies the chapel's founder whilst juxtaposing his name with that of the image of Christ - a potentially powerful intercessory tool (fig. 6).

Few medieval stained glass windows survive in parish churches. One unique example, however, is in the parish church of St. Mary in Fairford, Gloucestershire. Here, a rare set of twenty-eight large stained glass windows has remained virtually intact and constitute the only set in any English parish church to escape the ravages of the Reformation. At West Lavington, Wiltshire, the west window of the Dauncey chapel contains a small stained glass panel, which is of particular interest. Although the glass has been doubtlessly moved to its present position, its imagery is intact and depicts the ornate gothic "D" of the founder's family name juxtaposed with a chalice and Eucharistic bread (fig. 7). This may suggest an earlier intercessory function for what has been termed a post-Reformation private chapel for the local Dauncey family.

CHANGE AND CONTINUITY AT THE REFORMATION

The Reformation of the English church took place on four levels. *Prohibition:* proscription of the Mass, the official dissolution of chantries, legal proscription of lights, obits, intercession and prayers for the dead. *Iconoclasm:* the destruction of paintings, sculpture and glass. *Confiscation:* the appropriation of related goods of value as well as attached land endowments. Finally, *reorganisation*: the demolition or renegotiation of church space, including the obstruction and de-ritualising of former focal areas, ritual topography and communal accessibility (Roffey 2003). The effects of the Reformation were cataclysmic for traditional religion. At St. John's Glastonbury, Somerset, the loss included not just silver plate, vestments, carved seats and screens, but twenty-one chained books. At Nunney, Wiltshire, even the iron bars of the founder's tomb were considered for appropriation. At Bridgwater, Somerset, however, everything except a lone silver chalice had been spirited away by locals beforehand. The dissolution of the chantries at Mere, for example, meant that the dependent chapels at Zeals, Deverell and "Chadenwych" (Shapwick?) could no longer function (Godfrey, 100).

The Reformation therefore dramatically changed the nature of communal and individual piety at a local level. The color, sound, light, and spiritual vibrancy that parish churches had provided popular religious practice was extinguished. The emotive focus of the chapels and altars, adorned with burning lights and colorful images, and the elaborate and formal Eucharistic rituals were forbidden. The artifacts represented in this exhibition therefore offer a precious insight into a lost heritage. But more than this, they show the resilience of the human spirit when faced with overwhelming difficulties. These objects bear witness to the attempts made to try to sustain some link with a spiritual tradition whose vitality was being suppressed by the forces of perceived progress and change. They are therefore to be seen as not only works of art in their own right, but also as symbols of defiance, of resistance and of continuity rooted in long-standing religious tradition. And it is this, this new spiritual context, which can act as a source of inspiration in our modern world.

Bibliography

Blair, John and Golding, Brian, eds. *The Cloister and the World: Essays in Medieval History in Honour of Barbara Harvey.* Oxford: Clarendon Press, 1996.

Bossy, John. "Christian Life in the Later Middle Ages: Prayers," in *Transactions of the Royal Historical Society*, sixth series, 1 (1991): 137-48.

Brooke, Christopher, N. L. *Medieval Church and Society.* London: Sidgwick and Jackson, 1971.

Burgess. Clive. "For the Increase of Divine Service: Chantries in the Parish of Late Medieval Bristol," *Journal of Ecclesiastical History* 36 (1985): 46-65.

Burgess, Clive (1991) "Strategies for Eternity: Perpetual Chantry Foundation in Late Medieval Bristol," in Harper-Bill: 1-33.

Burgess, Clive (1996) "St Mary-at-Hill, London," in Blair and Golding: pp. 247-72.

Cross, Claire. *Church and People 1450-1660*, London: Collins, 1976.

Dobson, Barrie, ed. *The Church: Patronage and Politics in the Fifteenth Century*, Gloucester: Alan Sutton, 1984.

Foster, Andrew. "Churchwardens' Accounts of Early Modern England and Wales: Some Problems to Note, but Much to be Gained," in French, Gibbs and Kumin: pp. 74-94.

French, Katherine, *The People of the Parish: Community Life in a Late Medieval English Diocese*, Pennsylvania: University of Pennsylvania, 2001.

French, Katherine, Gary Gibbs, and Beat Kumin, eds. *The Parish in English Life 1400-1600*. Manchester: Manchester University Press, 1997.

Gaimster, David and Roberta Gilchrist, eds. *The Archaeology of Reformation.* Society for Post-Medieval Archaeology, Monograph 1, London: Maney, 2003.

Godfrey, Charles. "The Chantries of Mere and their Priests," *Wiltshire Archaeological Magazine* 55 (1954): 153-160.

Goodall, John, A.A. *God's House at Ewelme:. Life, Devotion and Architecture in a Fifteenth Century Almshouse.* London: Ashgate Press, 2001.

Harper-Bill, Christopher, ed. *Religious Belief and Ecclesiastical Careers in Late Medieval England.* Woodbridge: Boydell, 1991.

Horrox, Rosemary, ed. *Fifteenth Century Attitudes and Perceptions of Society in Late Medieval England.,* Cambridge: Cambridge University Press, 1994.

Hutton, Ronald. *The Rise and Fall of Merry England: The Ritual Year 1400-1700,* Oxford: Oxford University Press, 1994.

Jackson, James. "Wiltshire Chantry Furniture," *Wiltshire Archaeological Magazine* 22 (1885): 318-29.

Jones, William. "An Inventory of the Vestments and Belongings of "St Katherine's Ile" in the Church of Bridgwater," *Procs. Somerset Archaeological Society* 7 (1857): 100-105.

Kisby, Fiona, ed. *Music and Musicians in Renaissance Cities and Towns.* Cambridge: Cambridge University Press, 2001.

Kumin, Beat. *The Shaping of a Community: The Rise and Reformation of the English Parish, c. 1400-1560.* Hampshire: Scholar Press, 1996.

Kumin, Beat. "Mass, Morris and Metrical Psalms: Music in the English Parish Church", 1400-1600," in Kisby: pp. 70-82.

Peacock, Edward. *Instructions for Parish Priests, by John Myrc.* Early English Text Society Original Series 31, 1902.

Richmond, Colin (1984) "Religion and the Fifteenth-Century English Gentleman," in Dobson: pp. 195- 205.

Richmond, Colin (1991) "The English Gentry and Religion c.1500" in Harper-Bill: pp. 121-151.

Richmond, Colin (1994) "Religion" in Horrox: pp. 183-202.

Roffey, Simon (2003) "Deconstructing a Symbolic World: The Reformation and the English Medieval Parish Chantry," in Gaimster and Gilchrist: pp. 342-55.

Roffey, Simon (2004a) "Medieval Chantries and Chapels: An Archaeological Approach," *Church Archaeology* 5 (2004): pp. 62-68.

Roffey, Simon (2004b) *A Social Archaeology of Medieval Parish Church Chapels and Chantries: A Perspective from Southern and Western England,* Unpublished PhD. for University College Winchester.

Roffey (*in prep) Medieval Chapels and Chantries: An Archaeological Approach.* Boydell and Brewer.

Scarisbrick, Jack. *The Reformation and the English People.* Oxford: Clarendon Press, 1984.

Symons, Dom Thomas. *Regularis Concordia,* London: Thomas Nelson and Sons, 1951.

Tatton-Brown, Tim. "The Church of St. Thomas of Canterbury, Salisbury," *Wiltshire Archaeological Magazine* 90 (1997): 101-109.

Thomas, Ken. *Religion and the Decline of Magic.* London: Weidenfeld and Nicolson, 1971.

Warren, Frederick. *The Sarum Missal in English.* I and II, Alcuin Club Collection 11, 1913.

Weaver, Frederic. *Somerset Medieval Wills, 1383-1500.* Somerset Record Society 16, 1901.

Weaver, Frederic. *Somerset Medieval Wills, 1501-1530.* Somerset Record Society 19, 1903.

Wood-Legh, Kathleen, L. *Perpetual Chantries in Britain.* Cambridge: Cambridge University Press, 1965.

Picture and Policy: Contested Control of the Image

Virginia C. Raguin

In reviewing the tenacious nature of recusant attachment to the image, one may well reflect on the long tradition of Christianity and image making. From the third century, the image was an expected part of Christian self-identity as evidenced from the liberation themes in catacomb murals. With the official acceptance of the Christian religion under Constantine in the early fourth century, large scale mosaics proclaimed sacred history and doctrine. From the earliest years of Henry VIII's break with Rome, the visible external manifestation of English "otherness" was the repudiation of devotional images. Instances of iconoclasm had appeared in both official and transgressive circumstances in England for some time (Aston 1989; Davidson), but the attention that the monarchy brought to this question demonstrates how crucial picture became to national policy. Henry focused in 1538 on the image of the twelfth-century Thomas Becket (see in this catalogue "Relics and the Two Thomases) but all imagery was suspect, especially that of the pilgrimage and indulgence. The Royal Injunctions cautioned that "feigned images" that are "abused with pilgrimages or offerings of anything made thereunto" must be taken down and "henceforth no candles, tapers, or images of wax (ex votos) be set afore any image or picture" (Gee and Hardy, 277-78; for ex votos see Marks 2004, 212-15 and Marks and Williamson, 75).

With the ascent of Henry's son Edward VI in 1547, iconoclastic reformers became more influential in official policies towards the visual appearance of the old religion. Royal injunctions were issued, one explicitly mandating reformers to "destroy all shrines. . . pictures, paintings and all other monuments of feigned miracles. . . so that there remain no memory of the same in walls, glass-windows, or elsewhere within their church or houses" (Injunction 28: Marks 1993, 230). Some houses have explicit records of destruction. Norwich, the center of the wool trade of East Anglia, was wealthy enough to destroy rather than whitewash windows. (For whitewashing see Aston 1988, 260-61.) Faded whitewash remains on a fifteenth-century panel showing the symbol of the Trinity in the form of a shield (*scudum fidei*) now in the Walker Art Gallery, Liverpool. The 1547-52 Edwardian inventories for St. Mary Coslany in Norwich, for example, list "the glasying of fyften windows with new glass" (Cooper 368; Marks 1993, 231). Yet apparently enough remained to incur additional despoliation in the 1640s during the Commonwealth, necessitating window repairs to many churches, including St. Benedict, St. Gregory, St. Peter Mancroft, and St. Stephen (Cooper, 367-69).

During the reign of Elizabeth, whose own views were not iconoclastic, moderation often prevailed (Aston 1988, 294-342). In 1561, however, she acquiesced to pressure and issued an order against any surviving crucifixes by demanding that rood lofts must be taken down to the beam (Ibid., 312-3). Outright destruction was discouraged. Indeed many stained glass windows remain intact partially because of the expense of replacement. When repair was essential, however, the windows could then be replaced with clear glass. Thus, the espousal of progressive decay was recognized as an efficient means of removing imagery.

There was considerable divergence in practice. One need only look at the deeply moving poetry of George Herbert (1593-1633), arguably a committed member of the Reformed Church as a Fellow of Trinity College, Cambridge and Public Orator of the University for seven years. In *The Temple*, published 1633, he praised the British Church, where "beauty . . . takes up her place." Rome had too "long kissed her painted shrines" while the iconoclastic Protestant church "wholly goes on th' other side." The poems are symbolically arranged as ecclesiastic ritual and church furnishings, including porch, altar, floor, tombs, music, lock and key, and particularly windows, where it is clear that he is speaking about storied windows. Man is but a "brittle crazie glasse" who through the grace of God can "be a window." Herbert is clearly referring to traditional fired, painted windows as he states "But when thou (God) dost anneal in glasse thy storie, Making thy life to shine within" we are transformed. Herbert suggests that "colours and light . . . When they combine and mingle, bring Doctrine and life" more effectively than simple words that enter the ear but do "not conscience ring."

Herbert's verses reflect a brief revival, leading up to the so-called Laudian reform, under James I (reigned 1625-37), although Herbert is clearly distanced from the restoration-minded clergy of the era (Doerksen, 56-70). William Laud became archbishop of Canterbury in 1633 and clergy who shared his views on the centrality of the sacraments and liturgy redecorated many churches. In the trial of the politically rigid archbishop in 1644, he was accused of "countenancing the setting up of image in churches and the places of religious worship. That in his own chapel in Lambeth (London) he had repaired the Popish windows" (Marks 1993, 237). Two brothers, Bernard and Abraham van Linge, natives of Emden, Holland were active at this time. They supplied a number of windows, particularly in Oxford Colleges: Queens, 1635; Christ Church, ca. 1635; Balliol, 1637; and University, 1641. A panel by Abraham van Linge showing the Deposition from Hampton Court, Herefordshire displays both pot-metal and white glass with enamel paints (Victoria & Albert Museum C.62-1927). It is signed and inscribed: "The truth hereof is historicall devine and not superstistious Anno Domini 1629." Clearly the artist and his patron wanted to distance themselves from any suggestion of Popery or false religion. The image of Christ taken down from the cross is based on a fifteenth-century painting by the Lowlands artist, Rogier van der Weyden.

During the Civil War and the Commonwealth, (1640s-1660), vigorous elimination of imagery was again pursued, especially the imagery recently installed by the Laudian movement (Aston 1988, 93; Cooper). With the armed conflict, Oliver Cromwell's troops often engaged in random acts of destruction. The taking of Peterborough resulted in the almost complete destruction of the windows of the cloister and the church of the cathedral. Later, possibly exaggerated, accounts speak of Cromwell himself getting a ladder and breaking down a little image of the crucifixion he saw left over high up in the church loft. York was fortunate. When it was taken by Puritan troops under Sir Thomas Fairfax in July 1644, the Minster and parish churches were protected from destruction. Yet, more systematic campaigns were prevalent elsewhere. In 1643 laws mandated, again, the destruction of superstitious imagery, including crucifixes and pictures of the Virgin, the Holy Trinity and the saints. William Dowsing left a journal of his vigorous breaking of windows and other forbidden items such as the inscriptions on sepulchral monuments of "pray for us."

In Norfolk, at a parish church in Gorleston (Norfolk) near Yarmouth a vivid account remains of the work of Francis Jessup, Dowsing's deputy:

> In the chancel, as it is called, we took up twenty brazen superstitious inscriptions, *Ora pro nobis, &c.;* broke twelve apostles, carved in wood, and cherubims, and a lamb with a cross; and took up four superstitious inscriptions in brass, in the north chancel, *Jesu filii Dei miserere mei, &c.*; broke in pieces the rails, and broke down twenty-two popish pictures of angels and saints. We did deface the font and a cross on the font; and took up the brass inscription there, with Cujus animæ propitietur Deus, and 'Pray for ye soul,' &c., in English. We took up thirteen superstitious brasses. Ordered Moses with his rod and Aaron with his mitre, to be taken down. Ordered eighteen angels off the roof, and cherubims to be taken down, and nineteen pictures on the windows. . . .There were six superstitious pictures, one crucifix, and the Virgin Mary with the infant Jesus in her arms, and Christ lying in a manger, and the three kings coming to Christ with presents, and three bishops with their mitres and crosier staffs, and eighteen Jesuses written in capital letters, which we gave orders to do out. A picture of St. George, and many others which I remember not, with divers pictures in the windows, which we could not reach, neither would they help us to raise ladders; so we left a warrant with the constable to do it in fourteen days. We brake down a pot of holy water, St. Andrew with his cross,

and St. Catherine with her wheel; and we took down the cover of the font, and the four evangelists, and a triangle for the Trinity, a superstitious picture of St. Peter and his keys, an eagle, and a lion with wings. In Bacon's aisle was a friar with a shaven crown, praying to God in these words, Miserere mei Deus, - which we brake down. . . .We rent to pieces a hood and surplices. In the chancel was Peter pictured on the windows, with his heels upwards, and John Baptist, and twenty more superstitious pictures, which we brake: and IHS the Jesuit's badge in the chancel window (C. H. Evelyn White, 11).

What, if anything, filled this lacuna when imagery was suspect in religion? During Henry's reign and that of Edward and Mary, the Holbein-inspired Renaissance portrait gained great vogue. Holbein's majestic portrait shows Henry striding, corporeal, robust, and commanding three-dimensional space. The frail Edward is depicted with delicacy of youthful features. A portrait by Antonis Mor of Mary I, of 1554 (The Prado, Madrid: Howarth, 153) was executed a year after her accession to the throne. The artist was commissioned by Philip II of Spain as a prelude to the royal wedding, yet it follows Henry's strategy of self-representation. Its powerful realism depicting the broad forehead, resolute jaw, and undulating facial musculature proclaims Mary as her father's daughter. Given the lingering issue of Mary's birth from the discredited marriage with Catherine of Aragon (First Act of Succession, 1534: Gee and Hardy, 232-37) the paternal resemblance may have been an avowed goal. It was however, the style of portraiture repudiated by her sister Elizabeth.

Elizabeth adopted a deeply conservative, indeed even retrospective image: archaic, patterned, two dimensional, and hieratic, as Howarth phrases it, banishing "images of flesh and blood" (Howarth, 102). To the student of style and the concept of artistic progress, the backsliding during Elizabeth's reign, especially after the progressive work of Holbein whom Henry had rescued from commission-poor, Protestant Switzerland, the era seems a black hole of neglect. Her policies, however, articulate the traditional selection of style for its ability to serve the monarch. Philip II's patronage of Titian, or Henry's of Holbein was not different than Elizabeth's patronage of Nicolas Hilliard (1547-1619). The artist produced what was serviceable to the ruler: for Henry the cult of a male personality, for Philip, that of an international player, for Elizabeth, the substitution of the Virgin queen for the dethroned Virgin of Catholic tradition. Nowhere is this more evident than in Hilliard's *The Pelican Portrait* of about 1574 (The Walker Art Gallery, Liverpool). The queen is shown against a solid background, as in medieval miniatures, half length, and in three-quarter profile. Her face is a white mask, devoid of modeling. Her body, as well, is without spatial volume, allowing all attention to focus on the immensely complex

Abraham van Linge, *Deposition*, 1629, Hampton Court, Herefordshire. Victoria & Albert Museum, London. Courtesy of the Victoria & Albert Museum

embroidery, jewels, lace, brocade, and other fabrics of her costume. Pearls that drape her bodice became one of her cherished symbols, a motif demonstrated in the medieval poem *The Pearl*, where the purity and singularity are enhanced through both biblical and mundane cross references (Stanbury, 2-7, 11-17). For Elizabeth, the draping of the pearls recalls the manner in which statues were draped with rosary beads (Duffy 2002, 75-76), an association intensified by the Pelican Jewel. Elizabeth wears this image in the center of her chest, attention being directed to it by the position of her hand. The pelican was a highly recognizable medieval image, believed in times of stress to pierce its breast to feed its young with its own blood. It easily became a symbol of Christ's sacrifice during the Mass, giving his own blood to sustain his followers. Elizabeth adopted the symbol, placing herself as the pelican, sacrificing all, especially her virginity, to sustain her subjects.

Elizabeth's use of emblem and image, like her father's, was an official aspect of statesmanship. The spaces in the churches that traditionally held images of Christ and the saints, were "increasingly used to display images of royal arms or portraits of the Queen" (Tarlow, 112; Phillips, 118-21). The very nature of such paintings recalls devotional imagery, certainly depictions of the Virgin Mary, but also the even more potent image of Christ as Man of Sorrows. A rare surviving example from England dated about 1500 in St. Oswald's Church, Ashbourne (Derbyshire) (Marks and Williamson, 452-53, Cat. 345) shows the once ubiquitous devotional image with its indulgenced promise that veneration would reduce the time of Purgatorial suffering. The panel, probably one side of a folding altarpiece, shows Christ with hands folded across his chest, silhouetted against a gold and red tapestry background. This presentation derives

from a renowned mosaic icon in Santa Croce, Rome reputed to represent the miraculous image of the suffering Christ that St. Gregory saw when saying Mass (van Os, 106-13; DeLeeuw, 33-41). The paintings of Elizabeth would vary to emphasize different symbolic messages, but they unwaveringly present the timeless, unchanging image of medieval memory.

Elizabeth's portraits are ever youthful, as exemplified by *The Ermine Portrait* attributed to William Segar (1585, The Marquess of Salisbury, Howarth, 107-110). Although depicting the queen at the age of fifty, the portrait presents reddish curls framing a white, flawless face. The signature pearls are now massive, bunched strands across the bodice, encircling the waist, and branching out of the hair like the radiance of an aureole. The ermine is not a household pet but a symbol, playing on the belief that rather than accept uncleanness, the pure white ermine would rather shed its blood, obviously referring to Elizabeth's continued virginity.

Antonis Mor, *Mary I*, 1554, The Prado, Madrid. Photo: Art Resources

The Stuarts inaugurated a new policy in the arts, one more stylistically progressive and linked to the continent, where the monarchs sought to solidify legitimacy. James I patronized Rubens in creating the elaborate allegories for the ceiling of the new Inigo Jones Banqueting Hall at Whitehall to replace the one destroyed by fire in 1619. The paintings were finished after James's death, allowing his successor Charles I to execute an extraordinary cenotaph for the first Stuart monarch. Central to the program is the *Apotheosis of James I*, where the king enters the heavenly realm in a parallel to Christ ascending after his death witnessed by his followers. To the side are allegories of the union of the governments of England and Scotland and of the fruits of James's reign. The ceiling is one of the glories of any age and a triumph of Rubens's technical and organizational skills.

The funerary monument became a primary locus for England's political and aesthetic aspirations. Howarth comments that for families that rose as a result of the Tudor revolution over the medieval church, they saw within the "monuments to Norman or Angevin adventures lying in dusty silence in a parish church . . . reassurance and inspiration in the lethal world of the Tudor court" (Howarth, 153). Thus the increasing elaboration of the burial ceremony and the tomb monument, a tradition that continued under the Stuarts. Inigo Jones designed the *Catafalque of James I*, 1625, after Italian models, easily fusing the religious and the secular, the pagan and the Christian. Allegories of Religion and Peace as Roman matrons could easily have – given another course of history – functioned as saints Barbara or Katherine. The classical temple structure framed the life-size effigy of the dead king with moveable joints. The catafalque clearly resembled a tabernacle, but instead of the host, enshrined the represented body of the king.

This pattern of commissioning impressive funerary monuments can be seen in the Shireburn chapel in All Hallows Church, Mitton, some two miles northwest of Whalley. Images of the tombs that honor five generations of the family that built Stonyhurst were published by Thomas Dunham Whitaker in 1806 (CATALOGUE). The alabaster tomb with recumbent figures of Sir Richard and Dame Maude, daughter of Richard Bold, Sheriff

Nicolas Hilliard, *Elizabeth I: The Pelican Portrait*, ca. 1574, The Walker Art Gallery, Liverpool. Photo Courtesy The Walker Art Gallery

William Segar, attributed, Elizabeth I: The Ermine Portrait, 1585, Hatfield House. Marquess of Salisbury Photo: Courtesy The Marquess of Salisbury

of Lancashire has been attributed to Richard and Gabriel Roiley or Roiles of Burton about 1597. It continues the medieval format of husband and wife in elaborate dress "asleep." The four monuments along the wall were made by the sculptor William Stanton from the 1690s to 1703. These show a later style and fit with the tolerance for elaborate funerary imagery even as religious imagery was banished from worship space.

King Charles's level of patronage far exceeded his father's, and he early pursued a program of portraiture as carefully orchestrated as Elizabeth's. Anthony Van Dyck was the favored portraitist, established permanently at the court from 1632. Charles projected himself as sophisticated and virile, a man in control through images such as the justly famous *Charles I à la chasse*, 1635 in the Louvre (Howarth, 131). Here, as with Holbein, emblem could be fused with a bravura realism. *Charles I on Horseback* about 1637 (National Gallery, London) is directly inspired by the bronze equestrian sculpture of Marcus Aurelius, then still believed to be the first Christian emperor Constantine, recently relocated at papal insistence to Michelangelo's new Capitoline plaza. The imagery associated with Charles's beheading and subsequent martyr cult owes an enormous amount to Catholic tradition, but is a subject that can not be treated justly here. Suffice it to say that in a Europe still Catholic, and in a history still redolent with narrative of the life of Christ, this tradition reappeared in scenes that associated Charles with both Christ in the Garden of Gethsemane, the Presentation to the Jews (Ecce Homo), and his death.

Thus, we can contextualize the acquisition of oil paintings on copper in the Flemish manner by the Shireburn family of Stonyhurst. The family was distinguished and evidently as cultivated in their taste as they were loyal to Catholic tradition. In 1703, Sir Nicholas Shireburn, married to Catherine Charleton, received the Luttrell Psalter from Mary Widdrington Charleton, the wife of Sir Edward Charleton (Wormald and Wright, 167; Millar, 6, 7, 57). A lavishly illustrated manuscript, the Psalter was executed

Shirburn chapel, All Hallows Church, Mitton. from Thomas Dunham Whitaker LL.D. F.S.A., *An History of the Original Parish of Whalley and Honor of Clitheroe in the Counties of Lancaster and York,* London 1806.

PICTURE AND POLICY

shortly before 1340 for Sir Geoffrey Luttrell of Irnham in Lincolnshire. The manuscript had evidently been protected from royal censure by Catholic families beginning with Lord William Howard of Naworth (1563-1640) whose signature appears on the opening folio. Patronage and protection extended to the acquisition of new works as well as the preservation of the old.

Operating in seventeenth-century England, the Shireburns were part of a society where Lowlands' illusionism was accepted – indeed patronized – at the highest levels. Symbolic representation, in painting and masque were standard elements of royal policy. Churches, however, were embellished with plaques of the Lord's Prayer and Ten Commandments (for Elizabethan Commandment Boards, see Aston 1988, fig. 16 and Marks 2005, fig. 173), but pictures, except of the memorial portrait, were avoided. Catholic countries, such as the Southern Low Countries, France, and Italy were rich with images of the saints, miracles, and stories from the Bible. Stonyhurst, then the country seat of the Shireburn family, had a chapel that served a local populace as well as the family. Its 1713 inventory listed two "large black and white" images flanking the altar. These were presumably prints.

The only paintings in the Shireburn Chapel (as listed in the 1713 inventory) were of small dimension (about 12 x 10 in.), oil paintings on copper. It is tempting to surmise that they may have been acquired by Richard Shireburn (d. 1689) who had been educated on the continent at St. Omers. His Catholic sympathies were well known since he was imprisoned at the time of the Popish Plot and also arrested under William III, dying after a year of incarceration in Manchester jail. An alternative conjecture is that they were acquired as "antiques," older objects by Richard's son Nicholas (d. 1717) who spent lavishly on the embellishment of the

Anthony Van Dyck, *Charles I on Horseback,* ca. 1637, National Gallery, London. Photo: Art Resources

house and its gardens (Muir, 48-52). At the same time that Nicholas was devoting the staggering sum of £1547 on domestic renovations, he commissioned William Stanton (1639-1705) to carve the series of Shireburn funerary monuments in All Hallows, Minton. One of the most sensitive was that of his ancestor-founder of the chapel Richard and his second wife, Isabella, about 1699. Stanton was a part of family of sculptors located in Holborn who produced a large body of work, especially after the revival of decorative sculpture after 1660 under the Restoration. The monument of Richard and Isabella is an altar tomb, one of the last to continue the medieval tradition of recumbent figures of the deceased, a testimonial to Catholic memories of ancient forms (Whinney, 64).

The paintings show the influence of Anthony Van Dyck (1599-1641) and Flemish traditions of narrative painting. The subjects include the Life of Christ, beginning with the Adoration of the Shepherds, Circumcision, Flight into Egypt with the Holy Family Resting, Finding of the Boy Jesus in the Temple, Christ saying Goodbye to his Mother,

Christ Taken Down from the Cross, and Christ greeting Mary Magdalene after the Resurrection (Noli me Tangere). Veneration of the Virgin is seen in an image of the Assumption of the Blessed Virgin and Our Lady of Sorrows with seven swords piercing her breast, corresponding to the tradition of the Seven Sorrows. Pious tradition encouraged believers to try to empathize with the Virgin's human emotions when she participated in the Presentation in the Temple, Flight into Egypt, and Finding the Boy Jesus in the Temple, and as she witnessed Christ Carrying the Cross, the Crucifixion, the Descent from the Cross, and the Ascension when Christ finally leaves her. Above the suffering Virgin is Veronica's veil with the bloodied face of Christ carried by angels. Christ also appears as the Man of Sorrows. The saints' representations include two images of St. Jerome, and the Martyrdom of Thomas Becket, the feast removed from public devotion by Henry VIII, as demonstrated in the printed Books of Hours included in this exhibition. Many of the images seem to correspond to Jesuit traditions of spirituality. The importance of the Circumcision, the ritual at which Jewish males were given their names, relates to the veneration of the Name of Jesus by the Society of Jesus. At the top of the image, in a blaze of light is the sacred monogram the IHS, the emblem of the Society.

William Stanton, *Sir Richard and Isabella* ca. 1699, Shireburn chapel, All Hallows Church, Mitton. Photo: A. F. Kersting

PICTURE AND POLICY

CATALOGUE

Paintings of the Life of Christ, Saints, and Devotional Images

Oil on copper
333 Noli me Tangere 12 x 10 in. (30.5 x 25.5 cm.)
317 Flight into Egypt- Holy Family Resting 11 ¾ x 9 in. (30 x 22.9 cm.)
326 Finding of Boy Jesus in the Temple 11 ¾ x 9 in. (30 x 22.9 cm.)
332 Circumcision 11 ½ x 8 ½ in. (29.2 x 21.6 cm.)
325 Christ says Goodbye to his Mother 8 x 12 in. (20.3 x 30.5 cm.)
311 Adoration of the Shepherds 11 ½ x 8 ¾ in. (29.2 x 22.2 cm.)
370 Deposition 13 x 11 in. (33 x 28 cm.)
346 Assumption of the Blessed Virgin 6 ⅞ x 5 ¾ in. (17.4 x 14.6 cm.)
356 Martyrdom of Thomas Becket 11 ¾ x 8 ¾ in. (30 x 22.2 cm.)
312 Our Lady of Sorrows 11 ½ x 8 ½ in. (29.2 x 21.6 cm.)
32 Our Lady of Sorrows 15 x 12 in. (38 x 30.5 cm.)
357 St. Jerome 5 ¾ x 4 in. (13.5 x 10.2 cm.)
Low Countries, Antwerp? mid 17th century
Stonyhurst College, Lancashire

The Shireburn family may have been familiar with Van Dyck's style, as he was appointed the Court Painter of England in 1632. The works echo the artist's lesser-known historical and religious works, such as the *Lamentation over Christ* (Ashmolean Museum, Oxford, ca.1616) and *St. Augustine in Ecstasy* (Church of St. Augustine, Antwerp, 1628). The handling of flesh, pale round faces with chubby rosy cheeks, is most notably characteristic for both bodies of work. Limbs peek through flowing garments, exposing curvy, softly modeled musculature and a shiny pink glow. This is exemplified in the *Seven Sorrows of the Virgin*, particularly in the plump, rounded faces and bodies of the angels at the top that recall the cherubs in *St. Augustine*. We can see this same soft modeling in the *Circumcision*, echoing that in Van Dyck's *Lamentation*. Colors are muted; rather than bright reds or stark yellows, cool blues, greens and burgundies dominate a silvery pallete. This echoes the cool tonality of Van Dyck's works from his post-Italy Second Antwerp period of 1626-32 when the *St. Augustine* was painted. Although both sets of work often present us with darkly muddled, undefined backgrounds, neither uses the harsh lighting of Italian Baroque tenebrism. Instead, they often employ diffused white light with an unclear light source.

Coloring and plasticity of drapery are hallmarks of both the Shireburn and Van Dyck works, exemplified by Jesus's and Mary Magdalene's robes in the Shireburn *Noli me Tangere*, and Van Dyke's *Lamentation*. Both sets of drapery feature silvery highlights on jewel-toned material. The artists delight in the animated, flowing cloth as a dramatic and compositional device, using it to echo dynamic emotionality and to link figures together. The *Adoration of the Shepherds* and *Circumcision* feature a mass of dynamic figures in the bottom half of the frame centered around a sacred figure (the Christ Child in *Circumcision* and *Adoration*, the saint in *St. Augustine*), with a neutral dark background and a cloudburst of angels at top, and an ethereal glow above. Like Van Dyck's *Lamentation, the Deposition* presents a pale, limp Christ with visible wounds; he is portrayed rather realistically, neither idealized nor grotesque. The modeling of the wrapping cloth is much more delicately detailed in Van Dyck's, streaked with thin bright highlights, while the oil on copper uses thicker brushstrokes for broader shimmering effects. Although the artists share many similarities, Van Dyck lends more finesse to his paintings, flawlessly blending colors together in some areas, and letting individual brushstrokes stand out in others. An example of this can be found in the *St. Augustine,* where the realistic, detailed features of the saint stand in contrast to the more expressively conveyed angel wings above. **[Mallory Zeising]**

Hedley, Jo. *Van Dyck at the Wallace Collection*. London: Wallace Collection, 1999.

Larsen, Erik. *17th Century Flemish Painting*, Freren, Germany: Luca Verlag, 1985.

Shireburn Chapel, Mitton, from *An History of the Original Parish of Whalley and Honor of Clitheroe in the Counties of Lancaster and York*
Thomas Dunham Whitaker LL.D. F.S.A.
Second edition, London 1806
Stonyhurst College, Lancashire

The males of the Shireburn family passed down both first and last names. Sir Richard Shireburn (1523-1597) married Maude, daughter of Richard Bold, Sheriff of Lancashire. Maude remained publicly Catholic but Sir Richard followed the path of "Church Papists" professing the Queen's religion in public, and thus preserving his estates while supporting Catholics in his household and throughout his many estates. After Maude's death Richard married Isabella Wood. Richard bought up half the endowments of the Mitton chantry so that he could establish a family mausoleum on the north side of the chancel. Sir Richard and Dame Maude are shown as recumbent figures in an alabaster tomb attributed to Roiley of Burton. Sir Richard and Isabella are depicted in a later tomb carved in about 1699 by William Stanton. Their son Richard (d. 1629) married three times, each time choosing women with strong recusant backgrounds. He is portrayed in the family chapel with his wife Catherine, daughter of Lord Stourton. His son Richard (d. 1667) married first Elizabeth Molyneux, daughter of Sir Richard Molyneux of Sefton (no issue), noted as a recusant, for whom he was fined, and then Elizabeth, daughter of Thomas Walmesley of Dunkenhalgh. Their son Richard (d. 1689), educated at St. Omers, married Anne Cancefield. He was imprisoned at the time of the Popish Plot; he was also arrested under William III, the year of the Glorious Revolution of 1688, and died in Manchester jail the following year. His older brother Richard having died, Sir Nicholas Shireburn (d. 1717) inherited the Shireburn estate, marrying the wealthy Catherine Charleton, daughter of Sir Edward Charelton of Hesleyside. Their son Richard Francis died prematurely in 1702 at the age of eight, effectively ending the line. Their only surviving child, Mary, who married the

Finding of the Boy Jesus in the Temple, mid 17th century, Low Countries, Antwerp? Stonyhurst College, Inv. No. 326. Photo: Virginia Raguin

8th Duke of Norfolk, inherited Stonyhurst. She elected to be buried in the Shireburn chapel in Mitton. On her death in 1754, the estate passed to the family of Elizabeth Shireburn Weld (d. 1688), the sister of Nicholas who had married William Weld of Wilshire in 1658. The estate fell to Thomas Weld (1750-1810), who originally rented Stonyhurst to the Jesuits in 1794 for a peppercorn rent and then in 1809 made over the house and about 100 acres of land as a free gift "to the body" i.e. the Jesuits (Muir, 48-52; Stonyhurst Archives).
[Virginia C. Raguin and Janet Graffius]

Detail, candle bearer at Circumcision, mid 17th century, Low Countries, Antwerp? Stonyhurst College, Inv. N. 332. Photo: Virginia Raguin

Adoration of the Shepherds, mid 17th century, Low Countries, Antwerp? Stonyhurst College. Photo: Virginia Raguin

Martyrdom of Thomas Becket, mid 17th century, Low Countries, Antwerp? Stonyhurst College. Photo: Virginia Raguin

Trinity as Throne of Mercy, detail, Swansea Altarpiece, England, ca. 1450-80. Victoria and Albert Museum A.89-1919. Photo Victoria and Albert Museum

Narrative Altarpieces, Painted and Carved

Virginia C. Raguin

In the Middle Ages and the Renaissance, great art was public art. Even the most personal object, such as a prayer book, or apparel such as a vestment, was but one element in a coordinated public ceremony taking place within the most significant social locus of the community, the church (Marks and Williamson, 375-417). The development of Christian art was intimately tied to the liturgy, as the rituals changed to reflect the sequence of feasts during the liturgical calendar. This expectation of change extended to elements of fixed architecture within a building. Altarpieces, most commonly large pieces of church furniture raised up behind the altar, were designed to communicate imagery over long distances and to reflect changing aspects of the liturgy. Despite the fixed nature of painted panels or sculpted imagery as we view them in present-day museums, the altarpiece functioned as part of this changing and interactive display. They were built in sections, with folding doors that would be shut or open according to the seasons (Van Os, 136-56). Sculptors, painters, and architects most often worked together in planning and executing these large-scale decorative and didactic pieces.

England, with its considerable trade with the continent, apparently often relied on the painting tradition that flourished in the Low Countries and Germany, exemplified by the triptych showing saints and the donor couple Sir John Donne and his wife Elizabeth kneeling before the Virgin and Child (National Gallery NG 6275: Marks and Williamson, 79-80, 337, No. 213). Donne was frequently in the Low Countries on diplomatic embassies and commissioned the altarpiece in 1478 from Hans Memling who had settled in Bruges. The closed wings contain monochrome images of St. Christopher, patron saint of travelers, and St. Anthony Abbot, protector against the plague and other diseases, reasonable choices for a traveling diplomat. The interior is brilliantly festive with light blue wings for the angels and bright red for the Virgin and St. John the evangelist. Wall painting and stained glass, however, dominated domestic production for imagery actually set within buildings. Altarpieces, when not a flat panel, were frequently in alabaster, a medium for which England had become renowned (Cheetham 2003; Marks 2004, 234, 244). Whether three-dimensional or flat, however, the altarpiece was brightly colored.

Records have survived about the function of altarpieces within liturgical practice despite the heartbreaking level of destruction of these works. Often such descriptions do not appear to differentiate between

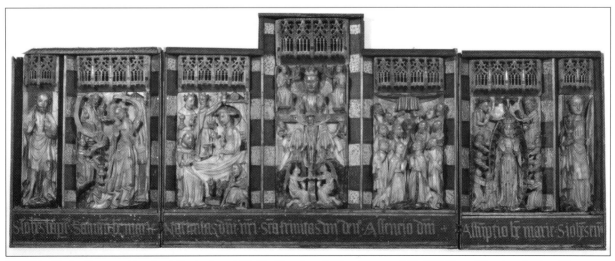

Joys of the Virgin, (Swansea Altarpiece), England, ca. 1450-80. Victoria and Albert Museum A.89-1919. Photo Victoria and Albert Museum

sculpture, painting, or a mixture of media. At Durham cathedral, for example, an altar dated to at least the early fifteenth century honored the cult of the Holy Name of Jesus (Pfaff 1970, 4, 62-83). On Fridays after evensong was sung "in ye quier" the monks added a special ceremony in the "bodye of ye church" stopping before the altar to sing the "Jesus Anthem." Situated in front of the rood screen that divided chancel from nave and in the space particularly accessible to the laity, the Jesus altar was equipped with special vestments. Its retable, the pictorial section above the altar table, had an elaborate series of images described as showing the:

> hole Passion of our Lord Jesus Christ most richlye and curiously sett furth in most lyvelie coulors all like the burni'ge gold, as he was tormented & as he honge on ye cross wch was the most lamentable sighte to beholde. The wch table was always lockt up but onely [seen] on principall daies. (Rites of Durham, written 1593, quoted in Pfaff 1970, 78-79)

The references to "lyvelie coulors all like the burni'ge gold" recall the alabaster altarpiece of the Joys of the Virgin, called the Swansea Altarpiece, probably executed 1450-80. The altarpiece was apparently an export to the continent and was bought in Munich by Lord Swansea in the 1830s (Victoria and Albert Museum A.89-1919; Marks and Williamson, 390-91, No 275). It consists of five narrative panels flanked by standing figures of John the Baptist and John the Evangelist. Traceried canopies in alabaster surmount all the panels and the wooden frame is provided with raised and gilded decorative gesso panels. The gilding of the alabaster and the bright color, however eroded, gives some indication of the original setting for the panel of the Adoration of the Three Kings from Stonyhurst.

Like a great deal of the imagery in the medieval church, the entire retable was only viewable on certain days. Its lavishness is indicated by the chronicler specifying that it presented the "hole Passion," exciting the imagination with rich color and narrative complexity – "curiously sett furth." By the ritual closing off of the image, the moment of viewing became a longed for and anticipated experience. Medieval imagery was enhanced through such interactive use. Veils were used during Lent, hung as Duffy explains: "within a foot of the ground, completely blocking the laity's view of the celebrant" performing the ritual of the Mass (Duffy 1992, 111). During seasonal liturgies such as the Passiontide, unveiling was a vital element of the ritual. On Good Friday a veiled Crucifix was presented to the people, and as the priests sang "Behold the wood of the cross" and the veil was lifted, three times, each time higher and higher creating the impression that Christ was appearing in the sacred space of the Church. The congregation then crept barefoot on their knees to kiss the foot of the cross (Duffy 1992, 29). The ceremony of "creeping to the cross" was a practice particularly condemned by Reformers beginning with the prohibitions under Henry VIII. Statues, as well, were given veils during Lent. Retable shutters, as described in the Jesus altar at Durham, could be folded to close off inner imagery, often the carved, three-dimensional elements invariably considered the most moving and the special target, therefore, for iconoclasts.

Narrative
Altarpieces

Adoration of the Three Kings, England, fifteenth century, Stonyhurst College, Lancashire. Photo Virginia Raguin

CATALOGUE

Adoration of the Three Kings
Alabaster, painted and gilded, 16 x 7 ½ in.
(40 x 24.7 cm.)
England, fifteenth century
Stonyhurst College, Lancashire, inv. no. 1794.22

This small panel once formed part of a large altarpiece, now lost, which would have comprised around a dozen or more such panels depicting pivotal scenes from the narrative of the Life of the Virgin, set into a painted and gilded wooden armature. This particular panel depicts the Adoration of the Magi, and is based both on the Gospels and on other medieval images. The post-partum Virgin, supine under an architectural canopy, props up a rather adult-looking Christ Child, who blesses the seated Magus at the right as he offers the Child a precious gift and doffs his crown in humility before the King of Kings. Below, the Ox and the Ass—representing the Old and New Testaments, respectively—feed from the manger, while the compressed figure of the ageing St. Joseph rests in the lower left corner of the composition. Two additional Magi gesture dramatically in conversation as they wait to present their gifts to Christ. This composition is typical of later fifteenth-century Adoration panels, and more than one hundred similar panels have recently been documented (Cheetham 2003, 83-87). There is some damage to the edges of the panel where it was pried out of its original setting.

Traces of paint remain in the contours of the panel, including red ochre on the inside of the kneeling king's crown and gilt on Mary's flaxen hair and the regal crowns of the two standing Magi. The attenuated, strangely elongated human figures, pulse-like eyes, and tight curls of head and facial hair are typical of late medieval English alabaster work, a vivid collective style that developed among the myriad sculptural workshops clustered in Midlands towns near alabaster quarries, particularly Nottingham. These centers were close-knit artistic milieus in which apprentices and journeymen circulated from shop to shop, master carvers inspected each others' wares informally and in guild settings, and artists sought to meet the visual expectations of demanding clients in a competitive marketplace. Alabaster altarpiece panels were mass-produced in large workshops that employed rote techniques, stock patterns (sometimes derived from Continental prints), and standard pictorial themes and color palettes to produce highly conventional products that varied little from decade to decade (Cheetham 1984, 18-20). Although, as with this example, such circumstances conspire to make surviving panels difficult to date and localize precisely—let alone attribute to an individual artist or workshop—this is not to say that Catholic viewers responded to these panels in purely conventional terms, or discounted them as mere ecclesiastical window dressing. In an age when most people lived their lives within a few miles of their birthplace, the painted, gilded altarpiece of the local parish church would have been one of the most salient visual narratives of biblical history, a natural focus of attention during the Mass.

The early provenance of the panel is uncertain, but it was displayed in an altarpiece in the private chapel of the Shireburn family whose mansion became Stonyhurst College in 1794. This was one of a group of 15 (?) when the Jesuit College took possession. The alabasters are mentioned in the 1713 inventory as being present in the chapel, a sumptuous and impressive room within the main house. It is possible that they were always located in the chapel, or they may have decorated the Shireburn chantry chapel nearby which was dissolved during the reign of Henry VIII. The Shireburns were among the most powerful of the Lancashire Catholic families and although frequently fined, they retained a certain level of immunity from more severe persecution by their status. During the English Civil War, the house was occupied briefly by Oliver Cromwell and it is highly likely that all external traces of Catholic worship would have been hastily removed and hidden prior to his arrival. There were a number of concealed hiding holes for priests in the house, including an escape tunnel leading from the sacristy of the chapel into the grounds.

Alabaster is a crystalline form of gypsum (hydrous calcium sulfate), the same material used in Plaster of Paris. Prized for its milky, translucent luster and its ease of carving—as well as its similarity to luxury media like Carrara marble and ivory—alabaster's fragility and solubility demanded that it be used exclusively indoors. In England, alabaster was used primarily for tomb effigies, altarpieces, and devotional sculpture. The earliest known alabaster tomb—that of Edward II in Gloucester Cathedral—has been dated to around 1330, and similar works continued to be manufactured well into the seventeenth century, largely escaping Reformation and Puritan iconoclasm. In contrast, Catholic altarpieces and devotional alabasters—produced in England from the mid-fourteenth century until the Reformation—were largely destroyed. No complete alabaster-panel altarpiece survives in situ in England, but exported examples have been found throughout Scandinavia, the Baltic, Germany, and southern Europe, demonstrating the fame and desirability of English alabasters during the fifteenth and early sixteenth centuries. More than fifty complete English alabaster altarpieces and around two thousand individual panels and figures survive to this day in public and private collections in Europe, North America, and Australia (Cheetham 1984, 11-12).

Stonyhurst College owns fifteen in total including a second panel of the Adoration—a horizontal composition featuring a midwife—dated to the second half of the fourteenth century (Cheetham 2003, "Life of the Virgin," fig. 47).

Cheetham, Francis. *English Medieval Alabasters, with a Catalogue of the Collection in the Victoria and Albert Museum.* Oxford: Phaidon and Christie's, 1984; reprint, Woodbridge, UK: Boydell Press, 2005

Hildburgh, W. L. "English Alabaster Tables of about the Third Quarter of the Fourteenth Century." *Art Bulletin* 32 (1950): 1-23, at p. 4, fig. 2; for photo

Illustrated Catalogue of the Exhibition of English Medieval Alabaster Work, Held in the Rooms of the Society of Antiquaries, 26th May-30th June, 1910. London: Society of Antiquaries, 1913, p. 57, no. 22, pl. XIII.

[Catalogue by Seth Hindin]

In elenatiõe cozpis rpi. fo.lrrriiij.

SACRAMENTŨ ALTARIS

Aue verum cozpus natum de ma
ria vgine. Uere passum immo=
latũ in cruce pzo homine. Cuius latus
perfozatũ vnda fluxit sanguine. Esto
nobis pzegustatũ moztis in eramine.

Monstrance with the Blessed Sacrament in procession: below, the Latin Hymn *Ave Verum Corpus natum de Maria Virgine. Vere passum immolatum in cruce pro homine. Cuius latum perforatum aqua fluxit et sanguine. Esto nobis praegustatum in mortis examine*. Hail, true Body, truly born of the Virgin Mary mild. Truly offered, wracked and torn, on the Cross for all defiled, from Whose love-pierced, sacred side flowed Thy true Blood's saving tide: be a foretaste sweet to me in my death's great agony. Book of Hours 1530 (Paris?), Stonyhurst College, S. 3/8, fol. 84

Liturgical Vessels

Virginia C. Raguin

Precious materials have been a part of Christian worship since at least the fourth century. One of the questions that a modern viewer inevitably asks is the value of such lavish expenditure on church vessels. Christ preached a simple life, he selected fishermen for his closest associates, and he clearly preached against vain display, calling the Pharisees "whitened sepulchers" for focusing on appearances, not internal purity (Matt. 23:27). The answer is complex and addresses the nature of organized religion however it might strive for spiritual goals, functioning in a material world with its accepted social norms. Christianity developed in a pre-modern society where dress and ritual were the primary signifiers of meaning. Thus it inherited a system where materials were a fundamental means of expressing value. Medieval aesthetics, furthermore, developed its material culture, ordering value according to three criteria: an object was worthy if it were constructed of important materials, displayed skilled workmanship, and was destined for an important function. The service of the liturgy, when Christ was present in the Eucharist, was the moment of ritual possessing the highest significance, thus it needed the most important materials (McLachlan, 369-80). Durandus, bishop of Mende (1285-1296), was one of many medieval commentators who justified precious materials by citing Scripture such as Exodus (35: 4-9), "Let everyone that is willing and hath a ready heart, offer them to the Lord: gold, and silver, and brass, violet, and purple, and scarlet twice died, and fine linen, goat's hair . . . and oil to maintain lights and to make ointment and most sweet incense. Onyx stones, and precious stones, for the adorning of the ephod and the rational." Durandus stated that God wishes the virtues of the priest to shine, but also his vestments and ornaments of the altar (Durandus, book 3, chapter 45, p. 92). English bishops, for example, made a concerted effort in the twelfth and thirteenth centuries to insure that all parishes had at least one silver chalice, endeavoring to displace the pewter chalices that were apparently in use for some of the less affluent congregations (Oman, 1962, 196).

The second and equally operative reason was economic. Precious metals and stones functioned as one of the rare elements of ready capital for pre-modern institutions. In times of need, often for repair or rebuilding of structures after natural disasters such as crop failure or floods, institutions sold their plate or gems detached from reliquaries, processional crosses or chalices for the necessary funds. In the twelfth century, Abbot Suger of St. Denis writes of buying "pearls and gems" at a bargain price from members of other Orders (Panofsky, 33). That this practice was employed in the Tudor era is attested by a review of the Crown's progressive despoilment of Church goods. In 1536 the smaller monasteries, those with income of less than £200 per year, were suppressed (27 Henry VIII, Cap. 28: Gee and Hardy, 257-68). Some were allowed to remain by paying a fine and forty-seven religious houses continued this way. For Dale Abbey in Derbyshire, the fine was £166. 13*s.* 4*d.*, clearly impossible to accomplish out of general revenues. Plate was certainly sold. At the end of the two years of reprieve, when in 1538 all houses were suppressed, those in this category had very little plate left. Dale had sold all but three chalices, the

Chalice, ca. 1495, Coombe Keynes, Dorset, after W. F. Cripps, *Old English Plate*, London, 1901, No. 5

plating of a processional cross, and eleven spoons (Oman, 112-113). The form of such Pre-Reformation plate is typified by a chalice made about 1495 at Coombe Keynes, Dorset, with deep bowl, a protuberance called a knop on the stem, and a sexfoil foot carrying an image of the Crucified Christ.

The survival of medieval church plate depends on circumstances similar to the survival of Catholicism itself. Laws were made, and commissioners nominated to enforce them, but invariably individual compliance varied greatly. An example of a conversion appears in the "Peacock Chalice" in the Museum of London whose base is the foot of a pyx (a container for the reserved Sacrament) dated 1507. In 1559 a bell-shaped cup was added, converting it for use in the Reformed Church (Platt, 101, fig. 72). The campaigns during Edward and Elizabeth's reigns to order Catholic service plate melted down for the creation of Reformation plate did not extend to the plate in colleges and private chapels with the end result that many Pre-Reformation chalices survive in Oxford Colleges (1 Edward VI, Cap. 14: Gee and Hardy, 328-57). These include Brasenose College's two chalices dating from the 1490s and Trinity's Pre-Reformation chalice given by Sir Thomas Pope, one of the Edwardian Commissioners. Corpus Christi has the renowned gold chalice of Bishop Fox (Oman, 45-46, pls. 18, 32; Marks and Williamson, 242, No. 105). When pressed, an institution, such as All Souls College simply reclassified altar plate, and the College's old plate appeared later in domestic plate lists (Glanville 1990, 376-77).

The shape of the Reformed church plate was distinctive and a communion cup of 1559, the second year of Elizabeth's reign, of St. Botolph, Aldgate, exemplifies the visual message. The cup's elongated bowl and

Communion cup, 1568 in a Norwich pattern, after W. F. Cripps, *Old English Plate*, London, 1901, No. 16

trumpet shaped foot are radically different from medieval models. Around the bowl, in large, upper case lettering is the English text taken from the *Book of Common Prayer:* AND HE TOKE THE CVP AND THANKED AND GAVE IT TO THEM, SAYING DRIKE OF IT EVERI ONE FOR TIS MI BLOVD OF THE NEW TESTAMENT, THAT SHALL BE SHED FOR MANY FOR THE REMISSION OF SINNES" (Oman, 194, pl. 55). Thus the repudiation of both Latin as the language of ritual and the visible connection of a medieval tradition is achieved. A similar strategy is seen on the Communion Cup dated 1568 in a Norwich pattern, a large squarish cup with the English text running around the lower potion of the bowl. The most visible similarities are to secular drinking vessels, an association used to define the Reformed communion as a commemoration and to distance it from the "superstitious" Catholic ritual of sacramental mystery. Such similarities can be seen in the tall communion cup, such as one hall-marked for 1551, in the last years of Edward's reign, a cup with a bell-shaped bowl and spool shaped stem over a bold ogee-molded base (Beddington church, Surrey: Oman, 192, pl. 49). The actual reuse of secular cups is also documented. An example is an early Renaissance drinking cup engraved with a band of scrolling foliage under the rim of the

LITURGICAL VESSELS

bowl from the era of Henry VII, gilt in 1545. The cup was presented to the church of St. Margaret Pattens, a wealthy congregation in the City of London and in 1649 the church commissioned a copy to make a pair (Glanville 1987, 283, fig 116; Platt, 103-106).

The size of communion cups also reflected their communal function since they were designed for the entire parish to imbibe. Immediately on Edward's accession in 1547, his councilors decreed that, "the said blessed Sacrament should be administered to all Christian people under both the kinds of bread and wine, than under the form of bread only" whereas for Catholics only the priest partook of the wine (I Edward VI, Cap. 1: Gee and Hardy, 322-28, quote 327). Two communion cups with paten covers in Cirencester, Gloucestershire, dated 1570 are very large, fourteen inches high and holding two and a half pints each (Oman, 198-99, pl. 62a). The paten is a closefitting cover with a circular handle for easy removal, not the flat dish simply sitting on top of the chalice familiar from medieval times. The silversmith Robert Taylboyes, used a pattern of a stem with a frill around it and a "hit-or-miss" ornamentation on the bowl.

Church plate after the Reformation continued to function in much the same ways as it had in Catholic practice. The precious objects, serving as a focal point of ritual attention, became a source of local pride for city, community, and individual. Communion cups, alms basins, and flagons were engraved with donors' names and localities. A notable example is a communion cup and paten of 1621-24 produced during the final years of James I. The bowl displays a large-scale image of the arms of Stuart impaling Howard, referring to Ludovic Stuart, Duke of Lennox and Richmond (1574-1624) who married Frances Howard in 1621. The cup is accompanied by a paten with the Stuart arms and earl's coronet (Glanville 1987, 213).

Communion cup, 1570, Robert Taylboyes, London, Cirencester, Gloucestershire, after W. F. Cripps, *Old English Plate*, London, 1901, No. 14.

The position of recusant Catholics was predictable, to cherish all that the national church had deemed illegal. Since the successive efforts to call in Pre-Reformation plate (see "The Daily Experience of Devotion," p. 15) were so much a part of public knowledge, the sequestering of the old chalices was viewed as a great act of piety. We now count only 80 medieval English chalices surviving, in contrast to 2,000 Elizabethan communion cups, a clear demonstration of the thoroughness of the Crown's efforts to convert usage (Glanville 1987, 374). The taking out of the hidden chalice and vesting in forbidden alb, chasuble, and stole must have created an intense communal experience for celebrant and worshipper alike. Such an experience appears associated with a Pre-Reformation chalice from Mains (or Monk's) Hall, the ancient seat of the Hesketh family (Camm, 379, ill. opp. p. 378). Edmund Campion (see essays on "The Society of Jesus" and the "Battle of the Books," pp. 135-37, 140-43) possibly said Mass with this chalice at Mains Hall in 1581 on his missionary journey to Lancashire. The knop has six lobes and the base is in the shape of a hexagonal star, the compartments IHC (a version of IHS) and XPC, monograms for the names of Jesus and Christ, discussed below, alternating; the sixth has a crucifix. It resembles the Hornby chalice, about 1490, from the parish church of Caton, four and a half miles from Lancaster, now in the Roman Catholic Church of Hornby, Lancashire (Blundell, 115-16; Oman, 45, 258, pl. 15b). The Hornby chalice is inscribed *Restore mee to Caton*, clearly the work of a recusant hoping for better days. For the

Mains Hall chalice, the calyx design at the base of the bowl is a modern embellishment but the chalice itself dates from the later years of the fifteenth century; thus it was close to a century in age when Campion is reputed to have used it. It was preserved at Claughton Hall, Claughton-on-Brock, Lancashire, and considered a relic in the early years of the twentieth century.

When bereft of a treasured ancient chalice, recusants understandably produced chalices as faithfully as possible modeled after the old medieval forms. Such an experience may have even had a particular resonance for "Church Papists", those individuals who attended the state services in order to avoid the heavy fines and confiscation of property, when returning to the "authentic" experience. Georgetown University preserves a recusant chalice (see p. 177), the earliest in this exhibition, dating from the Elizabethan era. It closely resembles the earlier Mains Hall chalice in being formed of three parts that are distinctly articulated: deep, rounded bowl, a hexagonal foot with an image of Christ crucified, and a stem interrupted by a rounded knop.

Chalice from Mains (or Monk's) Hall, about 1490, after Dom Bede Camm, O.S.B. *Forgotten Shrines* London, 1910, opp. p. 378.

Imagery associated with chalices is connected to earlier Catholic practices and those continuing after the Reformation. Chief among them are honoring of images of the Passion, including Christ crucified and his Sacred Name symbolized by the IHS or the more accurate IHC, the first letters of the name of Jesus in Greek. The late-medieval popularity of the cult of the "Holy Name of Jesus" is attested to by guilds dedicated to the name, the institution of a votive Mass and the evidence of designated altars for the celebration of the Jesus Mass, documented from 1388 (Pfaff 1970, 4, 62-83). The feast was established for all of England between 1488 and 1489 and gained popularity since it was associated with important indulgences. Typical is a Mass from the diocese of Norwich of the early fifteenth century promising that a believer who causes the celebration of the Jesus Mass, as well as the celebrant, will not die without sincere contrition for their sins and the comfort of the Sacraments, i.e., the Last Rites (Pfaff 1970, 63).

The honoring of the name with the sacred trigram was a common practice. One finds the IHS or IHC on funerary brasses, English pottery, imported Spanish glazed pottery plates, bowls, and vessels, and finger rings, as well as overtly religious objects. As a symbol, not an image, the trigram did not incur the same prohibition from Elizabethan Reformers. Yet, the Name of Jesus was deeply linked to Catholic piety and it was not common

Chalice, 1550-1600? Georgetown University Collections. Photo: Virginia Raguin

LITURGICAL VESSELS

after the 1540s. After 1600, despite a brief appearance associated with the Arminian movement in the established church during the early years of the century, the Name of Jesus appears to have become a symbol of recusancy (Block et al., 188-93). The trigram was frequently in place on Catholic objects in a form codified as the IHS in Roman capitals surmounted by a cross resting on the H cross bar with three radiating nails below. This is the form that was adopted by the Society of Jesus as its emblem, represented on a contemporaneous lead plaque with the inscription in Latin of the "Roman College of the Society of Jesus" (British Museum, MME 1856, 7-1, 2183: Block et. al., 190, fig. 12). In the symbol's application to church plate, recusant patens invariably bore the IHS below a cross (Oman, 272), as exemplified by patens connected to both the Elizabethan chalice and the two Petre chalices, 1640-60, in this exhibition. (CATALOGUE)

In the seventeenth century, the distance between medieval and Renaissance times had made memory more tenuous. Possibly the use of an overtly Catholic symbol of the IHS became more important as the visible form of recusant vessels became less definite. More varieties of chalice design appear although, unlike communion cups, the three separate elements of bowl, stem with knop, and foot were generally emphasized. The Petre chalices present a good example. The bowl is short and raised on a tall stem. The knop is quite prominent and pear-shaped, made even more notable by the application of molded images of cherubs. Cherubim are among the seven orders of angels, and, with the seraphim, are described as devoted to contemplating the splendor of the Divinity and thus are represented only with faces and wings. On one segment of the sexfoil foot is an engraved image of Christ crucified. The *Rookwood Chalice* of 1684 although considerably larger, also uses a seraph's head to embellish the knop. The *Constable Chalice* from the Bar Convent (see essay on the "True Cross," pp. 125-26), made during the same time, is much less undulating in profile. Its bowl is taller and its stem has sharp angles, continuing the sharp divisions in the segments of the foot. Its knop is a ring interrupting the verticality of the stem. The complex imagery of the signs of the Passion on the foot is unmistakably recusant.

Paten, 1550-1600 Georgetown University Collections. Photo: Virginia Raguin

CATALOGUE

Petre Chalice
England, 1650-1670, associated with the silversmith Albert Moore, City of London
Silver, with gilt interior of cup, 6 ½ in. (16.5 cm.)
Provenance: acquired in 1819 by Fr. Plowden, Rector and Provincial from the Petre family
Stonyhurst College, Lancashire

This chalice (Oman, 270, pl. 162b) is part of a series made for the Jesuit administrative division of mission activity called the College of the Holy Apostles, comprising the counties of Norfolk, Suffolk, Essex and Cambridge. When the English province of the Society of Jesus was authorized in 1623, England was divided into "Colleges" and that of East Anglia with its four counties given this designation. William, the fourth Lord Petre (1627-1683) apparently paid for a series of chalices for the use of the missioners (Taylor). The chalices do not have hallmarks but are identifiable by the molded head of the cherub shown with wings raised above its head on the knop. The knops may be in varying pear and oval shapes and the foot is in six sections with rather flat lobes. Oman identified the enterprise of Albert Moore of London with this group of chalices by comparison with a chalice with the maker's mark *AM in monogram* on a Church of England chalice in St. George's Chapel, Windsor (9 inches tall; Oman, 270-71, pl. 84c).

Very probably, all eighteen Jesuit missioners in the "College" were provided with these small chalices that could aid the itinerant nature of their services. Blundell identified three, at Great Eccleston, Goosnarah, and Downside (Blundell, 121-24, Nos. 8, 9, and 10, illustrated). He noted

Petre chalice, London, 1650-1670, associated with the silversmith Albert Moore, Stonyhurst College. Photo: Stonyhurst College

Petre chalice, London, 1650-1670, associated with the silversmith Albert Moore, Georgetown University Collections. Photo: Virginia Raguin

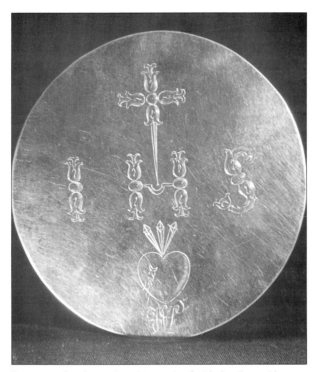

Petre paten, London, 1650-1670, associated with the silversmith
Albert Moore, Stonyhurst College. Photo: Stonyhurst College

Rookwood Chalice

England, dated 1684, associated with the
silversmith Albert Moore, City of London
Silver, with gilt interior of cup. 8 7/8 in. (22 cm.)
Provenance: Elizabeth Rookwood; Bury St.
Edmunds; Lady Catherine Ashburnham; Fr.
Martin D'Arcy, S.J.; Heythrop College, England;
The Loyola University Museum of Medieval,
Renaissance, and Baroque Art, Gift of Mr. and
Mrs. G. Arthur Stromberg in memory of Mr. and
Mrs. J. Hyland (acq. no. 2.72), Catalogue No. 83

The chalice is an unusually large one for recusant
times. The six-lobed foot is bordered with a
decorative geometric band gathered at the edges
of the lobes with fleurs-de-lis. On one lobe is a
simple image of Christ on the cross above which
is the inscription INRI. The knop bears front
and back an image of a seraph head, which would
suggest a similar maker as the Petre

their similarities but was apparently unaware of
their connection to Lord Petre's commission.
Taylor listed other chalices (Taylor). Of Blundell's
list he names only the chalice at Downside Abbey
but adds eight others, the chalice of Stonyhurst
College in this exhibition, and those at Ingatestone
Hall; Beaumont College; Broughton Hall,
Skipton; St. Dominic, Haverstock Hill; St. Mary
College, Sheffield; Gosforth Parish Church (CE),
Cumbria; Ushaw College; the Church at Clitheroe,
Lancashire, a Jesuit parish (8 inches tall; Oman pl.
163a); the National Museum of Dublin; and one
formerly at Sawston Hall, Cambridge (5 inches tall;
Oman, 270-71, pl. 162a) which has since traveled to
the United States with the heirs of the Huddleston
family. See chalice from Georgetown identified in
the exhibition as part of the Petre group.

Rookwood chalice, London 1684, associated with the silversmith
Albert Moore, The Loyola University Museum of Medieval,
Renaissance, and Baroque Art. Photo: John Buckingham

group, although it was made a year after Lord Petre's death. We do know its patron, Elizabeth Rookwood, whose family's primary residence until the late eighteenth century was Coldham Hall in West Suffolk. She caused the underside of the base to be inscribed: Col. Ap. S. J., Ex Dono Dna. Elizabetha Rookwood/ 1684. The abbreviated letters stand for Collegium Sanctorum Apostolorum Societatis Jesu (The College of the Holy Apostles of the Society of Jesus), the Jesuit administrative division of missions for the counties of Norfolk, Suffolk, Essex and Cambridge (see above). She added her name – "Given by Lady Elizabeth Rookwood 1684". Opposite the inscription is found the Rookwood arms showing six chess-rooks, three, two, and one impaling Elizabeth's family arms, a cross patée fitched surrounded by eight mullets, three, two and three. As is typical for most recusant plate, there are no maker's marks. The silversmith, who apparently had a long and successful practice that he handed down to a son, did not wish to be identified as having produced outlawed Catholic liturgical vessels. Since the Rookwood family was publicly known, and most probably already fined for its recusancy, the acknowledgement on the chalice would add little risk.

Rookwood arms, interior of chalice, London 1684, The Loyola University Museum of Medieval, Renaissance, and Baroque Art. Photo: John Buckingham

Chalice
Ireland, in the style of Thomas Lynch of Galway, dated 1724
Silver, with gilt interior of cup, 9 in. (22.5 cm.)
Provenance: Heythrop College, England
The Loyola University Museum of Medieval, Renaissance, and Baroque Art, Gift of Mr. and Mrs. Donald F. Rowe, Sr. (acq. no. 72.1), Catalogue No. 84

The chalice was made for the Dominican convent of Burisoule (Burrishool) founded in 1469 in County Mayo in the West Country of Ireland.

The form shows a deep bowl with splayed sides and slightly everted rim. An octagonal foot rises from several horizontal moldings. The stem is octagonal, interrupted by a bulbous knop with eight facets corresponding to the stem. The Crucifixion, apparently much worn from use, is engraved on one segment of the foot and the inscription runs around the lower part of the other seven. This chalice shows the Irish characteristic of a relatively tall foot compared to English models. See for comparison, the Mount Keefe chalice dated 1590 (Victoria and Albert Museum, M31-1929: Glanville, *Tudor*, 495, No. 142). Buckley notes, "The foot was almost invariably the most important member, from the historical point of view, as it was around the lower part of it that it was customary to engrave the dedicatory inscription" (Buckley, 4). Here the inscription reads "Orate pro anima Domini Petri Browne qui me fieri fecit pro Conventu de Burisoule Anno Domini 1724 (Pray for the soul of Mr. Peter Browne who had me made for the Convent of Bourisoule).

Peter Brown of Westport (1760-1724) owned the land on which both the priories of Bourisoule and Murisk were built, and he gave a similar chalice to the Convent of Murisk with comparable inscription (Buckley, 152-53). The Murisk chalice

Chalice, Ireland (Galway?), 1724, in the style of Thomas Lynch, The Loyola University Museum of Medieval, Renaissance, and Baroque Art. Photo: John Buckingham

survives with a paten and both chalice and paten bear the maker's mark "TL" for Thomas Lynch who worked in Galway between 1720 and 1740. This chalice also bears the letters "MF" presumably for Martin French who worked in Galway at the same time as Lynch. Another chalice given to the the Dominican convent of Burisoule is from Peter's first cousin, John Brown, inscribed: [orate pro] anima Joannis Brown qui me fieri curavit ad usum Conventus Burisowle [1723] (pray for the soul of John Brown who took care to have me made for use of the convent at Bourisoule). The chalice is also marked with an anchor and Lynch's initials "TL" (Buckley, 150). The Chicago chalice is also similar in form to several dated to the 1720s, especially the 1724 Fitz Peter-Fitz John Chalice (Buckley, 151-52, fig. 148) marked with the initials RI for R. Joyces or Joyce. The Joyces were a family of

silversmiths from Galway. Thus one might assume that Galway silversmiths worked in a similar style.

Throughout the recusant era in Ireland there was a consistent production of Catholic church plate, especially chalices. Sweeney's survey of the Stuart era lists 260 Roman Catholic chalices, only 29 whose makers can be identified, along with 20 patens, 3 ciboria, one crown for a statue, one cruet, two crucifixes, three monstrance's, six pyxes, and 10 reliquaries. The record of Communion Cups for the Church of Ireland is only slightly larger but of the 257 listed, the makers are identified on 168 entries. There are also a far great number of patens, 218 with the same proportion of makers identified (Sweeney, 221-42). The makers identified with Roman Catholic plate were not listed as having produced plate for the Church of Ireland. Thus there seems to have been a clear understanding of patronage that would not readily accept a silversmith crossing over to serve the rival faith.

The itinerary of the chalice is complicated. The chalices given to Bourisoule by Peter and John Brown were taken by the English from the convent in 1739 (Morain, 37-38). The John Brown chalice is now in the Catholic Church of Newport, which is located about two miles from the site of the Burrishool convent. The Peter Brown chalice given to Murisk was acquired from a Dublin dealer about 1874 and given by the Marquess of Sligo, a descendant of Peter Brown, to the Church of Ireland in Westport. The Peter Brown chalice from Bourisoule ended up a possession of Heythrop College, England, and from there was acquired by Loyola University.

Buckley, J. J. *Some Irish Altar Plate*, Dublin: John Falconer, 1943.
Morain, Padraig. *A Short Account of the History of Burrishoole Parish*, Tuam, 1957.
Sweeney, Tony. *Irish Stuart Silver: A Short Descriptive Catalogue of Surviving Church Plate. . . .1603-1714*, Dublin: Éamonn de Búrca for Edmund Burke Publisher, 1995.

Arrowsmith chalice, Lancashire? 1620s, Stonyhurst College. Photo: Stonyhurst College

Arrowsmith Chalice
England, 1620s
Pewter, 6 ¼ in. (15.9 cm.)
Stonyhurst College, Lancashire, gift of the Myerscough family

This small chalice is part of a cache of seventeenth-century artifacts for saying Mass associated with Edmund Arrowsmith. The vestments and other artifacts were found in a seventeenth-century box that was discovered at Samlesbury Hall in the nineteenth century (see "The Daily Experience of Devotion"). Edmund Arrowsmith was associated with the mission at Samlesbury Hall as was Edmund Campion some forty years earlier. The chalice is a small, sturdy type, of the early-seventeenth-century style, no longer so rigidly linked to a pre-Reformation form.

Pyx
England, 1st half of the 17th century
Silver gilt, 2 ¼" in. diameter (5.7 cm.)
Provenance: Stonyhurst College, Lancashire, England
The Loyola University Museum of Medieval, Renaissance, and Baroque Art, Gift of the Friends of the Gallery (acq. no. 2.71), Catalogue No. 71
Rowe, No. 71

The pyx or pyxis is a container for the reserved host (McLachlan, 396-98). The term means simply box, and such containers have been preserved from the Early Christian era, at that time most being in ivory. The reverence for the Eucharistic host is predicated on the belief that once consecrated by the words of the priest – Hoc est enim corpus meum (This is my body) the bread is transformed into the actual body of Christ. This process is called the transubstantiation, where the mystical body of Christ is present under the appearance of bread and wine. Catholics accepted the host as containing both the body and the blood, for the flesh can not exist without the blood as well. For the sacrament of Extreme Unction, the Last Rites, the consecrated host is brought to the sick. This pyx, able to contain a single host, may very well have been used for this purpose.

The decoration is significant for its retention of Latin for its doctrinal statement, as well as its injunction in English. On the obverse is the Crucifixion with the inscription: SACRO SANGUINE PXI PURGATI SUMMUS A CRIMINE (Through Christ's sacred blood we are purged of sin). Above Christ's head is the inscription INRI standing for Jesus of Nazareth King of the Jews (John 19:20). To the left (Christ's right) is the Virgin Mary, and to the right (Christ's left) is St. John the Evangelist. These two were traditionally depicted flanking the cross. The inspiration comes from the words of Christ to Mary as he hung on the cross, "Woman behold thy son," and similar words to John "Behold thy mother" (John 19:26-27). Significantly, here they actually face the cross in positions of adoration. On the reverse is the Agnus Dei, or Lamb of God, surrounded by the English text, LEARNE OF ME BECAUSE I AM MEKE AND HUMBLE OF (image of heart). The depiction of Christ as the sacrificial Lamb who atones for the sins of humanity comes from the Old Testament Passover Lamb, recalling the sacrifice of the Lamb when the Jews sacrificed and consumed a lamb and painted the sign of the Tau (a T, like a cross) with its blood on their doorways. The angel who struck the firstborn of the Egyptians could then recognize the believers and "pass over" their homes (Exodus 12:3-14), an event commemorated in the feast of Passover.

The style of the engraving is unsophisticated. Given the limited access of recusant patrons to sophisticated goldsmiths and engravers, it is likely that local metalworkers constructed the pyx.

Anatomical detail is nonexistent and shading of the robes accomplished through uniform hatch, particularly in Mary, or a "waffle" grid that suggests the use of a stamp as in John. The scale of the heads of John and Mary to Christ's is widely divergent. Yet, a very important spatial device is still evoked. Christ's cross pierces the borders of the image that contains John and Mary, intimating the Crucifixion is beyond time. Such visual differences might suggest to a viewer that his or her prayers are not confined by time, but can transcend the moment to mingle with those of Christians

Pyx, obverse with Crucifixion, England, 1st half of the 17th century, The Loyola University Museum of Medieval, Renaissance, and Baroque Art. Photo: John Buckingham

Pyx, reverse with Agnus Dei, England, 1st half of the 17th century, The Loyola University Museum of Medieval, Renaissance, and Baroque Art. Photo: John Buckingham

Confirmation with bishop wearing a mitre and cope, Book of Hours printed in Paris by Simon Vostre, 1512, Stonyhurst College, S. 3/3, fol. 85v

Priest at Mass, at the elevation of the host, wearing a chasuble, Book of Hours printed in Paris by Simon Vostre, 1512, Stonyhurst College, S. 3/3, fol. 84

LITURGICAL VESTMENTS

Liturgical Vestments

Virginia C. Raguin

The survival of vestments in contemporary collections is almost exclusively the result of religious resistance. The various Acts of Uniformity during the reigns of Edward VI and Elizabeth I, discussed in the chapter "The Daily Experience of Devotion," pp. 15-16, forbade the wearing of traditional Catholic vestments during worship service. As documented in the records of Morebath, vestments were sometimes restructured to serve as a covering for the altar table. In pre-modern times, dress, whether secular or religious, was a vital element of society, defining status as well as function. Each religious order was clearly recognized by distinctive dress; an order such as the Benedictines was referred to as the Black Monks while the Cistercians, who in the twelfth century changed to unbleached white, became known as White Monks. For Margery Kempe, the ability to wear white, for which she needed clerical approval, was the confirmation of her truly achieving the virginal state, and thus becoming eligible for Christ's espousal (ch. 44 and ch. 37; Windeat, lines 3417-48 and 3000-3002).

The sumptuousness of dress was an essential part of statecraft. Elizabeth I's careful use of elaborate jewelry, especially pearls symbolic of purity, is discussed in the chapter "Picture and Policy: Contested Control of the Image," pp. 34-35, and the sums spent on fabrics astound modern viewers. Every diplomatic mission necessitated sumptuous ceremonial, the wealth displayed by the delegation in dress being indicative of the political resolve and strength of the ambassadors. In 1520, when Henry VIII met Francis I on the "Field of the Cloth of Gold," outside of Calais, the name itself indicative of textiles as signifiers, Henry provided lavish dress. In addition to his personal adornment and that of his courtiers, he took with him the full set of vestments consisting of a chasuble and 29 copes commissioned by Henry VII for Westminster Abbey. The chasuble, from this set, now at Stonyhurst College, is discussed below. The original embellishment of the vestments is revealed in descriptions of the orphreys of the copes glittering with precious stones and pearls at the ceremonials (Marks and Williamson, 169).

The sumptuous display of fabrics in vestments was as important in the local parish as it was in royal performance. An example is the exertions of the priest Christopher Trychay beginning in 1529 and ending triumphantly in 1547 to acquire a set of black vestments for the small rural parish of Morebath (Duffy 2001, 38, 115-17). England, indeed, was famous for its production of vestments, especially for the kind of liturgical embroidery known as *opus anglicanum* (English work). The fame of the English workers was their ability to produce these gold backgrounds by a technique called underside couching. "In it the couching thread was drawn to the underside of the work so that the gold surface presented was smooth and almost uninterrupted" (Johnstone, 46-47). In a well-known passage, the chronicler Matthew of Paris described the admiration of pope Innocent IV for English vestments in 1246:

> . . . my Lord Pope, having noticed that the ecclesiastical ornaments of certain English priests, such as choral copes and mitres, were embroidered in gold thread after a most desirable fashion, asked whence came that work? From England, they told him. Then exclaimed the Pope, "England is for us surely a garden of delights, truly an inexhaustible well. . . . .Thereupon the same Lord Pope, allured by the desire of the eye, sent letters, blessed and sealed, to well nigh all the Abbots of the Cistercian Order established in England, desiring that they should send to him without delay these embroideries of gold which he preferred to all others, and with which he wished to decorate his chasubles and choral copes, as if these acquisitions would cost him nothing. This command of my Lord Pope did not displease the London merchants who traded these embroideries and sold them at their own price. (Johnstone, 36)

61

Liturgical Vestments

The Vatican had acquired more than 100 works of *opus anglicanum* by the end of the thirteenth century.

Throughout the Middle Ages, the style of textile design paralleled those of the other arts, such as architecture, manuscript painting, or stained glass. There was no division among the so called minor and major arts, a situation distinct from the hierarchy operative in modern times. Indeed, because textiles in their most lavish forms were so costly and were essential parts of sacramental ritual, they were often valued as particularly important manifestations of style. The Chichester-Constable Chasuble of 1330-50 (2.7 162.1, Metropolitan Museum of Art: King, 39, No. 78, pl. 16), possibly made under the patronage of Edward III, is comprised of gold and silver threads and colored silks with pearls on velvet. Its form is a quintessential example of the English Decorated style. The figural scenes of the Annunciation, Adoration of the Magi, and Coronation of the Virgin are framed by undulating, organic architectural forms characteristic of English Decorated Style architecture of the time, for example the Lady Chapel at Ely dated 1321-1330s. The chasuble, typical of the survival of church vestments, had been preserved in a Catholic family in Yorkshire until sold at auction in the early twentieth century.

Recusant Catholics preserved the pre-Reformation vestments but they also produced new vestments, such as the early seventeenth-century green set worn by St. Edmund Arrowsmith discussed in the chapter "The Daily Experience of Devotion," pp. 15-18. These were quite simple, green silk with white appliqué trim. The vestments embroidered by Helen Wintour in the 1650s, however, present tour-de-force embroidery with gold and silver threads and gems worthy of their medieval precedents. Wintour was the unmarried daughter of Robert Wintour who, with his two brothers, was executed as a conspirator in the Gunpowder plot of 1605 against James I. The vestments were named in her will of 1671 and in previous correspondence as being produced for use by the Society of Jesus. Among those that have been preserved at Stonyhurst are a set of white vestments for important feasts such as Christmas or Corpus Christi, and a red set for the feast of the Holy Spirit at Pentecost. A highly worked image of the Holy Spirit as a Dove appears at the intersection of the cross elements on the back of the red. Individuals associated with the Wintour vestments testify to the contentious issue of religion throughout the seventeenth century. The Wintour family lost three members in the aftermath of the Gunpowder plot. Fr. Anthony Turner, the Jesuit Superior who had received the vestments, lost his life in the anti-Catholic frenzy that was precipitated by Titus Oates's spurious "Popish Plot."

Even in a modern context, the religious aura associated with vestments was attractive. Isabella Stewart Gardner collected vestments, primarily from Italian provinces where she was able to acquire old and often worn vestments whose form was out of date. They are interspersed with the Italian paintings and sculpture displayed in the museum she created in Boston's Back Bay. Her motivation mixed both religious and aesthetic sentiments. Gardner was Episcopalian and an influential member of the Church of the Advent, Beacon Hill, Boston, Massachusetts where she donated the large, multi-tiered marble rerados. She also treated her Back Bay museum as a shrine for her son's memory; an only child, he had died before his seventh birthday. The chapel, located after the tapestry-and vestment-lined Long Gallery, and terminating in Gothic stained glass from Soissons cathedral, was the site of the Episcopal Mass dedicating the museum and where annual requiem Masses are held each year on Gardner's birthday.

LITURGICAL VESTMENTS

CATALOGUE

St. Dunstan Chasuble
Linen with gold metal and colored silk thread
embroidery, 45 x 26 in. (114.3 x 66 cm.)
England, 1450s and 1490s
Stonyhurst College, Lancashire

Chasuble of Henry VII
Cloth of gold with embroidered orphrey (gold
metal and colored silk thread on linen) and direct
embroidery, 44 x 27 ¼ in. (112 x 69.2 cm.)
Italy and England, 1499-1505, altered in the 17th
century, and late 1820s
Stonyhurst College, Lancashire

Two of the most important pre-Reformation art
objects owned by Stonyhurst College are chasubles,
the outermost vestment worn by a priest when
he celebrates Mass. Although during the Middle
Ages English chasubles were all-enveloping,
bell-shaped semi-circles of fabric, most surviving
examples—including these—have been radically
cut down at the bottom and at the shoulders to
form a flat, two-sided, tabard-like garment (V&A
Catalogue, xv) popular in the seventeenth century
and known as a fiddleback chasuble. Nevertheless,
each of these chasubles represents a remarkable
survival of fragile Catholic liturgical garb in the
face of hostile conditions, and each includes
fine examples of late medieval English orphreys,
independent strips of embroidered cloth that were
sewn onto clerical vestments.

The so-called *Chasuble of Henry VII* was made
sometime between 1499 and 1505 as part of a
vast set of luxurious Mass settings commissioned
by the English king and donated to Westminister
Abbey in his will. According to the records of
Westminster Abbey, the set of twenty-nine copes

St. Dunstan Chasuble, England, 1450s and 1490s, Stonyhurst College,
Lancashire

St. Dunstan pinching the devil's nose, detail of chasuble, England,
1450s and 1490s, Stonyhurst College, Lancashire

Chasuble of Henry VII, Italy and England, 1499-1505, altered 17th century and late 1820s, Stonyhurst College, Lancashire

Beauforts—as well as a seventeenth-century orphrey badge depicting the Holy Dove over the Sacred Name (IHS), a symbol of the Society of Jesus. The chasuble's back features a similar fabric column comprising additional pieces of cloth-of-gold, an orphrey badge of censing angels embroidered in England ca. 1500-5, and one of the Good Shepherd, sewn in the early seventeenth century. Clusters of grapes were embroidered directly onto the ground material in the late 1820s, when the chasuble was restored by Br. Houghton, the Jesuit Sacristan of Stonyhurst College, thus transforming the orphrey column into a symbolic cross shape (Monnas, 345-46; V&A Catalogue, xiii-xiv).

The other chasuble in this exhibition, known as the *St. Dunstan Chasuble*, is actually a modern reconstruction that combines orphreys from at least two separate late-medieval garments. The two outer strips on its back and the strips on its front all date to the mid-fifteenth century and depict scenes from the lives of saints associated with Canterbury Cathedral, for which these embroideries were probably made. On the back, the left strip portrays (top to bottom) saints Dunstan, Blaise, and Elphege, and the right strip portrays St. Odo and two miracles of St. Thomas Becket; the chasuble's front features embroideries of Saints Peter and Paul and of the Martyrdom of St. Thomas Becket. In contrast, the central orphrey on the back of the chasuble was made in the 1490s, and was added to the garment in 1829 to replace a damaged section. It depicts, from top to bottom, the solemn, standing figures of Saints Philip, Paul, John the Baptist, and Bartholomew, and may have once formed part of an altar frontal (*Stonyhurst Vestments*, 13-15; *To the Greater Glory of God*, cat. no. 4). Although he appears in only one scene, the chasuble is named for St. Dunstan, a tenth-century Benedictine monk who later became Archbishop of Canterbury. This is significant because early legends of St. Dunstan describe him as a talented embroiderer, making the luxurious garment both self-referential and self-justifying. Moreover, Dunstan was exiled to the continent by King Eadwig, only to return in triumph to restart monastic life there—a striking parallel to the peregrinations of Stonyhurst College itself. (For Dunstan's *vita*, see Farmer, 152-53, with further bibliography.).

had dwindled to twenty-four by 1563, and to eleven by 1608, when the Stonyhurst cope is first recorded at St. Omers. The remaining eleven at Westminster were burned during the time of Oliver Cromwell, and nothing appears to exist of the others that went missing. Stonyhurst College now owns the only three surviving pieces from this set, a chasuble, cope and chalice veil, which were removed from Westminster by 1608 and taken to the college of St. Omers the same year. (The other vestments donated by Henry VII disappeared gradually from Westminster, and in 1643 the last ones were burned by the Puritans.) The ground material of the chasuble is velvet on cloth-of-gold, depicting red Tudor roses with curving stems, and was woven in Florence in 1499 and 1500 expressly for the king. The front of the garment is decorated with square fragments of cloth-of-gold depicting a portcullis— the symbol of Henry VII's mother's family, the

LITURGICAL VESTMENTS

Medieval vestments were animated objects, viewed most often in motion. Gold thread caught the flickering light of candles and cloth took on projected color as the priest officiated beneath windows glazed with colored glass. Vestments made manifest the heightened sacrality of the Mass vis-à-vis the daily Office and quotidian non-religious activities; they separated the ordained body from the lay body, and distinguished visually among different grades or ranks of clergy. They could indicate chromatically the different phases of the liturgical year, and intimated the wealth and power of the Church and its supporters through their cost and luxury; indeed, recent studies confirm that embroidery and goldsmithwork, not painting or sculpture, were the most expensive artistic media of the fifteenth and sixteenth centuries (Belozerskaya, 76-145). Furthermore, during the Recusancy period vestments were a sign of resistance, garb which immediately and openly identified the celebrant as Catholic, opening him to summary arrest and persecution. Donning and doffing vestments became both a sacred and a political act.

The full appreciation of these chasubles requires several leaps of the visual imagination. First, vestments were typically commissioned and used as part of a complimentary set, often accompanied by matching altar hangings and similar liturgical textiles; this was certainly the case for the *Henry VII Chasuble*, and was likely so with the constituent elements of the *St. Dunstan Chasuble*. Thus, to view any one piece in isolation is to miss part of the effect intended by the orchestrating donor and the textile artists themselves. Second, while displayed today, by necessity, as static objects, in the Mass vestments were meant to be functional as well as decorative, and were a required element of an elaborate, performative ritual in which the body of the officiating priest and the body of Christ—the Eucharist—interacted intimately. As the priest performed the carefully choreographed motions and gestures of the Mass, different portions of his clothing solicited and receded from the viewer's gaze. Until Vatican II, most of the ritual was performed with the priest facing away from the congregation—hence the decorative emphasis on the back side of these chasubles. Contemporary depictions of the Mass in painting, prints, or sculpture invariably show the priest lifting up the elevated Eucharist as the deep folds of the chasuble hang down over his back. **[Seth Hindin]**

Belozerskaya, Marina. *Rethinking the Renaissance Burgundian Arts Across Europe.* Cambridge Cambridge University Press, 2002.
Farmer, David Hugh. *The Oxford Dictionary of Saints.* 5th edition. Oxford: Oxford University Press, 2003.
Monnas, Lisa. "New Documents for the Vestments of Henry VII at Stonyhurst College." *The Burlington Magazine* 131 (May 1989): 345-349.
Stonyhurst Vestments. Private publication, Stonyhurst College, undated [1957].
To the Greater Glory of God. Catalogue of an Exhibition Held at the Bar Convent Museum, Blossom Street, York, 4th July—4th October 1987 Wisbech: Balding & Mansell, 1987.
Victoria & Albert Museum Department of Textiles. *Catalogue of English Ecclesiastical Embroideries of the XIII. to the XVI. Centuries.* 4th ed. London: Board of Education, 1930.
Monnas, Lisa. "The Vestments of Henry VII at Stonyhurst College: Cloth of Gold Woven to Shape." *Bulletin de Liaison du CIETA* 65 (1987): 69-80.

Coronation of the Virgin
Linen with gold metal and colored silk thread embroidery, 11 5/8 x 12 ¾ in. (29.5 x 32 cm.)
England, late 15th century
Provenance: Heythrop College, London
The Loyola University Museum of Medieval, Renaissance, and Baroque Art, Gift of Mr. and Mrs. John V. Farwell III (acq. no. 1.76) Catalogue No. 95

This scene of the coronation of Mary is set under castellated arches against a background of diapered gold. Seated on a bench and holding an orb in her hand, Mary is crowned by God the Father. This is similar to the image from the north nave aisle of the cathedral, of 1508. The silk embroidery is in gold, green, white and blue while the gold background is couched to make its design. From the shape of the embroidery it can readily be assumed that it was the center panel of a cope hood and originally surrounded by various decorative

Coronation of the Virgin, England, late 15th century, The Loyola University Museum of Medieval, Renaissance, and Baroque Art, Chicago

bandings. This theme of the coronation became a popular imaged associated with honoring the Virgin; one of its most memorable examples is the central door of the North portal of Chartres cathedral, about 1215. The elaborate arch decorations were, perhaps, inspired by engraved designs by artists such as the Master of the Berlin Passion, a Lowlands engraver about 1460 (Hollstein, vol. XII, p. 90) whose works were widely distributed. **[Rowe, Catalogue]**

Crucifixion
Linen with gold metal and colored silk thread embroidery, 14 ¾ x 19 ½ in. (37 x 48 cm.)
England, about 1500
Provenance: Stonyhurst College, Lancashire, England
The Loyola University Museum of Medieval, Renaissance, and Baroque Art, Gift of Mr. and Mrs. John V. Farwell III (acq. no. 1.75) Catalogue No. 94

This image appears to have lost a segment extending the upper portion of the cross. Christ is displayed on a cross set in a two-stepped hexagonal base next to which a skull is shown. The skull is a traditional image referring to the word Golgotha – the place of the skull (Matt 27:33). The legends developed around the discovery of the cross evoke the notion that the cross was cut from the wood of the tree of paradise and that Golgotha was the site of Adam's grave. Thus we see Christ's position as the "new Adam," reversing the sin of the first parents: "And as in Adam all shall die, so also in Christ all shall be made alive" (Corinthans 15:22). On either side of Christ, two angels catch the blood flowing from his hands. Their holding chalice-shaped cups reinforces the concept of Christ's blood sacramentally present in the ritual of the Mass.

The figure of Christ is highlighted in a float embroidery stitch in silk against a plain linen background. His halo and loincloth are in couched gold thread while his hair and the blood from his wounds are in several shades of brown. The wings of the angels and the borders are in gold, green, blue, and cream-colored silk threads. Although the clothing of the angels and the diapered background pattern are embroidered in gold metal thread, the background threads are couched in a brick pattern while those of the angels' garments are laid down in pairs and affixed in a random pattern of threads. Crosses such as this often decorated the backs of chasubles. **[Rowe, Catalogue]**

The Crucifixion, England, about 1500, The Loyola University Museum of Medieval, Renaissance, and Baroque Art, Chicago

The Wintour Red Vestments: Chasuble, Stole, Maniple, and Chalice Veil
Velvet, with silk embroidery, Chasuble: 44 x 26 in. (112 x 66 cm.)
England, executed by Helena Wintour, 1650s
Stonyhurst College, Lancashire

This set of vestments is part of the rich bequest of Catholic liturgical embroidery worked by Helena Wintour over a lifetime. Helena's father and uncles had been conspirators with Robert Catesby and Guy Fawkes in the Gunpowder Plot against James I. They were executed in 1605 when she was only five year old. Unlike many female relatives of disgraced conspirators, she chose to remain on the family estate in Worcester and spent the rest of her life in works of charity, prayer, and needlework. She left these vestments, along with several other sets, money, and land to the Jesuits based at their secret mission in Worcester. In 1668, Fr. George Gray S.J., wrote to the Provincial, stating that he had visited Miss Wintour and seen her working on the vestments, still on the frame, and that she had been at work on them for many years. She evidently intended that her gifts would enable the Jesuits to found a school for Catholics- necessarily clandestine. She wrote a declaration to that effect on the day of her death on May 5, 1671, but immediately following her demise, the bequest was strenuously contested. In the end - this was a time approaching the "Popish Plot" hysteria - the Jesuits had to agree to divide the vestments with Helena's niece, Lady Wintour.

This set, as well as a parallel set in white, were rediscovered in Grafton Manor in 1820. The Manor had been part of the Jesuit mission, and it is presumed that the vestments had been stored away on the closure of Wintour's secret school some time in the mid to late eighteenth century and forgotten. They were in a poor state of repair, and this set has suffered at the hands of the restorers. Appropriate for a red vestment, it features the imagery of Pentecost, with the dove of the Holy Spirit on the back of the chasuble, surrounded by tongues of fire and clouds with torrents of rain perhaps representing the mighty wind encountered by the Apostles. It has the Jesuit monogram of the IHS, and Helena's family crest of the white falcon and the tower- a play on her surname, which was Welsh in origin- Gwyn, meaning white, and tour. Like the White set, it was richly embellished, with rubies, garnets and 471 pearls. **[Janet Graffius]**

Red chasuble, England, executed by Helena Wintour, 1650s, Stonyhurst College, Lancashire

Red chalice veil, detail, England, executed by Helena Wintour, 1650s, Stonyhurst College, Lancashire

RELICS AND THE TWO THOMASES: THOMAS OF CANTERBURY AND THOMAS OF HEREFORD AS BISHOP MARTYR AND BISHOP CONFESSOR

Virginia C. Raguin and Naomi Reed Kline

Venerated prelates, and the waxing and waning of their cults in England, can serve to profile shifting associations of religious loyalty, civic duty, and habits of piety from England's Middle Age through the nineteenth century. Church leaders, especially bishops, were not infrequently the focus of pious memory which developed a cult status. From the early days of Christianity in England, St. Cuthbert (635-687), bishop of Lindisfarne, attracted pilgrims to the cathedral of Durham, and St. Augustine (d. 604), first bishop of Canterbury and "Apostle of the English" whose remains were buried in the Canterbury monastery that bears his name, made the city famous even before Becket's assassination drew international attention.

Thomas Becket (1118-1170) was born to parents of undistinguished social rank, but was educated at Merton Abbey and Paris and in 1141 entered the service of Theobald, Archbishop of Canterbury, England's premier Episcopal seat. Becket subsequently served with distinction in the court of Henry II (1133-1189), who in 1162 appointed him to the see of Canterbury vacated by Theobald's death. Becket's loyalties to church privilege soon brought him into conflict with his patron, which involved exile in France and ultimately his return to England. Responding to the king's anger, in 1170, four knights accosted the bishop soon after his return, striking him down while he was at prayer in a side chapel of the cathedral. The incident was an immense shock to contemporaries; the news traveled across all of Europe and Becket was swiftly canonized two years later. Immediately, miracles, attested to by several monastic accounts, attracted pilgrims. The cathedral benefited from this popularity and is one of the most impressive religious edifices of the Middle Ages. The choir and transept were built in the Early English style from 1175 through 1220 after a devastating fire. The translation of Becket's relics into the new choir was a state occasion and became a commemorated feast day throughout England.

The focal point of the choir was Becket's shrine, designed by Elias of Dereham sometime between 1205 to1216. Faced with gold and decorated

Canterbury Cathedral, interior of choir with stained glass windows showing miracles of St. Thomas Becket, 1175-1220.
Photo: Virginia Raguin

Vision of St. Thomas Becket emerging from his shrine to cure the ill, window V:III(1), Canterbury Cathedral. Photo: Virginia Raguin

with jewels, it stood on an elevated base in the middle of the Trinity Chapel, at the east end of the church, as depicted in one of the stained glass windows. The pavement, of Cosmati work, survives. Pilgrims walked around the shrine, surrounded by a color-drenched backdrop of twelve windows illustrating Thomas's miracles. This carefully calculated experience was the goal of the pilgrim. Over the years, in time-honored practice, gifts added to the value of the shrine. Chief among them was a large ruby given by Louis VII of France in gratitude for Becket's good services in the cure of his son. In the sixteenth century, the shrine was protected by a wooden cover, which was drawn up by ropes to reveal the jewel-encrusted metalwork shrine. Desiderius Erasmus visited the shrine in 1514, leaving a valuable, if critical, assessment of the merchandising and veneration of relics shortly before the Reformation (Fleming, 148-51; Erasmus; Nichols). The description was early translated into English and often cited as an argument against the cult of relics. A fictive pilgrim asks his colleague "Dydste thou see hys bones?" The reply explains:

> That is not conuenient, nor we cowld not come to it, except we sett vp laders, but a shryne of wod couerede a shryne of gold, when that is drawne vp with cordes, thā apperith treasure and riches inestimable. . . . The vilest part and worst was golde, all thynges dyd shyne, florishe, and as it were with lyghtnynge appered with precyouse stones and those many and of great multitude: some were greater than a gowse egge. Dyuerse of ye monks stode ther aboute with greate reuerence, the couer takyn a way, all we kneled downe and worshyped. The pryor with a whyte rodde showed vs euery stone, addynge therto the frenche name, the value, & the autor of the gyfte, for the cheffe stonys were sent thyther by great princes (Erasmus).

The use of such "revelations" was common, from Eucharistic doves holding the host elevated with pulleys in the thirteenth century to the towering covers of fifteenth-century baptismal fonts lifted by ropes, as in Ufford and Hepworth (Suffolk) (Cautley, 77-79, 85-87).

Two Thomases

Canterbury became the most visited pilgrimage site in England. Pilgrim badges from the late twelfth through the sixteenth centuries recovered from datable deposits on the London banks of the River Thames reveal Thomas's popularity (Spencer, 37-128). An enormous variety of badges show Becket's death, the sword that struck him down, the saint in bishop's robes, Becket's head isolated, his shrine, Becket in a ship returning from exile, and Becket on horseback, among others. A series of ampullae designed to carry Canterbury water bear the Latin inscription: "Thomas is the best doctor of the worthy sick" (Spencer, 38, nos. 5-13).

Pilgrim ampulla designed to carry Canterbury water from shrine of St. Thomas Becket, Museum of London. London

Becket received ubiquitous commemoration in windows, wall paintings, vestments, statues, and prayer books where two days were allocated, the feast honoring his martyrdom on December 29 and the translation of his relics on July 7 (Borenius; Woolley; Caviness 1977). The Books of Hours in this exhibition all show both commemorations. This all came to an end in 1538 when Henry VIII abolished the cult:

> from hense forth the sayde Thomas Becket shall not be esteemed, named, reputed, nor called a sayncte, but bysshop Becket, and that his ymages and pictures, through the hole realme, shall be putte downe, and auoyded out of all churches, chapelles, and other places (Proclamation of Nov. 16, 1538 in Borenius, 109-110).

Devotional books were purged, such as the Book of Hours printed in Paris, 1526 whose December calendar shows the striking out of the name of Thomas Becket and his invocation in the suffrages. The following year Henry dissolved the Benedictine monastery and dismantled Becket's shrine, by which actions he was furthering several royal aims. The first was the continuation of policies that had routinely appropriated church goods, especially church silver and other negotiable objects for the royal treasury, and the suppression of designated religious houses in favor of other foundations (Oman, 112-14, 120-21). The second was the confirmation of the king as head of the Church, in particular by condemning the actions of any prelate to challenge royal authority, as Becket had done four centuries earlier.

Despite such royal censure, and the command to "put down and avoid" images of Becket, the miracle windows of Becket at Canterbury Cathedral were untouched. A twenty-first century visitor can view the entire stained glass program of miracles of Becket set in the eastern area of the cathedral of Canterbury

- the principle cathedral of the land then as now. The twelve stunningly complex lancets, each with different armature pattern (Caviness 1977, 146-50, Appendix fig. 2), present stories of the humble and the exalted helped through Becket's intercession. It is exactly such juxtaposition of promulgated rule and its application that challenges any complacent analysis of this period. Were these windows spared because they did not appear to present "idolatrous images" of the divine, but simply images of folk (with some appearances of Becket unrecognized)? Were they for the Early Modern period simply too archaic to even be read as a Catholic polemic, and the many small medallions somehow accepted essentially as a rich decorative fabric embellishing the architecture? These are the burning issues that motivate further exploration of this era.

December calendar showing the striking out of the name of Thomas Becket, Book of Hours printed in London, 1526, Stonyhurst College, S. 3/6, fol. 14

The practices of veneration of relics so abhorrent to the Reformers, however, continued in recusant tradition. Although denied the intensity of experience of the bejeweled shrine, the devout embellished what they could. The wood, cloth, and bead *Embroidered Reliquary Box* (CATALOGUE) is a poignant reminder of the honor given to heroic resistance for the faith. The reliquary contains part of the shoulder blade and upper arm of one of the four priests, Edmund Duke, Richard Hill, John Hog or Richard Holliday, who were together at Durham in 1590. Appropriately, the Latin inscription refers to Psalm 34:21: "He keeps all his bones; not one of them is broken," a prophecy that is associated with Christ's own death (John 19:36). Oral tradition locates the box in the possession of the pupil's Sodality in the Jesuit College of St. Omers in 1666. The hand-made reliquary box resonates with the description of an Italian woman, Beatrice Bocadiferro who had collected the remains of individuals who had been burnt by Catholics for heresy. In her own trial in 1307 she admitted to having retrieved body parts of a colleague that had been burned in the fire which she kept "in silken and precious cloths and covered with glass" (Rubin 1993, 181).

Thomas de Cantilupe (1218-1282), also known as Thomas of Hereford, is represented in this exhibition by a relic, a bone (CATALOGUE) that was rescued from destruction during the Reformation and given to Stonyhurst College in 1835. Cantilupe was a scholar, administrator, and cleric born at Hambledon, Buckinghamshire, who became the Bishop of Hereford in 1275. The major portions of his adult life were spent as scholar or professor in the faculties of Arts, Canon Law, Civil Law, and Theology at the Universities of Paris and Oxford. His family was well established and a powerful uncle, Walter de

Reliquary box, England, era of Charles I (1625-1649)? Stonyhurst College. Photo: Virginia Raguin

Cantilupe, Bishop of Worcester, facilitated his nephew's career. He died in 1282 near Montefiascone, Italy, on his return from an audience with the pope over a dispute with the Archbishop John Pecham of Canterbury. From all evidence available, Thomas was a model scholar and pastor, personally abstemious, generous to his flock, and tenaciously loyal, using considerable skills in the law to maintain church privileges against incursion by both secular lords and other ecclesiastics (Vauchez 1997, 296-304). Cantilupe's body was boiled to remove the perishable flesh from the bones, a means of "preserving" a body without embalming, and the bones brought back to Hereford where they were buried under a tomb slab before the altar in the Lady Chapel. The flesh and viscera were buried in Italy at the Abbey Church of San Severo near Orvieto (Strange, 206-207), and his heart received by Edmund, the Earl of Cornwall, a friend and admirer of Cantilupe. The following year Edmund founded a college of canons in Ashridge, Hertfordshire, giving it not only the relic of Thomas's heart but a vial of the "Holy Blood" of Christ similar to that which he had given to the Abbey of Hailes in Gloucester. In 1300, Edmund's body was similarly divided, his bones being kept at the abbey of Hailes and his heart kept in Ashridge with that of Cantelupe (Todd 10; Morris 121). As noted by Paul Binsky, such dismemberment for multiple burials was not unusual for noted individuals in the Middle Ages (Binsky, 58-69).

By the thirteenth century, the cult of relics and pilgrimage had become one of the most important sources of revenue for the construction and embellishment of buildings. Hereford's cathedral retained a good portion of its twelfth-century structure in the Norman style, despite some inspired building of the north transept under Cantilupe's predecessor Peter of Acqueblanche (1240-68). During Cantilupe's episcopacy, from 1274-1282, evidence suggests that "rebuilding and alterations were carried out slowly and that the chapter were struggling to raise money to meet the cost" (Morgan, 146). With the arrival of Cantilupe's remains in 1282, Richard Swinfield (episcopacy 1283-1316), his succeeding bishop and also Cantilupe's former chaplain, dedicated himself to the bishop's canonization which was approved in 1320. By 1287, Cantilupe's reputed sanctity had allowed Swinfield to transfer the bones to an elevated shrine in the north transept which became the focus of a popular cult for the next twenty years (Finucane, 171-88). Thirty-eight miracles were recorded for the canonization inquiry of 1307 (Vauchez 1997, 488-98). True to custom, the Archbishop of Canterbury granted an indulgence in 1283 to those who contributed to the building, followed by indulgences granted by other bishops between 1284 and 1291.

During Bishop Swinfield's tenure as bishop, Hereford Cathedral underwent architectural and decorative changes of significance that provided new possibilities for pilgrimages to Cantilupe's shrine. The new shrine unquestionably was part of the pilgrimage experience that helped fill the coffers of the cathedral

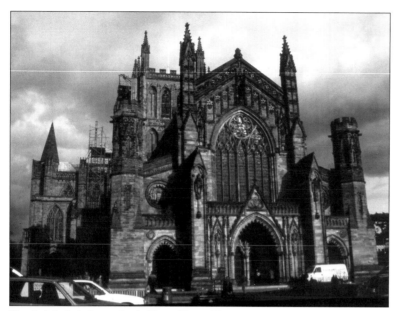

Hereford Cathedral, west façade. Photo: Naomi Kline

in the thirteenth and fourteenth centuries. Ensconced in the north transept, the newly sculptured shrine became the centerpiece along with an accretion of objects worthy of the pilgrim's attention. Included in the chapel was the famed Hereford Mappa Mundi (Kline, 76-83, 195-203). In fact, according to the account of the eighteenth-century antiquarian Stuckely, the north transept in which the shrine was located was additionally filled with items including banners, lamps, relics and the like (Stuckely, 67). His account suggests the appearance of the transept as early as the thirteenth century.

An analysis of the accounts by Penelope Morgan and review of the presumable construction of the time leaves the assessment that "Hereford cathedral was the centre of feverish activity with a small army of masons, stone cutters and other craftpersons and that much rebuilding was carried out in a comparatively short time" (Morgan, 147). By way of comparison with previous construction in the cathedral, only fourteen mason's marks (means of identifying individual masons) appear in the Lady Chapel and crypt, and two in the north transept, while from the 1280s through 1320s forty appear in the aisles, north-east transept and porch. The striking crossing tower was also built at this time. The popularity of the cult did not continue with the same fever from the 1330s onwards, a fact recognized in more economical and slower building.

Two items that were likely installed in the transept along with the shrine at the time of translation of Cantilupe's remains in 1287

Remnant of shrine of Thomas of Hereford, 1287, north transept, Hereford Cathedral. Photo: Naomi Kline

Two Thomases

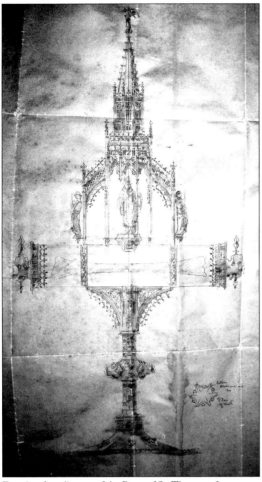

Drawing for reliquary of the Bone of St. Thomas of Hereford, England, ca. 1840, attributable to Augustus Welby Pugin, Stonyhurst College. Photo: Virginia Raguin

or shortly thereafter were the aforementioned Mappa Mundi of ca. 1300 and a thirteenth-century Limoges enamel chasse that contained relics of St. Thomas Becket. The map was the centerpiece of a triptych that could be didactically explained or simply open to interpretation by each visitor and pilgrim. Although embellished with images of church doctrine, the temporal material was of such fascination that it very likely became an attraction in itself. The painted side panels suggest that the ensemble could be opened or closed, adding to the dramatic possibility of the space, and the objects contained within this space were specifically meant to attract pilgrims.

The other object of note, the Limoges reliquary chasse of Thomas Becket of Canterbury suggests the synoptic relationship between Becket and Cantilupe. Becket was revered at Hereford as a precursor to Bishop Cantilupe. The connection between these two sainted churchmen, Thomas Cantilupe and Thomas Becket, enhanced the significance of the pilgrimage to Hereford. Hereford Cathedral was the unquestionable original destination for the chasse that was commissioned by William de Vere, Bishop of Hereford from, 1186-1198. Hereford was one of the few English sites that shared a close connection to the Plantagenets who were desirous of furthering the name of Becket by providing a number of English cathedrals with Limoges caskets containing relics of Becket. To testify to the relationship that the two saints held in the popular imagination there remains a fourteenth-century glass in Credenhill church near Hereford that contains the image of the two saints standing side by side.

Similar testimonials come from the art of music. A significant example of English "progressive music", testifies to honoring of Cantilupe after the hey-day of his veneration. About 1440, John Benet (1380?-1458?), a contemporary of John Dunstable, wrote a motet "Lux fluget ex Anglia, O pater pietatis – Salve Thoma." The manner of composition is isorhythmic, a sophisticated and highly contrived system using mathematical orders, highly prized by connoisseurs of musical art (Trowell and Wathey, 159-80).

Like the shrine of Thomas of Canterbury, that of Thomas of Hereford was destroyed in the reign of Henry VIII although the base remains. The bones, however, were apparently removed before its destruction and held in a clandestine location in Hereford. William Ely, a priest ordained during the Catholic restoration under Mary (1553-58) is noted in possession of the bones (Morris, 117-18). He went into exile under Elizabeth but later returned as a recusant priest and died in the Hereford jail in 1609. Subsequent Catholic custodians kept the bones and in 1665, according to some sources, Catholics engaged in a nocturnal procession carrying the relics in an effort to avert the plague (Morris, 114). That such veneration could take place is attributable to the considerable remnant of Catholic minority in Hereford; it is estimated that about one fifth of the population were recusants.

It was at this time, 1674, that Richard Strange (1611-1682) an English Jesuit living abroad, who was then a chaplain to a group of nuns, wrote an English account of the saint which was printed in Ghent, "at the sign of the Annunciation of our B. Lady." Strange's dedication to the Duke of Tuscany speaks of

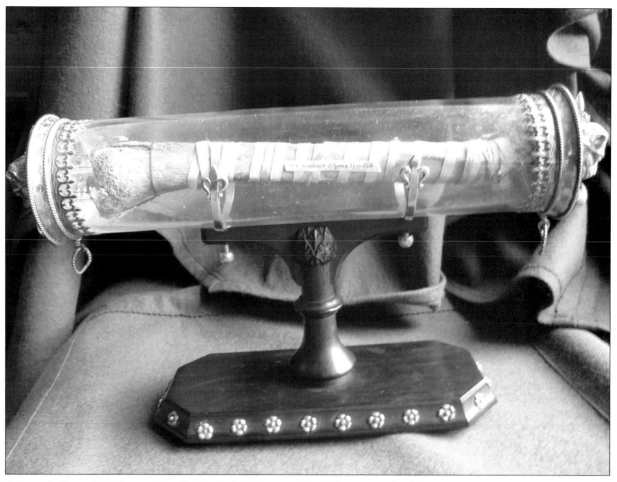

Reliquary for Bone of St. Thomas of Hereford, England, third quarter of the 19th century, attributable to Hardman & Company, Birmingham, Stonyhurst College. Photo: Virginia Raguin

the "Sufferings of Romane Catholiques even so farr" as in England, quoting the Duke's expression that "theyr invincible Constancy in Suffering persecution makes them meritt an eternall Crowne in the next [world]" (Strange, fol. 3v). The sense of a remnant preserving the "true England" is born out by Strange's characterization of his own efforts as home-bred sanctity: "And I hope, I do not disparage Sanctity of our lland by calling it home bred; the Sanctity of our land having bin in former times not onely the staple Commodity, as I may say, of the same, but of Christendome; illustrating the Church of God with as many and noble lights in that Kind as perchance any of its neighbouring Kingdomes" (Strange, fol. 7v). He notes that Cantilupe's "Sacred Corps" is interred in the abbey church of San Severo "neer the old Citty of Florence" (Strange, 203), and thus within the dominions of the Duke. His "Sacred Bones" receive frequent mention as well as meditation on his virtues. The volume in the Houghton Library, Harvard University, bears a handwritten line on the title page: "Given by the Authour to William Tunstall," and more than one hundred and fifty years later, a descendant, Charles Tunstall Esq., is noted on an end paper as having presented the book to the Reverend L. M. Gilbert in 1823.

During the same era as the biography, Cantilupe's relics were being dispersed, encouraged by the population of English in exile on the Continent as well as continued fears of Protestant desecration. An arm bone was given in 1651 by Rev. John Poyntz to his sister Mary Poyntz, then in Paris, one of Mary Ward's companions and the third superior of her Institute (Chambers, II, 512-13; Morris 123). The relic, now lost, was transferred to St. Omers in 1668 and installed in the Sodality chapel. About 1670, the skull was removed to Germany, to the English Benedictine house at Lamspringe in the diocese of Hildesheim, which became a parish church in 1803. In 1881 the skull was retrieved and brought to the Benedictine Abbey of Downside (Barrett, 183-84; Morris 121-23) where it is now enshrined in a reliquary "ark" designed by Ninian Comper in the Lady Chapel (*Downside Guide*, 11, 16). A shin bone was given in 1664 to Rev. Humphrey Brown (a.k.a. Mr. Evans, d. 1679), the Jesuit Superior of the mission of North Wales at Holywell. It is this relic that was transferred by Fr. Francis Lythgoe of Holywell to Stonyhurst in 1835 (Finucane, 216, fig. 15; Morris, 125-26).

In the nineteenth century, one finds a revival in interest in relics and reliquaries especially when they represented objects long suppressed or exiled, restored to honor. Thus the *Reliquary for a Bone of St. Thomas of Hereford* appears with distinction at Stonyhurst. The metalwork and glass reliquary was produced in the third quarter of the nineteenth century, and is attributable to Hardman & Company, Birmingham. This behavior is paralleled by the reintroduction or refurbishment of other objects associated with Catholic piety. The *Constable Chalice* in the Bar Convent (see in this catalogue "Veneration of the True Cross," pp. 125-26) of 1630-40 was embellished with jewels that appear to be from a single – or group - set of female adornments presumably in the early nineteenth century. The Wentworth Chalice in the Blairs Museum, Aberdeen, Scotland (Inv. 6138 BLRBM) carries a Latin inscription that proclaims a similar process of retention, testifying that Lady Harriet Wentworth restored the chalice after "many years in exile" to sacred purposes in 1888 (see in this catalogue "Mary Ward," p. 157).

Reliquary for bone of St. Thomas of Hereford, detail of end. Photo: Virginia Raguin

CATALOGUE

Reliquary Box
Wood with applied silk cloth, pearls, and glass
stones; in interior, human bones
4 ½ x 12 ½ x 6 ¾ in. (11.4 x 31.8 x 17.1 cm.)
England, era of Charles I (1625-1649)?
Stonyhurst College, Lancashire
In pearls the inscription reads: CUSTODIT DNS OIA
OSSA FORUM PS 33:21

During the recusant era, precious metals appear to
have been almost exclusively dedicated to liturgical
vessels such as chalices and patens. Reliquaries,
which in Pre-Reformation times would have been
in precious metals, crystal, gilt bronze, and enamels,
apparently used more mundane materials. This
wooden box covered with silk embroidery in a
floral work typical of its era is an example. The
decorated box contains part of the shoulder blade
and upper arm of one of the four priests, Edmund
Duke, Richard Hill, John Hog or Richard Holliday,
who were together at Durham in 1590. The
reliquary is believed to have been a possession of
the pupil's Sodality in the Jesuit College of St.
Omers in 1666. Psalm 33:21 reads: The Lord
keepeth all their bones, not one of them shall be
broken. In the Gospel description of Christ's
death, this psalm is referenced. The soldiers broke
the legs of the two thieves to hasten their deaths.
Christ was apparently already dead so that rather
than breaking his legs, they verified this by piercing
his side and saw water and blood run out. The
Gospel of John (19:36) explains: "For these things
were done so that the scripture might be fulfilled:
You shall not break a bone of him."

*Drawing for Reliquary of the Bone of St. Thomas of
Hereford*
Paper, ink, pencil, 19 ½ x 15 in. (49.5 x 38 cm.)
England, ca. 1840 attributable to Augustus Welby
Pugin
Stonyhurst College, Lancashire

Reliquary for Bone of St. Thomas of Hereford
Wood, silver, glass, 8 x 12 in. (20.3 x 30.5 cm.)
England, third quarter of the 19th century,
attributable to Hardman & Company, Birmingham
Stonyhurst College, Lancashire

The chief metalwork designer for Hardman &
Company was Augustus Welby Pugin's son-in-law
John Hardman Powell. Fr. Whitty (1817-1895),
the English Jesuit Provincial, completed this
commission which simplifies the first suggestion
of the A. W. Pugin drawing ca. 1840. The relic
was acquired in 1835 and thus available for Pugin's
inspection, when he first visited Stonyhurst
in 1837. The architect/designer had but little
success with the Jesuits, and was criticized as too
expensive for architectural work by Fr. Lythgoe,
the influential Provincial. The style and metal work
and chasing techniques suggest a date c. 1860.
The wooden plinth with applied metalwork is to a
form employed by E. W. Pugin, a son of Augustus
W. Pugin, both for furniture and other church
metalwork, as can be seen in related examples
at Belmont Abbey and St. Edmund's College,
Ware, where an E. W. Pugin mounted glass phial
reliquary is dated to 1862. Fr. Whitty joined the
Society of Jesus as a priest in 1857, so that is a
terminus post quem for the reliquary. **[Roderick
O'Donnell]**

Atterbury Paul, ed. *A. W. N. Pugin: Master of Gothic
Revival* [exh. cat. The Bard Center for
Studies in the Decorative Arts] New Haven:
Yale University Press, 1995.
Barrett, Dom Illtud. "The Relics of St. Thomas
Cantilupe," in Jancey: 181-85.
Finucane, pl. 15.
Morris, J. "English Relics I, St. Thomas of
Hereford," *The Month* 44 (Jan.-April., 1882):
124-26.
Wedgwood, Alexandra. *A. W. N. Pugin and the
Pugin Family: Catalogue of Architectural Drawings
at the Victoria and Albert Museum.* London:
Victoria and Albert Museum, 1985.

Two Thomases

Private Prayer and Books of Hours

Virginia C. Raguin

Books of Hours were the most popular works of "text" in the late Middle Ages and the Renaissance. The six books included in the exhibition reveal, as do all Books of Hours, the piety espoused by their users, the production and marketing of their makers, and, for the specific situation of England, their contested legitimacy as concepts of political and religious allegiance became intertwined. During their early stages, these books were individualized luxury goods, works of art purchased at great expense and indispensable for anyone of status. For example, the tiny (each page 3 ½ by 2 ¼ inches) Hours of Jeanne d'Evreux (Metropolitan Museum of Art, New York, Cloisters Collection, 54.1.2), 1325-28 is easily the most significant work of art of its generation. Illuminated by Jean Pucelle for the teen-age bride of King Charles IV, the images can be seen to construct a code of virtuous conduct for the young queen, whose role in producing a hoped-for male heir to the throne was of vital political importance.

During the fifteenth century, a rise in urban population and mercantile wealth encouraged a change in manuscript production that included mass-produced books (Duffy 1995, 209-32). Continental workshops in Paris and Bruges, to name the most important centers, sold Books of Hours to local and foreign clients. Those destined for the English market conformed to the English form called Sarum usage (Sarum is the Latin word for the diocese of Salisbury). With the use of the printing press and moveable type towards the end of the fifteenth century, Books of Hours became extremely widespread and were owned by almost all persons of means. As Eamon Duffy expressed it, "on the eve the Reformation [Books of Hours] were being produced in multiple editions in thousands, in formats ranging from the sumptuous to the skimpy," and varying considerably in price (Duffy 1995, 209).

The attraction of the Hours was multifaceted. First, the act of prayer was an ingrained social as well as religious practice in the Middle Ages. The most privileged members of society, which included the literate priests, monks, and nuns, were engaged in the act of prayer, for which a population honored them and transferred significant wealth to church institutions to guarantee that it would share in the merits of such prayers. The ability to pray directly to Christ, the Virgin and the saints from personalized prayer books would obviously have great value. The possession of books in itself was a mark of status.

A record of an Italian visitor a generation before the Reform left a vivid image of the gentry who frequented their family chapels daily but who attended their parish churches on Sunday:

> Although they all attend Mass every day, and say many Paternosters [Our Fathers] in public, the women carrying long rosaries in their hands, and any who can read taking the office of our Lady with them and with some companion reciting it in the church verse by verse in a low voice after the manner of churchmen, they always hear Mass on Sunday in their parish church and give liberal alms (Goldberg, 283).

The call and response method of the "office of our Lady" described by the visitor is conditioned by the alternate reading of elements of prayers called the Antiphon, Versicle, and Response in these exercises. This sense of intimacy, confirmed by interaction with a single or small group of companions in reading the Hours constituted an attractive element of this devotion.

These prayer books, sometimes referred to as primers, were also apparently essential elements in the acquisition of literacy. Many children learned their first letters from these books and graduated to simple and then more complicated prayers, thus reinforcing the position of devotion in family as well as clerical life. Chaucer's Prioress tells the tale of the youthful St. Hugh of Lincoln.

This litel child, his litel book lernynge,
As he sat in the scole at his prymer,
He *Alma redemptoris* herde singe
As children lerned hir anthiphoner;
And as he dorste, he drough hym ner and ner,
And herkned ay the wordes and the noote,
Til he the firste vers koude al by rote. (Prioress's Tale: lines 64-70)

Hugh is but seven years of age and hears the Latin text of the eleventh-century hymn *Alma redemptoris mater* (Kindly Mother of the Redeemer), one of the four Antiphons sung at Compline and Lauds in honor of the Virgin Mary at various times of the year. He is determined to master the text by heart so that he can sing praises to the Virgin as he walks to and from school, despite his neglect of any other obligation he has to learn the texts in the Primer.

Though that I for my prymer shal be shent
And shal be beten thries in an houre,
I wol it konne, oure lady for to honoure. (lines 89-91)

"Fifteen O's" with Renaissance secular decorative scenes in the margins, Book of Hours printed in Paris by Simon Vostre, 1512, Stonyhurst College, S. 3/3, fols.

Since the primary need for literacy was to enable individuals to enter clerical orders, and later civil service, as Thomas More would elect, the dominance of Latin was commensurate with function.

A review of the transformation of these texts is important for the history of the English Bible and for understanding the transition from a Latin culture to English as a language of worship and legal transactions as well as literature (Butterworth). Throughout the later Middle Ages English frequently mingled with Latin texts as in the Book of Hours printed by Wynkyn de Worde about 1494 with the "Fifteen O's" in English. The 1512 Books of Hours printed in Paris by Simon Vostre shows the "Fifteen O's" in Latin with secular decorative scenes in the margins (CATALOGUE). Other *Horae* included the Lord's Prayer or the Ten Commandments in English (Ibid., 305). The *Book of Hours of Sarum Usage* printed in Paris by François Regnault in 1526 (CATALOGUE) reserves folios at the back of the book for an English text to aid the examination of conscience and other essential Christian knowledge. A slightly later *Book of Hours* printed in 1530 (CATALOGUE) demonstrates the frequent device of English directions interspersed within the text to focus on specific Latin prayers such as those imploring aid for the sick or for the souls in purgatory, as well as closing folios in English.

The translation into English of substantial devotional texts appeared to wax and wane according to the orthodox or heterodox reception of the translation. During Chaucer's time, that is, the second half of the fourteenth century, there was a great growth in the use of English. Around 1400 a *Prymer*, now in the library of St. John's College, Cambridge, was written entirely in English with short titles of the Latin prayers used to locate the texts, for example, *Pater n'r* [pater noster] for the prayer of the Our Father: "Fader oure that art in heuene halwed be thi name" (Littlehales 1891, 20). In 1408 the influence of English connected to the anti-clerical Lollard movement associated with John Wyclif (d. 1384) who had made a translation of the Bible, culminated in the promulgation by Thomas Arundel, archbishop of Canterbury, of the "Constitutions of Clarendon" condemning any unauthorized translation of Scripture into English. Nicholas Love's approved English adaptation of the *Meditationes Vitae Christi* as *The Mirror of the Blessed Life of Jesus Christ* (Love) was published in 1410. The text of the *Prymer* at St. John's suggests that it did not follow the Wycliffite Bible but like Love, may have been associated with the desire to combat the Lollard challenges to the exclusivity of prayer in a clerical language (Butterworth, 100-101). The controversies over access to English language prayers and Biblical reading continued well through the Tudor era. Thomas More, for example, was opposed to the translation of the Bible into English and carried on a point-counterpoint attack on William Tyndale's Bible of 1525, in particular in his *Confutation of Tyndale's Answer* of 1528 (Martz, 31-41; Butterworth, 13-14). Even after Henry VIII's break with Rome and More's execution in 1535 councilors for Henry debated various editions of primers and the eradication of non-conformist books (Butterworth, 221-55). This was aided, however, by the publication in 1535 of the first complete English Bible, translated by Miles Coverdale as well as the English versions of the Our Father, the Creed and the Ten Commandments which were made compulsory for all parish churches (The Second Royal Injunctions of Henry VIII, 1538: Gee and Hardy, 275-76).

This exhibition contains a Primer in English published in 1541, *The Prymer in Englyssh and Laten after the use of Sarum*. The book has few illustrations, mostly simple initials set against a foliate square. Many items are simply in English, but for the better known sections, the familiar Latin is placed as a border text to the right and left. Significantly, there are no erasures in the text, for as printed by the King, the papal saints have been demoted to "bishop" and Thomas Becket no longer appears. The issue of uniformity and royal control is addressed in one of the opening pages. Having concern for the diversity of versions circulating of the Pater Noster, Ave Maria, Creed, and others, the king explains the need for a "uniform translacyon" so that all subjects in the realm would "learne and use the same." He thus commands every "Person, vicar, and curate to rede and teache the same to their paryssyoners. And that no man Imprynt, or set forth any other translacyon, upon payne at his hyghe dysplesure." Shortly thereafter, the king's Primer would become under Edward a matter of superstitious practices, and be replaced by the *Book of Common Prayer*.

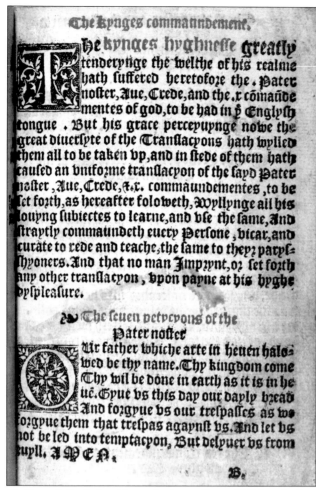

The kynges commaunndemenť.

The Prymer in Englyssh and Laten after the use of Sarum, 1541, introduction by Henry VII demanding adherence to a single English translation of prayers; Pater noster (Our Father), Stonyhurst College, S.3.26

By the seventeenth century, English was accepted, even for recusant piety. French and Flemish versions of the Hours were already available. In 1616 a *Primer, or Office of the Blessed Virgin Marie, in English* was printed by Henry Iacy, using the "latest edition" of the Roman breviary (Rogers). The Catholics had produced an official translation of the Bible, the New Testament in Reims in 1582 and the Old Testament in Douai in 1609. Accordingly, the Primer's opening pages explained that the "places of holy Scripture which are the principall part of the booke, are accorded with the Authenicall translation of the Bible in English, lately published in *Doway*." In a clear understanding of the Protestant position on intercessory saints, the Primer pleaded that if it "fall into the handes of any not Catholikes" the veneration given to the "mother of God, or any other Saint" is given because they are "Friends of God" but that God himself is "the only fountaine of all goodness." That the book was conceived as a true instructional manual is evident in the first matter after the calendar being the Apostles' Creed, the Lord's Prayer, the Hail Mary, the Ten Commandments, and then four pages listing Catholic beliefs and pious concepts including the Seven Sacraments, Seven Corporal Works of Mercy, Beatitudes, and so forth. The illustrations include: 26 Annunciation and Visitation, 44 Nativity, 62 Adoration of the Magi, 68 Flight into Egypt, 80 Assumption, 280 Resurrection of Lazarus beginning the Office of the Dead, 284 David at Prayer beginning the Seven Penitential Psalms, 312 Crucifixion beginning the Office of the Holy Cross, 323 Pentecost beginning the Office of the Holy Ghost, showing a man at prayer in a private chamber, 230 beginning A Daily Exercise, the Passion according to the four Gospels, each with a portrait of the Evangelists, 388, 406, 442 (labeled 242) and 436. The last quarter of the book is devoted to the manner of serving the priest at Mass (in Latin) and hymns and prayers for feast days and Sundays throughout the year.

Calendar

The calendar was an essential part of every Book of Hours because it allowed the owner to know which prayers to say on each day. The medieval church had constructed a sequence of commemorative feasts spaced throughout each year that recapitulated the dogmas of salvation. It began in Advent (penitential waiting), Christmas (Christ's Birth), Lent (penitential waiting), Easter (Christ's Death and Resurrection), Christ's Ascension, Pentecost (the Descent of the Holy Spirit on the Apostles) and the life of the Church under the Apostles. Furthermore, each day was dedicated to one or more saints. Some are familiar today, such as St. Patrick on March 17, or St. Nicolas (traditional gift-giving in Northern Europe) on December 5. Some saints were universally cherished, such as Katherine, Christopher, or Barbara. Different localities, however, invariably had saints of local devotion, such as Cologne's veneration of saints Gereon and Ursula as patrons of the city. These variations in the calendar can often help to determine the origin of a Book of Hours, or at least its destined owners. The most common images that accompany the calendar are the labors of the month and the signs of the zodiac. The former marked the passage of time according to human activities on earth, the later the changing configuration of the heavens. In the later Middle Ages the Calendar often incorporated allusions to the stages of human life and representations of the sacraments. The printed Books of Hours of 1530, (Stonyhurst S.3/6, fol. 12v), illustrates November with an old man sick in a chair and a doctor examining a urine flask. Sagittarius is framed on the wall behind them. Note in the list of feasts that both Popes Clement and Martin have been demoted; hand-written corrections by Henry's reformers designate them as merely "bishops." December

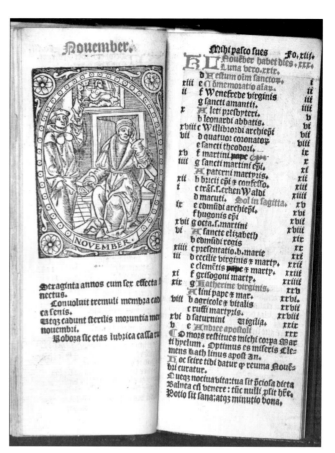

November Calendar showing an old man sick in a chair with a doctor examining a urine flask. Book of Hours printed in Paris by François Regnault, 1526, Stonyhurst College, S. 3/6, fols. 12v-13

Illustration for Gospel Lesson of John: after Albrecht Dürer, Emperor Domitian's attempt to execute St. John the Evangelist. Book of Hours printed in Paris by Simon Vostre, 1512, Stonyhurst College, S. 3/3, fol. 12v

terminates the year, and the man's life, with an image of his deathbed and Extreme Unction.

Gospel Lessons

Gospel Lessons were a standard element of Book of Hours by the fifteenth century. Excerpts from the four Gospel writers as found in the lessons read at Mass are presented in the chronological order of Christ's life. John's text (1:1-14) begins: "In the beginning there was the Word, and the Word was with God, and the Word was God," until the lines "And the Word was made flesh and dwelt among us, (and we saw his glory as it were of the only begotten of the Father,) full of grace and truth." Luke's text (1:26-38) relates the Annunciation and Matthew's (2:1-12) the Birth of Christ and the Adoration of the Magi. Mark's words (16:14-20) are the closing verses of his Gospel. Christ speaks to his disciples after his Resurrection, commanding them to go into the world and preach the gospel.

Hours of the Virgin

The central focus of the Book of Hours is a sequence of prayer called the Little Office of the Blessed Virgin Mary. Like the distribution of prayers across the hours of the day for the monastic life and for the clergy, called the Divine Office, the prayers are divided into eight parts: Matins, and Lauds, sometimes said at night and sometimes on rising, Prime, around 6 AM, Terce, at 9 AM, Sex, about noon, None, about 3 PM, Vespers, also called Evensong, in the early evening and Compline, normally before sleep. The authorship of the Hours of the Virgin has been associated with Benedict of Aniane, a major figure in the Carolingian reform of the church of the early ninth century. This sequence of prayers imposed greater uniformity on monastic life, importing the patterns begun in the sixth century with St. Benedict at Monte Casino. By the mid-eleventh century, the Virgin's Hours were a standard part of clerical and monastic prayer. Psalters, the group of the 150 psalms of the Old Testament continued in use primarily for monastic life. For the laity, by the mid-thirteenth century, the Psalters were to a considerable extent replaced by the Book of Hours and attached devotions.

By such a transformation, the lengthy sequence of 150 Psalms was supplanted by a more focused grouping of texts in the Hours. In the spirit of medieval Christianity that saw the entire Old Testament imbued with a hidden text prefiguring the New, the virtues of the Virgin were found amply announced in the eloquence and beauty of the psalms. At Matins, for example, Psalm 18: "The heavens shew forth the glory of God and the firmament declareth the work of his hands" is associated not only with the dawn,

but with the advent of Mary, whose spotless purity shines to God's glory. At Prime, after three psalms (53, 84, and 116) praising God's goodness, protection, and justice, the reader intoned lines from the Canticle of Canticles 6:9: "Who is she who cometh forth as the morning rising, fair as the moon, bright as the sun, terrible as an army set in array."

Hours of the Cross and Hours of the Holy Spirit

Many Books also contained the Hours of the Cross and the Hours of the Holy Spirit. These are shorter devotions that often follow each other and apparently functioned as a unit. For each of the seven hours (Lauds is not included), the reader says only a hymn and a prayer, introduced by a few short verses and responses. The opening image for the Hours of the Cross was almost always a Crucifixion.

Mary of Burgundy reading her Hours, Hours of Mary of Burgundy, Bruges, ca. 1477, Vienna Österreichische Nationalbibliothek, Cod. 1857, fol. 14v

Prayers Beeseeching the Virgin "Obsecro Te" and "O Intemerata"

These deeply moving prayers appear in almost all Books of Hours. They are referred to by their opening lines, or "incipits": "Obsecro te" (I beseech you) and "O intemerata" (O immaculate virgin). Mary is praised for her virtues; the reader reminds her of the immense joy of her bearing the messiah as well as commiserating with her as she contemplated Christ's Passion and death. Then the reader petitions the Virgin to "hasten and come to my aid and counsel," ending with the request that she insure that the petitioner fulfill the seven corporal works of mercy (feed the hungry, give drink to the thirsty, harbor the stranger, care for the sick, visit the imprisoned, and bury the dead), and believe in "the twelve articles of Faith" as listed in the prayer of the Apostle's Creed. The prayer concludes by asking: "At the end of my life show me your face." (For full texts see Wieck 1988, 163-64.)

Often the patron elects to have his or her portrait associated with this prayer. In an exquisite late fifteenth-century manuscript, Mary of Burgundy is represented reading her Hours within a well-appointed oratory complete with shutters equipped with bulls-eyes glass lattice, a glass vase with tall stalks of iris, and a pet dog (the Hours of Mary of Burgundy, Vienna Österreichische Nationalbibliothek, Cod. 1857, fol. 14v. Bruges, ca. 1477). She looks out into the church, in front of the high altar, a space into which Mary either projects or remembers herself, accompanied by her female companions, with a male devotee, possibly her husband Maximilian of Hapsburg, who prays before the Virgin, honoring her with a censor. The prayer she is reading has been identified as the Obsecro te (Inglis, 19-24).

Seven Penitential Psalms and the Litany

A long tradition associated seven specified Psalms with penitential expression. King David was presumed to have composed them to give voice to his sorrow for his adultery with Bathsheba, his sending her husband Uriah to be killed in battle, and also his later sins of pride. The Roman monk Cassiodorus in the sixth century referred to this group of psalms as a sevenfold means of obtaining forgiveness. Thus, an image of King David in prayer, confronting Goliath, and, especially in the sixteenth century, David looking with lust after Bathsheba bathing frequently illustrated this section of a Book of Hours (Costley). In the Printed Book of Hours by Simon Vostre, David is shown sending Uriah, Bathsheba's husband, to battle where he is sure to be killed (Costley, 1247, fig. 9). The printed Hours at Stonyhurst dated 1526 includes five images of David (fols. 65v-72), from his first lustful glance to his reconciliation with God by offering a holocaust.

David sends Uriah to his death. Book of Hours printed in Paris by Simon Vostre, 1512, Stonyhurst College, S. 3/3, fol. 63

Pope Innocent III (1198-1216) included the seven psalms in the rituals of Lent.

6. O Lord, rebuke me not in thy indignation, nor chastise me in thy wrath.
31. Blessed are they whose iniquities are forgiven, and whose sins are covered.
37. O Lord, rebuke me not in thy indignation, nor chastise me in thy wrath.
50. Have mercy on me, O God, according to thy great mercy.
101. Hear, O Lord, my prayer; and let my cry come unto thee.
129. Out of the depths I have cried to thee, O Lord.
142. Hear, O Lord, my prayer: give ear to my supplication in thy truth; Hear me in thy justice.

The Penitential Psalms are followed by the litany where the names of saintly intercessors are pronounced followed by the phrase "ora pro nobis" - pray for us. Such long, repetitive lists of invocations make a logical sequence to the confessional nature of the Penitential Psalms. The rhythmic eloquence of the invocation continues with a series beginning from: From lightning and tempest - O Lord deliver us." Switching to a series of positive images: "Through the mystery of thy holy Incarnation – Through thy Nativity – O Lord deliver us". It concludes with additional prayers of supplication.

David asking forgiveness from God, one of five images illustrating the Penitential Psalms. Book of Hours printed in Paris by François Regnault, 1526, Stonyhurst College, S. 3/6, fol. 69

ADDITIONAL TEXTS

Individual owners who commissioned Books of Hours and also publishers, aiming at a specific audience for printed books, customized the Hours. Additional texts could reflect the popularity of prayers concerning the fifteen Joys of the Virgin from the Annunciation to her Assumption or other such well-loved traditions. Some of the prayers said by the priest at Mass were often included. This allowed the owner to participate more fully at church where the priest was frequently far away, behind a grille or chancel screen. During Lent, the view of the celebrant was hidden by a veil that hung within a few inches of the floor. Prayers of pious reflection were encouraged at different moments in the Mass, such as on entering the church, at the moment of consecration, at the elevation of the host, or after taking communion.

INTREATIES TO SPECIFIC SAINTS OR SUFFRAGES

In a hierarchical society such as that of the Middle Ages, individuals routinely saw themselves represented by someone superior to them. They commonly accepted this division of status as divinely ordained; lords were born lords, and peasants, peasants. Yet, in God's mercy he raised up extraordinary persons, filled with grace, who transcended normal boundaries, often reversing expectations to conquer heaven and become saints. Often these individuals defined their loyalty to the point of martyrdom, such as Katherine, who defied an Emperor's demand of marriage, or Thomas Becket assassinated by the knights of King Henry II. The method of invocation involved three short segments, an antiphon, versicle, and response, and then a longer oration. An English suffrage to Thomas Becket, Archbishop of Canterbury, reads:

Antiphon: We pray you through St. Thomas's blood, which he for you did spend; cause us, O Christ, to climb, where Thomas did ascend. Versicle: You crowned him with glory and honor. Response: And placed him above your other creations. Oration: O God, for whose Church the glorious Bishop Thomas fell by the swords of ungodly men: grant, we beseech you, that all who implore his help may obtain for their salvation the grace that they ask. Through Our Lord Jesus Christ, who lives and reigns with you. (Pierpont Morgan Library, New York, Ms G9, Fol. 30V, Southern England 1440-50; see in this catalogue, "Relics and the Two Thomases."

Readers could call up these extraordinary persons to intercede for them with their

English suffrage to Thomas Becket crossed out after 1538 when Henry VIII abolished his cult. Book of Hours printed in Paris by François Regnault, 1526, Stonyhurst College, S. 3/6, fol. 26v

petitions. In the Late Middle Ages and the Renaissance, saints were often associated with power to cure specific ailments or effect certain kinds of rescue. St. Nicholas, whose tomb was in the Italian port of Bari, protected sailors at sea; Margaret, who emerged unscathed from the belly of a dragon, aided women in childbirth; and St. Christopher, who carried the Christ Child across a river, was invoked by travelers. A dozen or so saints were invariably included, often with their images, in this section of the Hours.

OFFICE OF THE DEAD

With the practice of burial in or around the church, the commemoration of the deceased was coordinated with the saying of Masses and other prayers for the welfare of their souls (Brown 1995, 92-110). Prayers and good works by those on earth were believed to be able to help the deceased shorten their time in purgatory and provide a speedier progress to heaven (Binski, esp. 25-28, 115-122). The Office of the Dead most often was the closing segment of a Book of Hours and was one of the longer sets of prayers. It consisted of only the three hours of Vespers, Matins and Lauds. Varying slightly from location to location, Vespers would generally include psalms of comfort. The Stonyhurst MS 57 begins Vespers with: In vigiliis mortuorum. Placebo. Dilexi quoniam exaudiet dominus vocem oracionis meii: "I have loved because the Lord will hear the voice of my prayer" (Psalm 114). This text is followed by the reading of Psalms 119, "In my trouble I cried to the Lord: and he heard me;" 120, "I have lifted up my eyes to the mountain from whence help shall come to me;" followed by Psalms 129, 137, the Magnificat (Canticle of the Virgin from Luke 1:46-55), Psalm 145, and final prayers. The illustration, typically, shows the coffin and mourners. In a Book of Hours from Stonyhurst College (MS 57, fol. 106v: see p. 97 in this catalogue) the coffin is draped with a blue cloth with a pattern of a cross in the center, and is flanked by four tall candlesticks with lit candles. To the left, two members of the family dressed in black look at the coffin while on the right three tonsured clerics sing from an open book set on a lectern. The clerics are dressed in cloaks of red, green and blue. Matins generally included extensive readings from the Book of Job on the shortness of human life and the promise of the resurrection as in 19:25, "For I know that my Redeemer liveth, and in the last day I shall rise up out of the earth;" as well as devotions such a Psalm 26, "The Lord is my light and my salvation, whom shall I fear." The Psalms for Lauds ended with the great "De Profundis" (129): "Out of the depths I have cried to thee, O Lord."

The Office was important not only for ceremonies of mourning and burial, but to commemorate the souls of the departed with daily prayers. The honoring of the dead was a central belief of Christianity, evident from the very earliest years. The Christian attitude, in distinction from the pagan treatment of the dead, characterized those who "slept in Christ" as members of an extended Christian community. Burial places were not outside the walls of cities, as prescribed in Roman law, but clustered around, in, and under places of worship. Those still living could affect the fate of those who were dead and through good works and prayers, could shorten the stay in Purgatory of their family of confraternity members.

Purgatory was a "place" where the souls underwent suffering for sins committed in life before being able to enter heaven, worthy to look upon the face of God. To aid the passage of the soul, the socially privileged founded chapels where family members were interred within churches and where funerary Masses would be said (see, in this catalogue, "Devotional Objects and Cultural Context: The Medieval Parish Church"). Viewed as almost as efficacious was the Praying the Office, by the clergy but also by laypersons.

PRIVATE PRAYER

Two Books of Hours: The Gold Scrolls Group, England, and Internationalism in the Fifteenth Century

Amanda Luyster

The two manuscript Books of Hours selected for this exhibition, Stonyhurst MS 35 and MS 57, are noteworthy in various ways. First, intentional damage to selected images and text bears witness to the religious and political turmoil in Reformation England. Second, these codices suggest the particular structure of English Books of Hours, distinct from that of manuscripts manufactured for use on the Continent. Third, both show evidence of having either been executed on the Continent or by artists with substantial knowledge of Flemish styles (in particular, that of the so-called Gold Scrolls Group). Therefore both manuscripts reflect not only the religious practices in the fifteenth century -- and the effect of the Reformation upon these practices -- but also the dynamic role of internationalism and commerce in a pre-Reformation world.

The Face of God: Manuscripts and the Reformation

In Stonyhurst MS 35, the face of God has been erased (literally "defaced"), both in the Trinity as the Throne of Mercy, where God the Father holds the bleeding figure of the crucified Christ (fig. 1) and in the Commendation of Souls, in which we see a soul carried by angels heavenward where God the Father awaits (fig. 5). Perhaps counter-intuitively, this defacement implies respect, not disrespect. It was a general tenet of Reformation thinking that veneration of religious images might supplant contemplation and love of the true nature of God (Duffy 1995). Indeed, such concerns had been present within Christianity for many centuries, exemplified by thinkers as varied as Byzantine iconoclasts and England's Lollards (Scott 1996, vol. I, 44).

In England, Henry VIII's break from the Catholic Church was accompanied by a series of dictates. One commanded that "ymages and pictures" of Thomas Becket, a twelfth-century saint who was martyred after asserting church authority against the English king "shall be putte downe, and auoyded," and former papal saints be commemorated under the title of bishop of Rome (see in this catalogue "Relics: the Two Thomases"). In Stonyhurst MS 35, Becket's name has

1 Trinity as Throne of Mercy, *Book of Hours, Use of Sarum*, ca. 1430-50, Belgium, possibly Bruges. Stonyhurst College, Lancashire, MS 35, fol. 7

2 Trinity as Throne of Mercy, *Book of Hours, Use of Sarum*, ca. 1410-20, Flemish and English, assembled in London? Stonyhurst College, Lancashire, MS 57, fol. 7v

been scratched out on fols. 22v-23, evidence that the manuscript was in England at the time of this proclamation. Under Henry's successor, Edward V, iconoclasm became more extreme, proscribing any image of the divine or a saint. The faces of God the Father and Christ in the Throne of Mercy on fol. 7 have been washed out. The faces of the angels in the Commendation of Souls also show signs of smearing, characteristic of washing. The defacement of Becket's name and that of the images may have occurred at separate times. One can only imagine how the owner of a Book of Hours must have felt in attempting to erase the face of Christ (frightened that despite the king's assertions, such an act might bring divine retribution? Or relieved, knowing that with these adaptations having been made, the book would now be deemed "corrected"?). Such scoring-through and washing-out were, paradoxically, the actions of those concerned to safeguard manuscripts which would otherwise have been destroyed or discarded during the frequent visitations by the Reformed ecclesiastical commissioners (Brennan, 14).

Intriguingly, Stonyhurst MS 57 was only partially defaced. Commissioned in the mid-fifteenth century by an unknown patron, these Hours were believed from the seventeenth century to have been the property of Cardinal Wolsey. Thomas Wolsey was one of the most powerful officials of Henry VIII, but he fell from grace when he was unable to arrange Henry VIII's divorce from Catherine of Aragon. In the 1520s, when Wolsey was still at the height of his power, he had been twice a candidate for the papacy. One wonders whether the opening miniature of MS 57, the Trinity as the Throne of Mercy on fol. 7v (fig. 2) might have resonated for Cardinal Wolsey: God the Father in this image wears a three-tiered crown topped by a cross. This is the papal tiara, in use from the fourteenth century. Thomas Wolsey died in 1530 on a long and slow journey toward London where he was to be held under a charge of high treason. Wolsey apparently remained Catholic to his deathbed. These Hours were in England at the moment that Henry demanded the demotion of Becket in 1538. Both the calendar page and the commemoration of Becket were carefully removed by scraping off the inked letters. Of small size, it is likely that the manuscript was hidden and thus escaped further damage by Reformers; its purported owner, Wolsey, had not been so fortunate.

Two Books of Hours

Books of Hours in Fifteenth-Century England

Both Stonyhurst MS 35 and MS 57 were produced during the fifteenth century, a time when native English traditions of miniature-painting, according to many art historians (at least in the first half of the twentieth century), were not at their height (Marks and Morgan). Fifteenth-century English painting is often more difficult for today's viewer to appreciate because it lacks the interest in realism more common on the Continent. Kathleen Scott has suggested that English styles of painting were affected by the earlier Lollard concerns about image-making at the end of the fourteenth century, and that the result of these concerns was to turn English artists away from the Continental trends of realism. The English painted image, according to Scott, was meant to be a sign, to deliver meaning, rather than to tempt its viewer toward too much admiration of the image itself; it embodied a new commandment, "Thou shalt not lead us into aesthetic temptation" (Scott, I, 45).

There was a large and growing demand for illuminated Books of Hours in fifteenth-century England, probably arising from an increased emphasis on private devotion (Arnould and Massing, 113). Much of this demand came to be met with the help of imported manuscripts and illustrators from France and Flanders (and elsewhere). Why the English market did not meet this demand on its own remains uncertain; it has been suggested that there were not enough trained English artists (Scott 1996, vol. I, 62). It is also possible that foreign styles held their own allure (perhaps book-owners preferred images which were more sensuous than sign-like?). In any case, the popularity of the illustrated Book of Hours in fifteenth-century England was such that there was a need to import from overseas both manuscripts and artists who worked specifically for the English market, often in conjunction with English artists. As we shall see, such exchange between the Continent and England seems to have been important (albeit in different ways) for both of these manuscripts.

Books of Hours made for the English market are usually distinct from those made for other locations in Europe. The order of prayers is nearly always that of Sarum, the diocese of Salisbury, which was generally accepted throughout England. The calendar contains English saints (sometimes misspelled if recorded by a non-English scribe; see Arnould, 113). Books of Hours of the use of Sarum tended to be illustrated by a fairly standard cycle of images which is, in general, followed by the two Stonyhurst manuscripts. The iconographic cycle for the Hours of the Virgin, often depicting the Life of the Virgin in continental manuscripts, is frequently replaced in England by scenes of the Passion of Christ (Ibid.). An image accompanying the Commendation of Souls (a series of psalms following the Office of the Dead) such as that discussed above, in which one or a small group of souls are carried heavenward in a cloth, is also a typically English inclusion (Wieck 1988, 131).

Both Stonyhurst MS 35 and MS 57 contain prayers following the use of Sarum, as well as other typical features of manuscripts manufactured for the English market, such as the depiction of the Commendation of Souls. Both manuscripts were, therefore, intended for use in England. However, they also both contain evidence of either manufacture on the Continent or contributions from foreign-trained artists. Intriguingly, both codices can be related to the so-called Gold Scrolls Group, a group of artists who were active about 1410-55 (for references, see below). These artists worked in various workshops but may have been substantially based in Bruges (in modern-day Belgium, but in the fifteenth century, this and surrounding areas in Belgium and northern France were part of the county of Flanders; medieval manuscripts produced there are therefore termed Flemish). While at first it may seem too much of a coincidence that both of these manuscripts bear evidence of a relationship to the same group of artists, this circumstance is not as surprising as it might first appear. Although France produced the greatest number of Books of Hours in the fifteenth century, Flanders was the second-largest producer (Wieck 1988, 30), and the area was well-known for its export of Books of Hours to England (Orr, 620; Rogers 1982; Arnould, 113-31; Colledge). The Gold Scrolls Group produced great numbers of manuscripts, many of which were Books of Hours intended both for local use and foreign markets.

The Gold Scrolls Group and the Stonyhurst Codices

The style of the Gold Scrolls Group was first identified early in the twentieth century by Winkler and assigned to a single artist, the "Master of the Gold Scrolls" (for a concise summary and a history of scholarship, see Cardon; recent publications include Bousmanne 1987; Bousmanne 1989; Dogaer, 27; Orr; Tanis, 94; Wieck 1988, 30). Since then it has been recognized that there are many more manuscripts which can be categorized under this style than could have been accomplished by a single artist; moreover, there are also variations within the Gold Scrolls style which suggest that the style was practiced in multiple workshops. The practitioners of this style were probably based in Bruges, although Bert Cardon has suggested that some (especially in early stages) may have been based in Paris. The Gold Scrolls style does draw from some of the Parisian masters of about 1400, such as the Boucicaut Master. In addition, at least one artist practicing in the Gold Scrolls style is known to have been working in England about 1420, as is witnessed by the Hours of Elizabeth the Queen (British Library MS Add. 50001; see Orr). So although members of the Gold Scrolls Group were quite probably producing in Bruges, they were also responsible for work done elsewhere; hence these manuscripts, despite Gold Scrolls-style images, were not necessarily executed in Bruges. To determine the likely place of manufacture of the Stonyhurst manuscripts, more information must be taken into account. First, however, the elements of both codices which relate to the Gold Scrolls Group should be articulated.

3 Last Judgment - Son of Man on rainbow, *Book of Hours*, early to mid 1440s, Ghent or Tournai. Baltimore, Walters Art Gallery, MS W.263, fol. 94. Courtesy of the Walters Art Gallery

The Gold Scrolls Group was named after a characteristic background in which gold scrollwork, often including sunbursts and other flourishes, is painted over a wine-red ground. This background is sometimes related to the figures, either by outlining figures in gold at a slight distance away from their edges, or by surrounding a figure with a halo created by radiating gold spokes. A good example of the characteristic red ground and haloes can be seen on fol. 135v, the Commendation of Souls, of MS 57 (fig. 6). Other characteristic motifs of the Gold Scrolls Group include a half-length angel and a star-shaped cloud, sometimes used together, as on fol. 62 of MS 35, another Commendation of Souls (fig. 5). Here two angels, one clothed in fiery orange with feathered wings of acidic green and the other with the reverse coloration, grasp the corners of a white cloth cradling a naked female figure, visible to the waist with long, chestnut hair and a gently downcast gaze. The angels carry her above a landscape made up of sharply sloping hills, bare on top, with lush greenery below. The bare hillocks visible both in the Commendation in MS 35 and MS 57 are also frequently found in Gold Scrolls miniatures. Furthermore, both folios 7 and 48 of MS 35 show a distinctive type of decoration made up of small adjacent circles, each with a dot in the center, used to ornament textiles and furniture. These folios show such ornament over a green ground suggestive of a rich textile, used to ornament both the throne of the Trinity and a piece of furniture in the funeral service which is presumably the altar. This decoration of small circles is also characteristic of the Gold Scrolls Group.

One might note that despite the above examples, there are other grounds used within both these manuscripts which are not the characteristic gold scroll type. Furthermore, the angels in the MS 57 Commendation of Souls (fol. 135v; fig. 6), although half-length and presumably resting on clouds, certainly do not seem to be accompanied by star-shaped clouds. In the case of the Gold Scrolls Group, however, Bernard Bousmanne has rightly suggested that an identification should be made not on the basis of any single motif alone, but rather on the preponderance of motifs - and compositions – used (Bousmanne 1987, 127). (I will show below an example of one composition in a Stonyhurst manuscript which is

4 Last Judgment - Son of Man on rainbow, Book of Hours, Use of Sarum, ca. 1430-50, Belgium, possibly Bruges. Stonyhurst College, Lancashire, MS 35, fol. 38

closely echoed in a previously-identified Gold Scrolls manuscript.) There is much variation within the style, and sometimes even manuscripts without a single "gold scrolls" background can be shown to be connected with the Gold Scrolls Group. Indeed, although the grounds in MS 35 do not tend to depict gold scrolls, the ornamental grid patterns of gold on wine-red can be matched closely if not exactly in another previously-identified Gold Scrolls manuscript in Brussels (Brussels, B. R., 18270, fol. 49v; for reproduction, see Dogaer, fig. 7). It has been noted that from about 1440 onward, the gold scroll motif gradually disappears (Ibid., 27). To further complicate attribution, some motifs, for instance the decoration of small circles, were used in other schools. It is unwise, therefore, to connect a manuscript to the Gold Scrolls Group without multiple justifications. Since, however, the Stonyhurst manuscripts manifest so many characteristics of the Gold Scrolls Group (gold scrolls grounds, half-length angels, star-shaped clouds, stony hillocks, small circle decoration, as well as the compositional similarities to be discussed below), an attribution to the Gold Scrolls Group appears more than justified.

STONYHURST MS 35

Indeed, the Book of Hours known as Stonyhurst MS 35 contains a composition which closely resembles that of a previously-identified Gold Scrolls manuscript, Walters MS W.263, also a Book of Hours. The Walters manuscript was probably completed in Ghent or Tournai in the early to mid 1440s, a time and place consonant with that which we will suggest for Stonyhurst MS 35. The scene of the Last Judgment

5 Commendation of Soul (female torso), *Book of Hours, Use of Sarum*, ca. 1430-50, Belgium, possibly Bruges, Stonyhurst College, Lancashire, MS 35, fol. 62

in both cases, Stonyhurst MS 35, fol. 38, (fig. 4) and Walters fol. 94, (fig. 3) shows Christ as the Son of Man on the rainbow, and the dead rise from their graves from the ground beneath him. Half-length angels on star-shaped clouds blow curved horns to either side of the haloed Christ, who spreads his arms wide to show the stigmata. Christ's mantle covers his shoulders and falls behind the outstretched arms, revealing a bare chest, and is gathered together across the lap to cover the lower torso and legs. The mantle then cascades for some length down the rainbow, revealing, however, Christ's feet, which are perched on a globe. The mouth of hell, a literal mouth, gapes in the lower right corner, dark and fiery. The dead rise from scattered holes in the grassy ground, and the ground extends slightly less than halfway up the picture. The resemblances are such that one imagines that both artists were using a similar or even identical model. The re-use of compositions is another characteristic of the Gold Scrolls Group. They manufactured large numbers of manuscripts and were known to use various techniques of copying, possibly from model-books or previous exemplars, to speed the process (Bousmanne 1987, 141). After a survey of Gold Scrolls Group half-length angels, many of which are similar in size and gesture, Bousmanne has even suggested the use of tracing (Ibid., also Bousmanne 1989, 260).

Stonyhurst MS 35, then, contains miniatures which are linked to the Gold Scrolls Group. There are other image-fields to consider, however. In the margins of MS 35, multicolored (green, blue and pink) acanthus leaves extend from the corners. The remainder of the marginal space is inhabited by scrollwork from which sprout both abstracted vegetal motifs in gold leaf and painted leaves and flowers. Such marginal decoration is fairly common in France and Flanders in the first half of the fifteenth century. The most distinctive features in the margins are trumpet-shaped flowers seen in profile, some of which have a green calyx (small leaves underneath the flower) extending beyond the flower petals (e.g. fol. 62; fig. 5). Other flowers, again shown in profile, have a tripartite color structure (as in the upper right), and fol. 62 also contains a red strawberry-shaped object, again with a visible calyx. Similar flowers, frequently but not always in profile, as well as occasional strawberries, were included in at least five manuscripts also attributed to the Gold Scrolls Group. These manuscripts have been attributed to Bruges, Ghent or Tournai, or Belgium more generally, between about 1430-50 (see New York City, Pierpont Morgan Library MS M.19 [Book of Hours, Belgium, perhaps Bruges, ca. 1440], fol. 50v, available online from http://corsair.morganlibrary.org/; Prague, Czech State Library, Ms. XXIII.F.198 [Book of Hours, probably Ghent or Tournai, 1440s], fol. 187, reproduced as fig. 58 in Clark; Free Library of Philadelphia, Rare Book Dept. Lewis E99 [Book of Hours, Bruges, 1430s], fol. 59v, reproduced as fig. 27-1 in Tanis; Cambridge, MA, Houghton Library MS Lat 132 [Book of Hours, Belgium, mid-fifteenth-century],

TWO BOOKS OF HOURS

reproduced as fig. 28, p. 149, in Wieck 1983; Baltimore, MD, Walters Art Museum MS 239 [Book of Hours, Belgium, perhaps Bruges, ca. 1430], fol. 101v, reproduced as fig. 110 in Wieck 1988). Two other manuscripts contain flowers which are more distantly related to those in MS 35; these manuscripts have been attributed to northern or eastern France or southern Belgium, about 1450-70, and it is plausible that these are later copies of a tradition earlier made popular by the Gold Scrolls Group. Evidence suggests, then, that the margins of MS 35 were accomplished either by Gold Scrolls artists or by others who habitually worked alongside Gold Scrolls artists, most likely in Belgium. Although the Gold Scrolls group was active, then, about 1410-55, the marginal decoration of MS 35 suggests that this manuscript would most likely have been produced within the second half of that period, about 1430-50.

The evidence of both the miniatures and the margins of Stonyhurst MS 35, then, suggest that it was likely to have been produced in Belgium about 1430-50 by artists related to the Gold Scrolls Group. It was intended to be exported to England and was in England at the time of the Reformation. Although this Book of Hours could well

6 Commendation of Souls, *Book of Hours, Use of Sarum*, ca. 1410-20, Flemish and English, assembled in London? Stonyhurst College, Lancashire, MS 57, fol. 135v

have been sent overseas without being intended for a specific recipient, there are certain details which suggest that this manuscript was manufactured with a female patron in mind. The strongest piece of evidence is the female depicted in the Commendation of the Soul (fol. 62; fig. 5). Much more common is an ungendered, childlike rendering of the soul, or, frequently, souls, who are being carried heavenward. (This more typical rendering is used in Stonyhurst MS 57, fol. 135v; fol. 137). Scott also states that the concentration on a single female figure is unusual, suggesting in her survey that a Princeton manuscript is to be "specially noted" because it does depict a female in the Commendation (Princeton Univ. Lib. Scheide 127, ca. 1420; see Scott 1996, 57, vol. I). The image accompanying the Commendation of Souls draws on a long tradition of blessed souls being taken to heaven in a cloth of honor. Pamela Sheingorn describes how this tradition began with respect to the souls of martyrs and spread to all Christians, and how, at first understood as a recognition of the piety of martyrs, it grew to be understood as a scene in the subjunctive, an expression of a wished-for future for all Christian souls (Sheingorn, 163). It appears, then, that the wished-for future in MS 35's Commendation could have been intended to apply to an explicitly female figure, presumably the patron or purchaser.

There are other intimations that MS 35 was commissioned by a woman, or at least manufactured with the goal of attracting a female patron. The program of the Hours of the Virgin, frequently in England illustrated by a pictorial cycle of the Passion of Christ, in this manuscript shows instead a cycle from the life of the Virgin. Scott's analysis of Books of Hours manufactured in England for English use shows that of 20 complete sequences included, only five contain a set from the life of the Virgin for the Hours of the Virgin (Scott 1996, vol. I, 56, see also Table III, vol. II). Two of these cycles are merely subordinate imagery, co-existing alongside larger miniatures illustrating the Passion, and two are known to have been made for women (Ibid.). The unusual choice of the Virgin cycle and the fact that other such choices are known to have been connected to a female patron implies that the same may be true for MS 35.

One further detail is only suggestive. The funeral service depicted in MS 35 shows two lay onlookers, both with identical headgear characterized by a high-rising bulb over the top of the head. The height and shape are characteristic of the more general class of headgear worn by women in the first half of the fifteenth century (Scott 1986, 17). Men, by contrast, frequently wore lower headgear, usually hoods with or without the padded roll known as the *bourrelet*. Comparing the funeral service in MS 35 (fig. 8) to that depicted in MS 57 (fig. 7) we note that 57 also shows two lay onlookers, but in this case one individual is wearing the high headdress in MS 35 (presumably a woman) and the other (presumably a man) sports a lower-profiled hood. The same is the case in the funeral service in Morgan MS M.19, fol. 100v, and is also the case in other representations of funeral services. This raises the question of whether the two onlookers in MS 35, wearing the same headgear, are meant to be understood as belonging to the same gender, that gender being, presumably, female. Why would MS 35 depict two women, rather than the customary woman and man? One hypothesis would suggest that the presumed female patron of MS 35, if it is she we are meant to see in the funeral service, might also have been an older unmarried woman or a widow, since she is unaccompanied by a husband. Whether or not MS 35 was actually commissioned for a specific English female patron, many women did own Books of Hours. Indeed, Catholic women were among the most public and steadfast in their refusal to give up their faith during the English Reformation; in some cases they were notably more militant in their refusal to do so than their husbands (Brennan, 12).

STONYHURST MS 57

The second Stonyhurst manuscript, MS 57, does not contain such evocative clues as to its original patron, although it was, as mentioned above, owned by Cardinal Wolsey at a later point in its existence, at least according to an inscription on the flyleaf. While MS 35 is a fairly standard or "trade" production, MS 57 is clearly a luxury product. Yet at the same time MS 57, because of its small size, remains poignantly intimate. The many prayers are contained in a compact format, one which could easily be slipped in a purse. In an era that still held beauty and goodness to be the primary attributes of God, might this compact, ordered example of beauty intensify the act of worship? One more personal addition was a pasted-in image of the Holy Rood of Bromholm (see in this catalogue "Veneration of the True Cross, the Holy Rood of Bromholm, and Passion of Christ).

MS 57 also contains miniatures executed by artists associated with the Gold Scrolls Group. However, its margins tell a different story, one which reminds us of the importance of international exchange in fifteenth century manuscript production. For the margins in this case are quite characteristic of native English production. Examining the opening at fol. 106v-107 (the funeral service; fig. 7) the two pages at first appear to have been executed in two completely different pictorial languages. To the left, the margin is inhabited by pen-and-ink scrollwork suggestive of vines, enlivened by small painted motifs reminiscent of leaves and acorns in blue, red, pink and green. The inner margin is instead ornamented by four star-like motifs in black ink with a gold leaf center. The page to the right, however, is much more distinctive. Its margins are structured by thick tendrils creating a boxy shape, from which emerge a profusion of fleshy leaves and flowers. The leaves, some of which are trifoliate and some of which, elongated and multi-lobed, resemble oak leaves, fold and wrap around corners and nestle into the enclosed shapes formed by the climbing tendrils. The center of the bottom margin is enlivened by knotwork formed by tendrils which then emerge in a flourish at the base of the page. Ornamental black penwork, often in a series of

TWO BOOKS OF HOURS

7 Funeral service, *Book of Hours, Use of Sarum*, ca. 1410-20, Flemish and English, assembled in London? Stonyhurst College, Lancashire, MS 57, fols. 106v - 107

short parallel lines terminating in a sort of curlicue, repeats in various locations within the margins of both these pages. A shared palette of azure blue, red, pale pink and sap green also links both pages suggesting that despite some differences in format, the same artist was indeed responsible for both margins.

Although the margin to the left (fol. 106v) is not necessarily distinctive, that to the right (fol. 107) is, and its attribution can then be used to further illuminate the circumstances of this manuscript's production. A near match can be found in two manuscripts currently in London, one in the British Library (MS Royal 2.B.VIII, the "Princess Joan Psalter") and one in Lambeth Palace Library (MS 474). These two manuscripts share the boxy frame of thick tendrils, the trilobed leaves nestling inside circles, four-petaled flowers, pen-and-ink squiggly stars, and a knotwork motif in the center of the bottom margin, from which emerges a flourish of flowers and leaves. The elongated oak leaves which fold in three dimensions can also be seen here, for instance in the upper right corner of fol. 101v of the British Library manuscript. Indeed, that same manuscript even contains ball-like motifs and abstracted leaves of similar shape and distribution to that found on the left side of the opening in the Stonyhurst manuscript, suggesting again that a single artist was capable of working in multiple decorative languages. This comparison suggests that the margins of Stonyhurst MS 57 should be related to those of manuscripts which were executed in England, probably in London. The British Library manuscript was executed about 1405, and the Lambeth manuscript has been dated about 1415. The margins of the Stonyhurst MS 57, then, could have been executed in London about 1405-1415, or at least by an artist who had trained in that locale.

While the miniatures of Stonyhurst MS 57 are attributed to a Flemish-trained artist in the Gold Scrolls style, therefore, its margins were apparently executed by an English (or English-trained) artist. The

8 Funeral service, *Book of Hours, Use of Sarum*, ca. 1430-50, Belgium, possibly Bruges, Stonyhurst College, Lancashire, MS 35, fol. 48

manuscript itself contains prayers for use in England and was designed for use there. Various possibilities arise for the manuscript's production: it could have been produced in Belgium, perhaps in Bruges, with the margins left blank so as to be illuminated in a style popular in England once it reached that country. Some manuscripts were known to have been manufactured in this way (Arnould, 126). It could have been manufactured either on the Continent or in England by a workshop employing artists of both nationalities (or artists trained in both the Gold Scrolls and native English styles). This was a common situation, and many foreign-trained artists were working in London in the first half of the fifteenth century (Scott 1996, vol. I, 62). Or it could have been manufactured in England with imported miniatures, another known method of production. In this case, painted leaves, imported from overseas, would be inserted at the appropriate location in a codex being made up in England. A patron could choose which miniatures he or she wanted (Arnould, 113; Tanis, 122).

This latter scenario seems to have been the case for Stonyhurst MS 57; at least, it was manufactured with inserted single folios. These inserted leaves are blank on the reverse and are made of a smoother vellum, visible in the sheen of the page and also because the paint from the marginal decorations does not adhere well. The inserted leaves in Stonyhurst MS 57 resemble those of another Book of Hours, Morgan M.76, also created by means of inserting imported leaves. The similarity exists first between the miniatures, both products of the Gold Scrolls Group and both manifesting nearly identical details, such as the obliquely tiled and patterned floor (which suggests recession but does not actually recede), set on a platform with a three-sided protruding "stage" upon which a figure is placed: compare fol. 7v of Stonyhurst MS 57 (fig. 2) with fol. 265v of Morgan M.76. Moreover, the border immediately surrounding the miniature is also nearly identical on these two folios. The similarity of the tiled stage and the border is sufficiently striking to suggest a close relationship between these two folios. The Morgan manuscript M.76 has been dated to ca. 1420. This dating is consistent with that indicated by the English margins in the Stonyhurst manuscript. Probably, then, the miniatures in Stonyhurst MS 57 were painted in Belgium, possibly in Bruges, and subsequently shipped over to England (probably London), where the codex was assembled and its margins painted. The evidence of the margins and miniatures then suggests that this manuscript was executed toward the beginning of the period in which Gold Scrolls artists were known to be active, that is, about 1410-20. (Cardon's estimate of about 1415-1455 is a rough estimate, and should not be taken to preclude Gold Scrolls activity about 1410; Dogaer suggests that the Group became active in Flanders "by 1410 or a little before:" see Dogaer, 27).

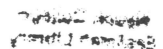

CONCLUSION

Both Stonyhurst Books of Hours, then, witness the movement of painted miniatures and manuscripts across cultures and across seas. Stonyhurst MS 35, demonstrably linked to the Gold Scrolls Group (which was probably based in Bruges), may bear witness to the particular desire of a female patron or purchaser for a Continental Book of Hours, possibly manufactured in Belgium ca. 1430-50. The manuscript was in any case intended for English use and was in England at the time of the Reformation, when certain of its images and texts were rubbed out in conformance to the government's new dictates. Some of its miniatures can be shown to relate to compositions frequently used by Gold Scrolls artists, suggesting that mechanisms of copying that might be termed early mass-production were used for this codex.

Stonyhurst MS 57, also demonstrably linked to the Gold Scrolls Group, was the result of a cooperative effort between at least one English artist (responsible for the margins) and one or more Gold Scrolls artists (responsible for the miniatures). This cooperation may not have been undertaken in person, and the leaves painted by the Gold Scrolls artist(s) were probably imported to England. The codex could have been constructed in London, where its margins, certainly by an English artist, would have been illuminated, probably about 1410-20. The insertion of imported leaves which could be individually selected by a patron is another technique recalling present-day manufacturing, in which the process of choosing one or more preset options, rather than entirely free choice, streamlines production.

Books of Hours, despite their standard format, have often been described as highly personal manuscripts. For many men and women, their Book of Hours was the only, or at least the most important, manuscript they owned. As such, Books of Hours became the repositories of family histories, and births, marriages, and deaths were recorded in their calendars alongside the feasts of the saints (Brennan). Although no such recordings have been found in the Stonyhurst manuscripts, they remain evocative testaments to their time. Both Stonyhurst MS 35 and MS 57 were intended for English use and were partly executed by artists from the Gold Scrolls Group, but their creation and histories remain distinct. A close examination of the pages of these two Books of Hours, however, vividly brings to life the importance of international trade in books for private devotion, the changes in theology and practice brought about by the Reformation, and the working habits of artists, more international and more attuned to the requirements of mass markets than we might have assumed. Finally, even minute details – the female soul in the Commendation, the papal tiara worn by God in the manuscript thought to have belonged to Wolsey, the care taken in washing out the faces of God and the angels – evoke both larger religious concerns and the more personal hopes and fears of some of the men and women who owned these manuscripts throughout their long histories.

CATALOGUE

Book of Hours, Use of Sarum
Vellum, 8 x 6 in. (20.3 x 15.2 cm.)
Belgium, possibly Bruges, ca. 1430-50
Miniatures associated with the Gold Scrolls Group
Stonyhurst College, Lancashire, MS 35

1-6 Calendar
7 Trinity as Throne of Mercy (fig. 1)
9 Pietà
25 Nativity
28 Annunciation to Shepherds
31 Presentation
33 Massacre of Innocents
35 Flight into Egypt
38 Last Judgment - Son of Man on rainbow (fig. 4)
48 Funeral service (coffin before altar) (fig. 8)
62 Commendation of Soul (female torso) (fig. 5)
73 St Jerome in study with lion - both defaced
74 last folio

Binding and flyleaves are not original. Sewing and endbands are sufficiently tight to obscure details of many gatherings. Findings below are made on the basis of observable evidence only and should be revised if the manuscript is ever re-bound. No catchwords extant.

Gatherings	*Folios*
1 (6)	1-6
2 (6 + 1)	7-13
3 (10)	14-23
4 (6)	24-29
5 (8 + 1)	30-38
6 (6)	39-44
7 (8)	45-52
8 (6)	53-58
9 (6)	59-64
10 (4)	65-68
11 (6)	69-74

Book of Hours, Use of Sarum
Vellum, 5 ¼ x 3 ⅝ in. (13.3 x 9.2 cm.)
Margins by an English artist, miniatures by a Flemish-trained artist of the Gold Scrolls Group, ca. 1410-20. Possibly assembled in London
Stonyhurst College, Lancashire, MS 57

7v Trinity as Throne of Mercy (fig. 2)
40v Agony in the Garden
41 Annunciation (illuminated initial), beginning of Matins
76v Virgin and Child, beginning of hymn Salve Regina
89v Last Judgment
106v Funeral service (draped coffin with mourners) (fig. 7)
135v Commendation of Souls (fig. 6)
158v St. Jerome and lion
174 pasted in prayer card with image of
The Holy Rood of Bromholm (see in this catalogue "Veneration of the True Cross, the Holy Rood of Bromholm, and Passion of Christ")

Binding and flyleaves are not original. Catchwords extant. Gatherings 1-5 display catchwords without ornament at the base of the page; gatherings 6-21 display catchwords ornamented with faces, animals, and other humorous motifs at the base of the page.

Gatherings	*Folios*
1 (6)	1-6
2 (8 + 1)	7-15
3 (8)	16-23
4 (8)	24-31
5 (8)	32-39
6 (8 + 1)	40-48
7 (6 + 1)	49-55
8 (8)	56-63
9 (8)	64-71
10 (8 + 1)	72-80
11 (8 + 1 + 1)*	81-90
12 (8)	91-98
13 (8 + 1)	99-107
14 (8)	108-115
15 (8)	116-123
16 (8)	124-131
17 (8 + 1)	132-140
18 (8)	141-148
19 (8)	149-156
20 (8 + 1 + 1)*	157-166
21 (8)	167-174

* This notation is used to suggest that two singletons have been added (not a bifolio).

Bibliography

Arnould, Alain, and Jean Michel Massing. *Splendours of Flanders*. New York: Cambridge University Press, 1993.

Bousmanne, Bernard. "Deux livres d'heures du Groupe aux rinceaux d'or," *Revue des archéologues et historiens d'art de Louvain* 20 (1987): 119-44.

Bousmanne, Bernard. "Remarques sur la décoration marginale d'un Livre d'heures de la Bibliothèque Ambrosienne (Milan, Bibliothèque Ambrosienne, ms. S.P. 12)," *Aevum* 63, No. 2 (1989): 252-64.

Brennan, Michael G., "The Book of Hours of the Braddyll family of Whalley Abbey (University of Leeds, Brotherton MS. 15)," *Transactions of the Historic Society of Lancashire and Cheshire* 146 (1996): 1-30.

Cardon, Bert. "Gold Scrolls Group," in *Dictionary of Art*, ed. Jane Turner, London: Grove, 1996, pp. 681-83.

Clark, Gregory, *Made in Flanders: the Master of the Ghent Privileges and Manuscript Painting in the Southern Netherlands in the Time of Philip the Good*. Turnhout, Belgium: Brepols, 2000.

Colledge, E. "South Netherlandish Books of Hours made for England," *Scriptorium Gand* 32, No. 1 (1978): 55-57.

Dogaer, Georges, James H. Marrow, and Friedrich Winkler. *Flemish Miniature Painting in the 15th and 16th Centuries*. Amsterdam: B.M. Israël, 1987.

Marks, Richard, and Nigel J. Morgan. *The Golden Age of English Manuscript Painting, 1200-1500*. London: Chatto & Windus, 1981.

Orr, Michael T. "The Hours of Elizabeth the Queen: Evidence for Collaboration between English Illuminators and an Artist from the Gold Scrolls Group," in *Flanders in a European Perspective: Manuscript Illumination Around 1400 in Flanders and Abroad: Proceedings of the International Colloquium, Leuven*, 7-10 September 1993, Leuven: Peeters, 1995: pp. 619-33.

Rogers, N. "Books of Hours Produced in the Low Countries for the English Market in the Fifteenth Century" (M. Litt. dissertation, University of Cambridge, 1982).

Scott, Kathleen L. *Later Gothic Manuscripts, 1390-1490*. 2 vols. vol. 6, *A Survey of Manuscripts Illuminated in the British Isles*. London: H. Miller, 1996.

Scott, Margaret. *The Fourteenth & Fifteenth Centuries, Visual History of Costume*. London: Batsford, 1986.

Sheingorn, Pamela. "'And flights of angels sing thee to thy rest': the soul's conveyance to the afterlife in the Middle Ages," in *Art into Life: Collected Papers from the Kresge Art Museum Medieval Symposia*. East Lansing: Michigan State University Press, 1995: pp. 155-82.

Tanis, James, Jennifer A. Thompson, and C. W. Dutschke. *Leaves of Gold: Manuscript Illumination from Philadelphia Collections*. Philadelphia: Philadelphia Museum of Art, 2001.

Wieck, Roger S. *Late Medieval and Renaissance Illuminated Manuscripts, 1350-1525, in the Houghton Library*. Cambridge, Mass.: Dept. of Print and Graphic Arts, Harvard College Library, 1983.

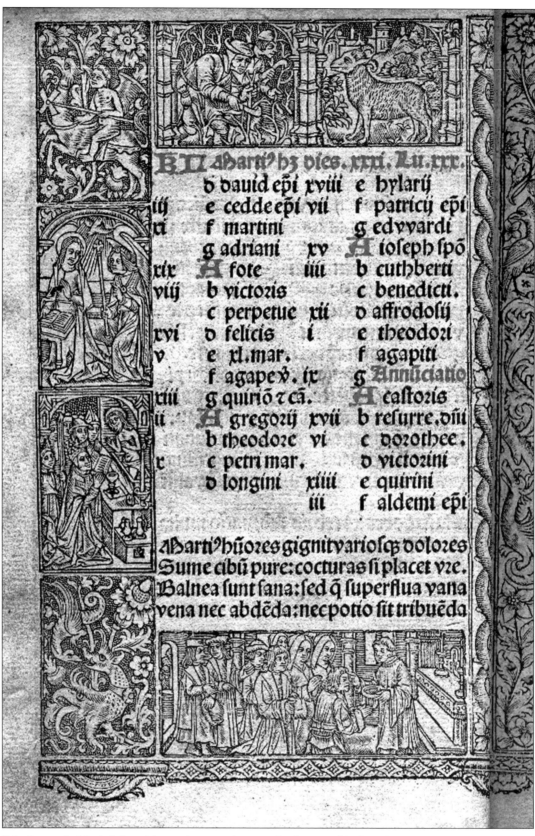

Calendar page for March: Labor of the month pruning the vine and zodiac sign of the Ram; Side: putto riding a horse-griffon, Annunciation, Miracle of St. Gregory, and hybrid beast; Below: Distribution of Ashes at the beginning of Lent. Book of Hours printed in Paris by Simon Vostre, 1512, Stonyhurst College, S. 3/3, fol. 2v

Four Printed
Books of Hours

Four Books of Hours: Paris, London, and Sixteenth-Century Print Culture

Virginia C. Raguin

The four printed Books of Hours in this exhibition demonstrate many of the same concepts exemplified by the manuscripts of the Gold Scrolls Group discussed in the previous essay. They are also part of an international trade of books, which in the sixteenth century particularly focused on the great printing houses of Paris and their partners in London. Employment of many small plates that could be grouped with any text made it possible for printing houses to customize works for foreign clients, and Parisian presses published Books of Hours of foreign rites such as Sarum and Roman usages - as well as those of specific dioceses of France. Printing also introduced the dissemination of multiple copies of the same image. More images were incorporated into any given book because they were now so readily reproduced; many became "popular" images resulting in a common stock of familiar illustrations. Although sometimes vellum was used, most books were printed on paper, significantly reducing cost and therefore reaching a broader clientele for this devotional practice. The condition of these Books of Hours, like that of manuscripts, demonstrates the changing views concerning religion in the first half of the sixteenth century. Their pages show successive defacement of the sets of prayers and ultimately a "Reformed" edition authorized by Henry VIII.

In densely-packed pages, these new books reveal the tension between one-of-kind luxury manuscripts, such as the manuscript later owned by Cardinal Wolsey with its colorful, gold-embellished illuminations, and the competitive strategies of mass-produced printed Hours. Pioneering French printers who emerged in the 1480s under the reign of Charles VIII relished the facility with which numerous illustrations could be presented on a page. In the early years of the sixteenth century, these printing houses continued to reedit the books, retaining and rearranging many of the border plates, and commissioning newer, more stylistically up-to-date full-page illustrations. Often the Italian Renaissance and the lingering Late Gothic were face to face. In a Book of Hours of 1512, now at Stonyhurst, for example, the image of Job speaking to the three false comforters (74v) shows volumetric figures and classical architecture in contrast to the facing page where ogee arches frame small vignettes showing death confronting the living who are dressed in garments delineated by sharp Gothic folds. In addition, the margins allowed the designer to present many narratives only sparsely depicted in manuscripts. The tribulations of Job present a compelling story, apparently of great interest to Early Modern patrons. These scenes were rare in medieval manuscripts; nine such scenes, an unusually high number, are included in a French Book of Hours

Job and the Three False Comforters, Book of Hours printed in Paris by Simon Vostre, 1512, Stonyhurst College, S. 3/3, fol. 74v

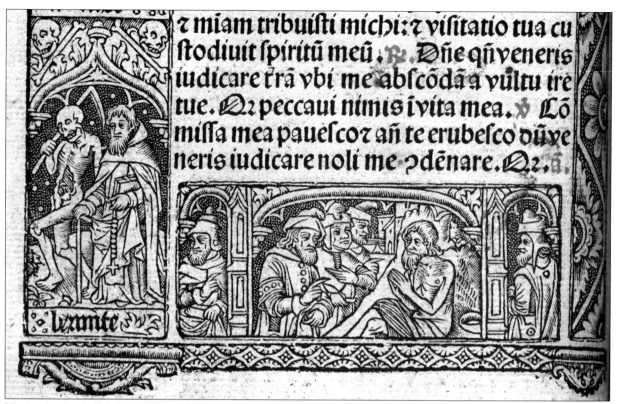

Margins showing the Tribulations of Job and Death coming for the living, Book of Hours printed in Paris by Simon Vostre, 1512, Stonyhurst College, S. 3/3, fol. 79v

dating to the mid 1480s (Walters Art Gallery MS W. 245; Wieck 1988, 201). In the Stonyhurst Hours of 1512 (fols. 75-83), a full 16 lower border images show the story of Job from prosperity, through the series of calamities, including God's permission to allow Satan to afflict his health, God's message to Job, and finally the reinstatement of Job's good fortune. Such lush complexity also continued the manuscript tradition of marginalia of hybrid beasts, hunters, sporting monkeys, putti, or shepherds at work and play, now reaching a whole new audience.

Some of the best known and most lavishly illustrated of the printed Horae were by the Parisian house of Simon Vostre; one published in 1498 met with particular success (Soleil, 25-85). Many of the illustrations for that printing were provided by the Master of the Apocalypse Rose of the Sainte-Chapelle of Paris, which was reworked shortly after 1482. He contributed images to Parisian books printed by Thielman Kerver and Anthoine Vérard as well as Simon Vostre. Most of the smaller images and borders in Stonyhurst's 1512 work come from these earlier plates, for example, the Virtues (fols. 60v – 62), which retain their French labels: foy, charite, iustice, esperance, etc. (Nettekoven, fig. 229). The page facing the depiction of Job with illustrations of death as a skeleton seizing a pope, emperor, and cardinal, and the sacrament of marriage flanked by sibyls are also taken from the Vostre's publication of 1498, where they framed an image of Lazarus approaching Dives as he feasts (Soleil, 59-60, fig. IV).

The 1512 Hours of Stonyhurst also incorporates more contemporary images, including some borrowed from a later Vostre Book of Hours and others copied from Dürer woodcuts. Simon Vostre published another landmark Book of Hours, undated, but with an almanac dated 1508 – 1528 (Soleil, 86-150; see also edition owned by John Hopkins University, Baltimore, Maryland), reusing many small motifs but with many new full-page illustrations in an Italianate style, with classical decorative motifs and three-dimensional spatial compositions. In the Massacre of the Innocents, for example, the charged composition and drama as well as classicizing setting and costume suggest an exposure to the prints of Andrea Mantegna (Renouvier, 18). The 1512 Hours of Stonyhust incorporates many of these but also adds newer types. The 1512 depiction of the Emperor Domitian's attempt to execute St. John the Evangelist by immersion in the cauldron of burning oil at the Porta Latina in Rome (12v; Voragine, 58) is a close copy of the woodcut by Albrecht Dürer of 1497-98 (illustrated p. 83). Significantly, this image is large and fills the page without a border. The same is true for the eloquent representation of the Crucifixion, consonant with both illustrations being created after the 1508 work.

Made for an English client, the 1512 Hours employs several strategies to relate to its designated audience. The standard modification concerns the sequence of prayers and veneration of local saints, such as prayers addressed to Thomas Becket. In addition, the increasing democratization of the practice of the Hours is seen in the clustering of designated prayers at the beginning of the book, just after the Calendar. Frequently English phrases point out the moment to use these Latin prayers, such as just before and after receiving Communion: "Whan thou shaltre receive the sacrament." At this time, the lay worshipper did not follow a written text of the Mass and so could attend Mass while praying privately or using the Hours. Subsequent prayers are further qualified: "To get he grace for synnes, For the kyng; For ty frend lyving; For wayfaring men." Others point to the concern for health and for the souls in purgatory. Such sensitivity to the client is continued in the work of the Parisian printer François Regnault.

Two Books of Hours (Stonyhurst S. 3/6 and S.3/8), are similar; one dated 1526 is labeled from the press of François Regnault who produced many works for England. Most famous is Regnault's printing of the Great Bible of 1539, the first royally authorized English translation of the Scriptures. In 1538, the printing of the Bible was interrupted by the decree of the Inquisitor General for France who labeled the enterprise heretical. The English rescued many of the finished sheets, condemned to be burned, and transported presses and workmen to London where the publication was achieved. Texts reappear in the English Primer of 1541 (Stonyhurst S.3.26).

Regnault's long narrow Books of Hours is liberally illustrated with embellished initials and small images as well as 55 larger illustrations. A later book of 1530 (S. 3/8), in a squarer format, shows almost the same illustrations. These images are similar to a Book of Hours for the use of Paris by the Parisian printer Theilman Kerver of 1525 (Soleil, 151-237). Most striking is the similarity of the Calendar cycle between Kerver's 1525 publication and Regnault's of 1526, a cycle of life ending with December, where a dying man receives Extreme Unction. At the top of each calendar scene is an image of the appropriate zodiacal sign. The books are highly visual and simple to follow. In addition, both show an unusually rich illustration of the Penitential Psalms; seven scenes show David catching sight of Bathsheba, Uriah killed in battle, David and the prophet Nathan, David in prayer, and David offering a holocaust, Nathan absolving David, and Nathan giving the crown of Rabbath to David. Three are subjects repeated in Kerver's Hours. In particular, the opening scene shows David and Bathsheba in an uncommon format where David sees her as she bathes on a balcony, while below his envoy knocks at the door to deliver his letter of assignation (Soleil, 174; Costley, 1261).

English guide phrases for Latin prayers: "For frendes in syknes or in necessite; For thy frende tat is deed; For the lyuyng and deest." In the side margins are scenes from a long narrative of Joseph and his Brothers in Egypt, and below a Renaissance secular scene. Book of Hours printed in Paris by Simon Vostre, 1512, Stonyhurst College, S. 3/3, fol. 11v.

FOUR PRINTED
BOOKS OF HOURS

Bibliography

Hindman, Sandra, and James Douglas Farquhar. *Pen to Press : Illustrated Manuscripts and Printed Books in the First Century of Printing.* College Park: Art Dept., University of Maryland, 1977.

Nettekoven, Ina. *Der Meister der Apokalypsenrose der Saint Chapelle und die Pariser Buchkunst um 1500.* Turnout, Belgium: Brepols, 2004.

Renouvier, J. *Des Gravures sur bois dans les livres de Simon Vostre, Libraire d'Heures.* Paris: Auguste Aubry, 1862.

Soleil, Félix. *Les Heures gothiques et la littérature pieuse aux XVe et XVIe siècles.* Rouen: E. Augé, 1882.

Catalogue

Hours of the Virgin – Sarum Usage
Paper, 7 ½ x 4 ¾ in. (19 x 12 cm.) 121 folios
Printed in Paris by Simon Vostre (fl. 1486-1518), 1512
Stonyhurst College, Lancashire, S. 3/3

All pages have a full outer border composed of two to three small picture-cuts with text and upper and lower border with one or two small pictures. The text is black with red special texts. Compare to Book of Hours for the use of Rome, printed on vellum (no date – almanac 1507-1527), initials and capitals added in gold on a red or blue ground (Harvard University, Houghton Library, Typ 515.07.263).
Full Page Illustrations: *Same as Hours of the Virgin, use of Rome 1507 (Harvard University, Houghton Library, Typ 515.07.263)

1 Skeleton and jester* (1507: fol. 2)
12v St. John in the boiling oil
22 Augustus and the Tiburtine Sibyl* (1507: fol. 23)
28 Crucifixion
30 Circumcision* (1507: fol. 36)
32 Massacre of the Innocents* (1507: fol. 38) (Vespers for Hours of the Virgin)
34 Death of the Virgin* (1507: fol. 41) (Compline for Hours of the Virgin)
63 Uriah being sent into Battle* (1507: fol. 48) (7 Penitential Psalms)
74v Job confronted by the three friends* (1507: fol. 56v) the facing page fol. 57 uses the same borders as fol. 75: Sacrament of Matrimony at bottom and the dance of death, with pope, emperor, and cardinal

Selected borders

2v March
   Top: Labor of the month pruning the vine, sign of the Zodiac, the Ram
   Side: putto riding a horse-griffon, Annunciation, Miracle of St. Gregory, hybrid beast
   Below: Distribution of Ashes at the beginning of Lent
5v November
   Top: Labor of the month feeding pigs, sign of the Zodiac, Sagittarius
   Side: death seizes pope, pope at prayer, St. Katherine, wildman with harp
   Below: Men congregating
42 Pentecost and Adoration of the sites in Jerusalem where Christ walked
53v Sacraments of Confession and Matrimony
68v – 71 Litany surrounded by depictions of the 15 Last Days of the World (1507: fols. 53-55)
77 Job family and destruction at table; death takes theologian, bourgeois, canon
79v Job's three false friends; death takes infant in cradle, cleric, hermit
84 Sacraments of Holy Orders and Eucharist
84v Sacraments of Confession & Matrimony
85 Sacrament of Extreme Unction
85v Sacraments of Baptism and Confirmation
111 Rosary

Hours of the Virgin – Sarum Usage
Paper, 6 ½ x 3 in. (16.5 x 7.6 cm.)
Printed in Paris by François Regnault, 1526
Stonyhurst College, Lancashire, S. 3/6

The book shows signs of censorship presumably under Henry VIII: on 26v suffrages for Thomas Becket are crossed out (see in this catalogue p. 87); on 129 English indulgences are crossed out; and on 134v -135 English explanations of the values of prayers are crossed out.

Calendar 2v-14 (Soleil, 154-59, fig. XI)
2v January: playing with tops
3v February: at school – lessons
4v March: hunting
5v April: one man and two women well dressed
6v May: people on horseback and walking
7v June: marriage with priest officiating (Soleil, fig. XI).
8v July: family of man and woman and little boy
9v August: return from labor with donkey; a worker receives his salary from his master
10v September: dog keeping beggar away from door
11v October: feasting
12v November: old man sick in a chair with a doctor examining a urine flask
13v December: deathbed and Extreme Unction
14v Trinity as Shield of Faith (Soleil, fig. XIX)
18v Tree of Jesse
19 Annunciation
12 Visitation
28 Agony in the Garden
29 Nativity
31 Christ before Pilate
33v Ecce Homo
34v Adoration of the Magi
36 Christ Carrying the Cross
37 Presentation in the Temple
39 Flight into Egypt
41 Deposition
42 Coronation of the Virgin
44 Entombment
49v Procession with the Blessed Sacrament
61 St. George slaying dragon
64 Trinity as Shield of Faith
65v David spying Bathsheba (Soleil, 174)
66v Uriah killed in battle (Soleil, 175)

67v David is lectured by the prophet Nathan (Soleil, 176)
69 David in prayer
70 David offering a holocaust
71 Nathan absolves David
72 Nathan gives crown to David
80v and 81 Confrontation of the three living and the three dead (Soleil, figs. XIV and XV)
85 Adam and Eve expelled from Paradise (Soleil, 185)
86 Adam seated and Eve nursing a child (Soleil, 189)
87 Adam kneeling before God the Father (Soleil, 189)
89 Clergy in choir praying over draped coffin (Soleil, 189-90, fig. XVI) – Story of the deceased Parisian canon calling out after death that he was damned for his vices (French quatrain under the image)

Annunciation, Book of Hours printed in Paris by François Regnault, 1526, Stonyhurst College, S. 3/6, fol. 19

90 Man dying and a child born (Soleil, 192-93, fig. XVII)

91 Souls in purgatorial fire (Soleil, 193)

93v Man receiving Last Rights (Soleil, 200)

94v Job visited by wife and false friends (Soleil, 200-201)

95v Infant before World Flesh and the Devil (Soleil, 201)

101 Lazarus and the Rich Man

106v Christ with the Instruments of the Passion

120v Crucifixion

131v Virgin on Crescent surrounded by rosary

137v Pietà

142v Kiss of Judas

159v Trinity as Shield of Faith

162-65V in English – the last four folios before the table of contents

"Here folowe certayne questyons hat synne is: with the order of confession"

- 7 deadly sins: pride, envy, wrath, sloth, covetousness, gluttony, lechery
- 10 commandments
- 5 senses (Wyttes): sight, taste, hearing, smell, touch
- 7 corporal works of mercy
- 6 spiritual works of mercy
- 7 gifts of Holy Spirit
- 7 Sacraments
- 8 beatitudes

168 In edibus Francisci regnault vici diui Jacovi /Ad Signum Elephantis commorantis iuxta templum Mathurmorum . . . . MCCCCCXXVI. Die vero XI Mentiis Januarii.

Hours of the Virgin –Sarum Usage
Paper, 4 ½ x 3 in. (11.4 x 7.6 cm.)
Printed in Paris? 1530
Stonyhurst College, Lancashire, S.3/8

The Hours are truncated and begin with fol. 33, the Gospel lesson of Mark. The illustrations are essentially the same as those printed by François Regnault in 1526. Several prayers are explained as particularly effective, exemplified in the Hours of the Passion for Compline (fol. 37): Benedict XII made this prayer and gave them that devoutly sayeth it as many days as Our Lorde had wounds, that is V1 M.V1.C. 1X and VI. Pfaff

notes that "it was common in the middle ages to augment the verisimilitude surrounding a grant of indulgences with the names of popes, more or less indiscriminately bestowed without regard for historical fact" (Pfaff 1970, 63). The Mass of the Name of Jesus, for example, had a large number of spurious indulgences associated with its practice. Benedict XII (1335-42) the third Avignon pope, was formerly Jacques Fournier, a Cistercian monk who held bishoprics in France and was named cardinal in 1327. His association with such an indulgence is unverified. Important illustrations follow:

38v Tree of Jesse

39 Annunciation

50v Suffrages to St. Thomas Becket

52v Christ with Signs of the Passion

54 Nativity with English text below: How Jesu Chryst ryght poorely borne was./ In an olde orybbe layde all in poverte./ At bethleem by an oxe & an asse./ Where Mary blyssed his natyvite.

57 Christ before Pilate

58v Annunciation to Shepherds

59 Ecce Homo

62v Adoration of the Magi

64v Christ Carrying the Cross

69 Flight into Egypt

76 Deposition with English text below: How our lorde at tyme of even-song / By Joseph Nychodeme was take downe/ Layde in his moders lap he screched a long/ Whiche for pure sorow fell in a swoune.

84 Procession with the Blessed Sacrament

90 St. Brigid praying for souls in purgatory

105 Trinity as Shield of Faith

107 David spying Bathsheba

108 Uriah killed in battle

109 David is lectured by the prophet Nathan

110v David in prayer

112 David offering a holocaust

113v Nathan absolves David

114v Nathan gives crown to David

126v and 127 Confrontation of the three living and the three dead

132v Adam and Eve expelled from Paradise

133v Adam seated and Eve nursing a child

134v Adam kneeling before God the Father

Ad primam.   Fo.liiij.

GLORIA — IN EX — CELSIS — DEO

¶How Jhesu Cryst ryght poorely
borne was. ¶In an olde/oryybbe/layde
all in pouerte · ¶At bethleem/by an
oxe & an asse. ¶Where Mary blyssed
his natyuite.

Nativity with English text below: How Jesu Chryst ryght poorely
borne was./ In an olde orybbe layde all in poverte./ At bethleem by
an oxe & an asse./ Where Mary blyssed his natyvite. Book of Hours,
1530, (Paris?), Stonyhurst College, Lancashire, S.3/8, fol. 76

137v Clergy in choir praying over draped coffin
    – Story of the deceased Parisian canon calling
    out after death that he was damned for his vices
    (French quatrain under image)
138v Man dying and a child born
138v Souls in purgatorial fire
143 Man receiving Last Rights
144 Job visited by wife and false friends
145 Infant before World Flesh and the Devil
152v Lazarus and the Rich Man
140v Christ with the Instruments of the Passion
181 Crucifixion
197 Virgin on Crescent surrounded by rosary
206 Pietà
213 Christ before Pilate
237 Trinity as Shield of Faith

The prymer in Englysshe and Laten, 1541
Paper, 6 1/8 x 5 1/8 in. (15.5 x 13 cm.)
London, Thomas Petyr, St. Paul's Church Yard
Stonyhurst College, Lancashire, S.3.26

The first entry after the calendar is a proclamation
by Henry VIII that the book is an authorized
translation of the Latin, and that it is to be
used to instruct parishioners and that no other
English translation will be tolerated.   Notably,
it includes the popular prayer of The Fifteen O's
before the Seven Penitential Psalms. There are
very few illustrations: Annunciation, Visitation,
Annunciation to Shepherds, Flight into Egypt,
and Coronation of the Virgin. Beginning the
Seven Penitential Psalms, David looking down
at Bathsheba as she bathes in the garden tended
by a serving woman, Death striking a seated man
that begins the Office of the Dead. The Hours
are bound with an English text (almost half the
book) introduced as: An exposicion after the
maner of a cotemplacyon upon the ll psalm called
Miserere mei deus: whiche Hierom of Ferrarye
made at the latter end of his dayes. Psalm 55
begins "Have mercy on me O God, for man hath
trodden me under foot." The treatise also extends
to an analysis of the 30th psalm, "In thee O Lord
have I hoped, let me never be confounded." This
text is followed by an English translation of the
Epistles and Gospels for the Sundays and Holy
Days. Concluding the book is a table of contents
in the last 4 folios. The verso of the last folio
defines the printer: Printed at London in Paules
church yearde. At the sygne of the maydens heed
by Thomas Petyr MDXLI.

Ruins of Whalley Abbey, Lancashire. The Cistercian abbey was founded in 1296 and the last abbot, John Paslew was executed March 10, 1537 for support of the Northern Rising, the "Pilgrimage of Grace" against Henry VIII's policies of confiscating the monasteries. The recusant Towneley family kept a set of cloth-of-gold vestments made between 1415 and 1435 from the abbey as well as books. After Thomas Dunham Whitaker, *An History of the Original Parish of Whalley and Honor of Clitheroe in the Counties of Lancaster and York,* London 1806

The Rescue of Books from the Suppressed Religious Houses

A. I. Doyle

As institutions dedicated to both piety and learning, England's medieval monasteries possessed rich libraries. Founded with books of worship at their core, they acquired through the centuries religious and secular works through the monks copying texts, but also by gifts from donors, purchases, and inheritances from other monasteries. These houses were great prizes for ambitious administrators. Cardinal Wolsey effected the suppression, with papal authority, of twenty-nine chiefly small monasteries, male and female, between 1524 and 1528, largely for the benefit of his own collegiate foundations at Oxford and Ipswich. He had plans of more extensive reforms which were only realized after his own downfall and England's break with Rome. These were accomplished by Henry VIII and Thomas Cromwell between 1536 and 1540, starting with the smaller houses and ending with the mendicant friaries and the largest monasteries and nunneries (Knowles III, 161-64).

As the dissolution was looming, it is clear that some individuals were planning their roles as the beneficiaries of monastic library treasures. About 1533, John Leland, claiming a royal commission, had inspected many houses, taking particular notice of their libraries by listing unusual books. Another agent had listed monastic possessions in Lincolnshire intended for, and ultimately entering, the king's own collections. Other sharp-witted observers might have been equally preparing to salvage what they could from the anticipated destruction. In retrospect, their concern was justified.

No matter what their status, monastic libraries were fair game to Henrician administrators. A number of the major monasteries, such as Canterbury, were already also cathedrals. Under Henry's policies they and several more were converted into secular cathedrals staffed by deans and canons, partly recruited from former monks. It might have been expected that at least these great libraries would have been kept intact *in situ*. This did not generally happen. The case was much worse for the majority of houses dissolved without having institutional heirs. In both cases some of the continuing or dismissed members appropriated what had been communal books,

View of ruins of the monastic church, Mount Grace Priory, Yorkshire, established in 1398 by Thomas de Holand, Earl of Kent and Duke of Surrey. Like many Carthusian foundations, it was renowned for its intellectual achievements and its library before it was suppressed in 1539.

while others were acquired by the new owners (often former patrons or lay officers) of the adapted or partly demolished monastic buildings. Very many must have been destroyed as having no future use: these included the multiple books for church services and religious rules which the Reformers wholly abolished.

We have only patchy early evidence of what, where, when and by whom books were saved. There were some people with historical interests who, after Leland had pleaded the opportunity for public benefit, took advantage of their positions in different localities to make small collections of their own. Some of this activity seems motivated partly by piety and partly in hope of eventual restoration (Wright, 148-75). One notable instance of the latter is the prime copy of Thomas of Elmham's history of St. Augustine's abbey, Canterbury, acquired years after its dissolution by Robert Hare, a recusant gentleman (ca.1530-1611), and given by him to Trinity Hall, Cambridge, with the proviso that in the event of the restoration of that monastery it should be returned there. It seems from other cases that books may have remained at St. Augustine's for years after its dissolution (as late as 1565). Manuscripts from Winchester Cathedral Priory were acquired by Thomas Dakcomb (1496-ca.1572), a minor canon from 1541 in the secular

refoundation. Dakcomb's sympathies are suggested by his intending one of them to go to the Marian refoundation of Sheen Charterhouse in 1558, a hope destroyed by the Queen's death that year (Watson 2004, III). The Ingleby family, on whose lands the Charterhouse of Mount Grace (North Yorkshire) had been founded in 1399, after its suppression in 1539 owned more than one of its manuscripts; while the unique *Book of Margery Kempe* which had belonged to Mount Grace and was annotated by its monks, survived in the hands of the Catholic Butler-Bowdon family until the 1990s. A remarkable illustrated devotional collection written at one of the northern charterhouses, now in the British Library (MS Add.37049), went abroad and was only brought

Reconstruction of Carthusian cell at Mount Grace Priory; materials for copying, illuminating, and binding manuscripts have been excavated in the site. Photo: Virginia Raguin

back in the nineteenth century. A manuscript of the Latin translation of Walter Hilton's *Scale of Perfection* copied by a mid-fifteenth-century monk of Sheen, later lent to the Benedictines of Bury St. Edmunds (Suffolk), also went to the continent before coming back to England in modern times. The copy of the *Cloud of Unknowing* in the hand of B. William Exmewe, a Carthusian martyr of London, was treasured by Dom Maurice Chauncy of the restored Marian community of Sheen that was subsequently exiled under Elizabeth. The great illuminated Sherborne Missal, made for that abbey in Dorset between 1400 and 1407, was taken overseas by someone before 1700 (Backhouse 1999, 58-61). There are still a few other outstanding books from English religious houses now in continental libraries which were probably exported by exiles, rather than merely being sold, for example, the St. Albans Psalter now in Hildesheim (Wormald 1960, 6), and the *Sanctilogium Salvatoris* from Syon Abbey now at Karlsruhe (Doyle 1997a). There are about 200 theological manuscripts in the Vatican Library from several Cambridge friaries and other English sources which have been in Rome since shortly after the closure of those houses (Ker).

The prior, sub-prior and two other monks of the Cluniac house of Monk Bretton (West Yorks.), still living together in a nearby village almost twenty years after the dissolution, had 142 listed books (mostly printed) which the prior, like other ex-monks, provided in his will in 1557 for return to the house if it were to be restored. The bequest, like others of this sentiment, was made in Mary's reign (Cross; Sharpe, 266-88). At Durham the new secular Cathedral Chapter was at first staffed entirely by former monks, but in the reign of Edward VI (1547-1553) under Protestant deans, some of the most important manuscripts such as the Lindisfarne Gospels were alienated. When Queen Mary was succeeded by Elizabeth, a number of the canons refused to accept her ecclesiastical supremacy and took away books which they had had from monastic times and from communal collections. Two of the canons gave them to their relatives, a branch of the local Tempest family, persistent "Church Papists" or recusants. The Tempest family retained a large number, over fifty, mostly printed, until after the end of the seventeenth century and later, many passing into Catholic clerical collections (Doyle 1984). Major manuscripts of Durham chronicles were acquired from the Cathedral in the later sixteenth century by William Claxton (1530-97), a local antiquary from another Catholic family, who was probably responsible in part for the *Rites of Durham* which describes the former life there (Doyle 1997b).

A number of the expelled Brigittine nuns of Syon Abbey (Middlesex) went on living together in small groups after the suppression in 1539. In 1560 under Elizabeth's rule, the Marian nuns sought exile in Flanders and apparently brought their service books with them. We have the evidence of those books which survive carrying their user's names. Certain of these books were carried with the nuns through France, to Portugal and back to England in the nineteenth century (De Hamel, 109-50).

Books were collected by John Nettleton of Hutton Cranswick (East Yorks.), particularly from the Cistercian houses of Byland, Fountains and Rievaulx. Nettleton was a recusant, who died in prison in 1597; books had been bequeathed to him in 1581 by a namesake of the last prior of Byland (Cross; Hicks; Watson 2004, IX, Addenda, 8-9.). Through his own relatives, the Saviles of Banke, they were eventually added to larger collections such as Cotton's, now in the British Library. Lord William Howard (1563-1640) of Naworth Castle (Cumberland) was a major collector, and a stalwart of aristocratic Catholicism, who obtained former monastic manuscripts from many different sources, such as the unique Middle English verse life of St. Cuthbert certainly from Durham (Mathew). In the Midlands, Thomas Allen (1540-1632) of Oxford obtained the (later Stonyhurst) Gospel of St. John from Durham, given to the Jesuits at Liege in 1769, via a Catholic Jacobite nobleman (Mynors). Allen left most of his books to his co-religionist Sir Kenelm Digby (Watson 1978), whence they are now in the Bodleian Library, Oxford.

Further attention to this question would surely result in the identification of many more sixteenth-century Catholic owners of books from former religious houses and privately-owned Psalters, Books of Hours and Missals. Such an inventory should also include the relics, vestments and altar vessels which remain in present-day Catholic churches, colleges and religious houses, as well as the many which over the last century and a half have been sold or lent to public museums. Those adherents of the "old religion" preserved many pre-Reformation works of art and literature whose significance is gradually being understood.

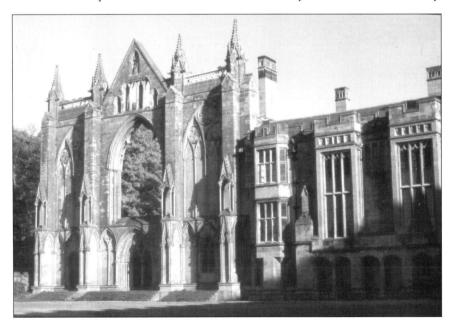

Newstead Abbey (Nottinghamshire) suppressed under Henry VIII by the order of 1538, was given to Sir John Byron of Colwick (1487-1567). Like many of the Tudor nobles, he let the church deteriorate, but converted the adjacent buildings for a house for his family. Photo: Virginia Raguin

BIBLIOGRAPHY

(also see General Bibliography)

Backhouse, Janet. *The Sherborne Missal.* London: British Library, 1999.

Cross, Clare. "A Medieval Yorkshire Library," *Northern History 25* (1989): 281-90.

De Hamel, Christopher. *Syon Abbey the Library of the Bridgettine Nuns and their Peregrinations after the Reformation.* Ottley: priv. pr. for the Roxburghe Club, 1991.

Doyle, Anthony Ian 1984. "The Library of Sir Thomas Tempest: Its Origins and Dispersal," in *Studies in Seventeenth-Century English Literature, History and Bibliography*, ed. G. A. M. Janssens and A. M. Aarts, Amsterdam: Rodopi, 1984: pp. 83-93.

Doyle, Anthony Ian 1997a. "Stephen Dodesham of With and Sheen," in *Of the Making of Books: Medieval Manuscripts, Their Scribes and Readers, Essays Presented to M. B. Parkes*, ed. P. R. Robinson and R. Zim, Aldershot: Scolar, 1997: pp. 98-101.

Doyle, Anthony Ian 1997b. "William Claxton and the Durham Chronicles," in *Books and Collectors 1200-1700: Essays Presented to Andrew Watson.* ed. J. P. Carley and C. G. C. Tite: British Library, 1997: pp. 335-55.

Hicks, Michael A. "John Netleton, Henry Savile of Banke and the Post-medieval Vicissitudes of Byland Abbey Library," *Northern History* 26 (1990): 212-17.

Ker, Neil R. "Cardinal Cervini's Manuscripts from the Cambridge Friars," in *Xenia Medii Aevi Historiam Illustrantia Oblata Thomae Kaeppeli.* Rome: Storia e Letteraturea, 1978: pp. 437-58.

Mathew, D. "The Library at Naworth," in *For Hilaire Belloc: Essays In Honour of His 72nd Birthday.* London: Sheed & Ward, 1942: pp. 117-30.

Mynors, Roger A. B. "The Stonyhurst Gospel," in *The Relics of St. Cuthbert.* ed. C. Battiscombe, Oxford: University Press, for the Dean and Chapter of Durham, 1956: pp. 360-62.

Sharpe, Richard. *English Benedictine Libraries: the Shorter Catalogues.* ed. R. Sharpe et al. Corpus of British Medieval Library Catalogues 4; London: British Library, 1996.

Watson, Andrew G. 2004. *Medieval Manuscripts in Post-Medieval England.* Aldershot: Ashgate, 2004.

Watson, Andrew G. 1978. "Thomas Allen of Oxford and his Manuscripts," in *Medieval Scribes, Manuscripts and Libraries: Essays Presented to N. R. Ker*, ed. M. B. Parkes and Andrew G. Watson, London: Scolar, 1978: pp. 279-314.

Wormald, Francis. *The St. Albans Psalter.* intro. Otto Pacht et al. London: Warburg Institute, 1960.

Wright, Cyril E. "The Dispersal of the Libraries in the Sixteenth Century," in *The English Library before 1700*, ed. Francis Wormald and Cyril Wright, London: Athlone, 1958: pp. 148-75.

Veneration of the True Cross, the Holy Rood of Bromholm, and the Passion of Christ

Virginia C. Raguin

The death of Christ on the Cross is attested by all four Gospel writers, and thus has been an article of faith since the beginning of Christianity. Its significance to the common believer, however, varied considerably across the centuries. In the earliest imagery, the cross was noticeably absent; focus devolved rather on Christ's triumph over death and themes of deliverance: Jonah rescued from the Lion's den, the three Hebrews unscathed in the midst of the fiery furnace, the Good Shepherd with errant lamb, and the youthful and triumphant image of Christ. The Crucifixion appeared in symbolic form, exemplified by the sarcophagus with Scenes from the Passion from the mid-fourth century, probably from the Catacomb of Domitilla where the cross is surmounted by the Chi Rho, the monogram of Christ, encircled by the victor's laurel wreath. The relic of the "True Cross" itself entered veneration through its purported discovery by Helena, the mother of Constantine, the first Christian emperor as illustrated in the 1584 *Ecclesiae Anglicana Trophaea* (see p. 142). Voyaging to Jerusalem, she excavated the hill of Golgotha where the True Cross was distinguished from those of the two thieves when it miraculously resuscitated a dead person. This is commemorated as the feast of the Invention (Discovery) of the Cross, celebrated the 3rd of May. A portion of the True Cross enclosed in a silver reliquary was venerated in the church of the Holy Sepulchre in Jerusalem. Another portion and the nails were apparently sent to Constantine who incorporated them into his construction of the city of Constantinople. Helena's relic was not without its drama. Removed to Persia by Chosroes II after his conquest of Jerusalem in 614, it was returned to the city by the Emperor Heraclius in 629. It is this restoration that is commemorated on September 14th as the Feast of the Exaltation of the Cross.

Fragments of the Cross were apparently distributed from the earliest times. One of the first arrivals in the west was a fragment of the True Cross given by Constantine to the basilica now known as Santa Croce in Gerusalemme in Rome. In 569 Queen Radegund, the wife of Clothair, ruler of the Frankish Kingdom, roughly present-day France, received a relic from the Byzantine Emperor Justin II. Radegund, very much a dynastic pawn in territorial disputes, had withdrawn to convent life and founded a monastery in Poitiers named in honor of the Holy Cross. Literary and visual works of art were inspired by the relic. Venantius Fortunatus, Bishop of Poitiers and a confidant of the queen, composed several hymns for its reception. His *Pange Lingua* (Sing, my tongue) and *Vexilla Regis Prodeunt* (The banners of the King go forth) became part of Good Friday liturgies, feasts of the Holy Cross, and the Divine Office throughout the Middle Ages. The relic was arguably the motivation for the immense image of the Cross in the central window of Poitiers Cathedral installed about 1175. The richness of the treatment of the cross and the royal purple cloth worn by Christ transcend generic images to evoke the presence of the relic in the Holy Cross Abbey adjacent to the cathedral. Venantius' *Vexilla Regis Prodeunt* proclaims "Hail Cross! On which the Life Himself/ Died and by death our life restor'd." One of the verses describes the cross as *arbra decora et fulgida/ ornata Regis purpura* (shining tree adorned with splendor, decorated with royal purple).

The Anglo-Saxon Poem the *Dream of the Rood*, dated to the early eighth century, has also been associated with a relic of the True Cross as inspiration. Although a specific relic has yet to be identified, the poet's references suggest his meditation on a reliquary shaped in the form of a cross. The poet declares his hope that "my Lord's Cross, which here on Earth I had earlier beheld, will from this fleeting life carry me off and bring me . . . (to) perpetual bliss." He also describes viewing an image that is strikingly similar to reliquaries that enshrined fragments of the cross: "covered with gold; jewels studded lovingly at its Earthen base, while likewise there were five upon that shoulder-span." A modern reader can easily construct an image of a medieval cross with jewels at its four points and crossing similar to the Gertrudis's cross from the Guelf Treasure now in the Cleveland Museum of Art. A hypothetical base could be seen as a circular form with jewels, "four gems were set where it met the earth," marking the cross axes, and thus aligning the cross with the four compass points and giving testimony to Christ's dominion over creation. The poem was honored in its own time, evident in the presence of verses of the *Dream of the Rood* carved on the side of a great stone wayside cross carved about 730-750 in Ruthwell, Scotland (Cassidy, 70, 85-93).

A documented relic of the True Cross originating from the imperial collection in Constantinople did come to England much later. The relic, a part of the plunder taken during the Fourth Crusade's Sack of Constantinople in 1204 was acquired by the Cluniac priory of Bromholm in Norfolk about 1220. A contemporary chronicler, Roger of Wendover, recorded miracles increasing at Bromholm in 1223 and gives as well the history of the acquisition of the relic. Roger's account was widely circulated and it was taken over practically verbatum by Matthew Paris in the *Chronica Major*. The story of the acquisition includes the topos of the "neglected treasure" that justifies the transfer of ownership. The relic at Bromholm is identified as a portion of the True Cross which was customarily carried before the Emperor in battle. An English priest was returning from a pilgrimage to the Holy Land and remained after the fall of Constantinople, becoming the keeper of relics under the new emperor, Baldwin Count of Flanders. Baldwin, however, in the year after his coronation, leaving the relic behind, engaged the Bulgarians in the battle of Adrianople and defeated, was led off to imprisonment and death. During the confusion in the city, the priest took this and other relics from the treasury and fled to England, settling in his native county, Norfolk. Francis Wormald has carefully sorted through the several accounts to explain the convoluted story of the priest's initial secrecy and efforts to provide for his two sons by offering the relic for sale (Wormald).

The plunder of Constantinople was unprecedented. Steven Runciman has excoriated the decision of Crusaders to attack a Christian city as a "crime against humanity" whose "effects were wholly disastrous" (Runciman, 122-31, quotes 130). Although a modern historian might lament "the destruction or the dispersal of all the treasures of the past that Byzantium had devotedly stored" (Ibid, 130), a contemporary would justify ownership as God's will. No more vivid proof of righteousness could be found than miracles. Soon after its arrival at Bromholm, the

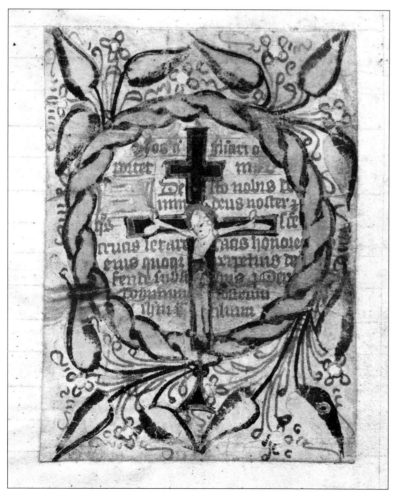

Pasted in prayer card of the Holy Rood of Bromholm, late 15th century, Book of Hours, ca. 1410-20, Stonyhurst College, MS 57, fol. 174

TRUE CROSS

relic gained renown for its many miracles, in particular the healing of the sick. It is probable that the days of organized pilgrimage were associated with the days of devotion to the Cross, Passion Sunday, and the Feast of the Exaltation of the Cross, September 14. The conjecture is strengthened by the documentation of the monks' privilege of a three-day annual fair that took place before and after the September 14 feast from 1226 onwards.

Bromholm is located on the coast, almost directly north of Norwich and in proximity to the region of Walsingham and the pilgrimage site of the Virgin's house. The Walsingham shrine centered around a small house that was believed to have been built in 1061 by a noblewoman named Richeldis under the Virgin's direction. It was Mary's loving wish that English Pilgrims, unable to go to Jerusalem could have access to a replica of the house where she received Gabriel's message that she would give birth to Christ. The site was patronized by royalty as well as humbler folk. All English kings journeyed to Walsingham with petitions and thank offerings. It was still one of the major pilgrimages of England when Erasmus wrote his critical *Pilgrimage of Pure Devotion* describing the shrine as " a lytle chapell seelyd ouer with wodde, on ether syde a lytle dore wher ye pylgrymes go thorow, ther is lytle light, but of ye taperes, with a fragrant smell . . . (with) all thynges be so bright in gold, syluer, and precyous stones" (Erasmus).

Apparently the Holy Rood of Bromholm early on also enjoyed a similar fashionable notoriety, with the powerful and wealthy paying attention. In 1226 King Henry III made his first visit to honor the relic and he later gave significant ex votos, one a silver model of the King's great ship in Portsmouth given in 1225 and another Henry's own image in silver gilt produced in 1234. It remained a popular pilgrimage site through the end of the Middle Ages, although decidedly less important than Walsingham. In the late fourteenth century, the poem *The Vision of Piers the Ploughman* has Avarice speak of a petition to the "Rode of bromeholme" to be free of debt and Chaucer includes a reference in the *Reeves Tale*. The miller's wife cries out for help to the Holy Rood of Bromholm when she is sat upon in her sleep.

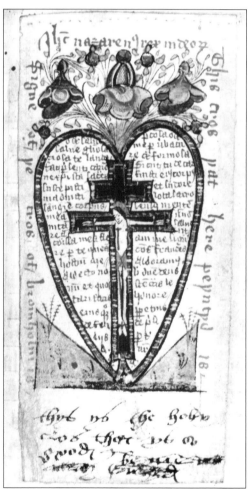

> And with the fal out of hir sleep she breyde.
> "Help! hooly croys of Bromeholm," she seyde,
> *In manus tuas!* Lord, to thee I calle! (lines 431-33)

In the fifteenth and sixteenth centuries, "holy card" souvenirs were produced by pilgrimage sites (Wormald, 124-26). The Stonyhurst Book of Hours once owned by Cardinal Wolsey shows a pasted-in prayer card of The Holy Rood of Bromholm on fol. 174 (CATALOGUE). The image shows the relic's distinctive shape, a fragment of wood almost as long as a man's hand which had two transverse pieces with a corpus attached (referred to as a patriarchal cross). The cross is enclosed by a green wreath sprouting flowers. Behind the rood appears a prayer "Adesto nobis Domine Deus noster, et quos sancte cruces letari facis honore ejus quoque perpetuis defende subsidies. Per Christum Dominum nostrum tuum filium." Two late fifteenth-century manuscripts provide parallels. A Bromholm prayer card is similarly glued into the Lewkenor Hours on fol. 136v (Lambeth Palace Library MS 545;

Bromholm prayer card glued into the Lewkenor Hours, England, 1490s, Lambeth Palace Library MS 545, fol. 136v. Courtesy Lambeth Palace

Marks and Williamson, 435, No. 326). The manuscript was begun in the 1390s and expanded in the 1490s probably for Sir Thomas Lewkenor, a member of the entourage of Lady Margaret Beaufort. The card presents the rood enclosed by a heart-shaped frame with flowers sprouting from the heart. It is inscribed at the top: Ihesus nazarenus rex Iudeorum, on the left: Thys cros that hryr peyntd is', and on the right: Syng of the cros of bromholm His'. An imitation of a prayer card is painted on fol. 57 of a Book of Hours made for the diocese of Norwich (Cambridge, Fitzwilliam Museum, 55 fol. 57). In the background are verses from a hymn associated with the rood of Bromholm. The full text of the hymn is found on fol. 184 of the Lewkenor Hours:

O crux salve preciosa	Hail, precious cross!
O crux salve gloriosa	Hail, glorious cross!
Me per verba curiosa	I will praise the beautiful cross
Te laudere crux formosa	Through earnest words
Fac presenti carmine	With this present song.
Sicut tu de carne Christi	Just as you are a holy, consecrated object
Sancta sacrata fuisti	By carrying the flesh of Christ
Ejus corpus suscepisti	You held his body
Et sudore maduisti	And you became purified with his sweat
lota sacro sanguine	And sacred blood.
Corpus sensus mentem meam	You redeem my body, my senses, my mind.
Necnon vitam salves ream	But you do not yet save my soul.
Ut commissa mea fleam	So I weep for my sins
Me signare per te queam	And I am marked as human,
Contra fraudes histium	Susceptible to the evil of others
Me defendas de peccato	You keep me from sin
Et de facto desperato	As the enemy, pushed down
Hoste truso machinato	Is weakened.
Reconsignas dei nato	You recognize me
Tuum presidium	As a child of God.
Adoramos te Christi	Let us adore you Christ
Quia per crucem, etc.	Through the cross.

Oratio. Adesto nobis Domine Deus noster, et quos sancte cruces letari facis honore ejus quoque perpetuis defende subsidies. Per Christum Dominum nostrum. Amen.

Spoken. Come to us, Lord, our God, and may the holy cross which we praise with his (Jesus's) honor be forever our courage and aid. Through your son, Christ Our Lord, Amen.

Translation by Lisa Litterio

Like most cult objects from high-profile pilgrimage sites such as Canterbury (see in this catalogue "Relics and the Two Thomases") the relic was removed early in Henry's campaign against "popish" associations. The rood was described in 1536 with the explanation "Hic apparuit multa superstitio circa crucem quam vocant the holie Crosse of Bromholme" (Wormald, 134). It was delivered by agents to Thomas Cromwell in 1537 and presumably destroyed and its metal covering melted down.

Devotion in the later Middle Ages gravitated to meditation on the Cross as the site of Christ's sufferings with an effort to empathize with these painful moments (Van Os, 104-28). Such piety characterized all of Europe and of all devotions, those connected to this subject were early phrased in the vernacular. The Arma Christi Scroll (CATALOGUE) is in English, in rhymed verses for easier recall. The text and images construct meditations on the Instruments of the Passion and the Wounds of Christ. A "constant representation" of the Instruments of the Passion and the Five Wounds appears in fifteenth-century stained glass, often on shields in tracery lights (Woodforde 1954, 26). One such example from Great

Witchingham, now in King's College Chapel, Cambridge (Wayment 1988, 91, pl. 1*e*) silhouettes yellow and white symbols and a green Crown of Thorns against a vivid red shield. The scroll carrying such imagery is an unusual form of prayer-book which must have been designed for public instruction. The verses are interspersed with images such as Christ laid out on the grave, the Holy Face, the nails that pierced Christ's hands and feet, the spear that pieced his side, and the thirty pieces of silver received by Judas. Over fifteen examples of the scroll survive, most probably made to be displayed in churches to stimulate the devotion of the unlettered parishioner.

A Mass honoring the Wounds of Christ was introduced into late-medieval England in the first half of the fifteenth century although prayers including the Wounds appear in English manuscripts from the late twelfth century (Pfaff, 84-91). The Pearl poet, for example, writing in the 1380s gives Sir Gawain a pentangle on his shield since, among other justifications "all his fealty was fixed on the five wounds" (line 643). Like other votive Masses, the Mass of the Five Wounds was associated with indulgences, if, in this instance, said five times. The texts are similar to those used at Passiontide. In 1536, the Pilgrimage of Grace (Knowles, 320-35), the name given to the Northern rebellion against Henry's policies, took the emblem of the Five Wounds of Christ (Van Os, 116, pl. 36). This emblem shows at its center a heart with a side wound, and radiating from the top, two disembodied and pierced hands, and below the pierced feet. This was an image found in England for some time, as exemplified by the stained glass in Great Malvern Priory of about 1440. Its use for the armed uprising of a major portion of the country reiterates the great link between religion and public policy.

Meditation was aided by texts as well as images. A long tradition of literature calling on the empathy of the reader/listener focused on the themes of the Passion (Bennett) and lamentations of the Virgin (Keiser). Chief among the pious texts was the Franciscan *Meditationes Vitae Christi*, written about 1375 (Van Os, 164-65; Ragusa). About 1410, the Carthusian Nicholas Love of the monastery of Mount Grace, Yorkshire, produced a vernacular adaptation, *The Mirror of the Blessed Life of Jesus Christ*. The overall structure of the text places the meditation on the life of Christ over the seven days of the week and apportioned at canonical hours of the day. Love's introduction makes it clear that he is writing not only to "clerkes in latyne but also in Englyshe to lewde men & women & them that be of simple understanding" (Love, 10: lines 5-7). The Passion of Christ from the entrance

Instruments of the Passion in stained glass, Great Witchingham (Norfolk), 15th century. King's College Chapel, Cambridge. Photo: Virginia Raguin

Five Wounds of Christ in stained glass, Great Malvern Priory (Worcestershire), ca. 1440. Photo: Virginia Raguin

into Jerusalem to the lamentation after his death and the veneration of the Cross was the subject of meditation from late Thursday through Saturday. Love prescribes devotional attitudes, especially to the objects of Christ's suffering. In the closing meditation on Friday, for example, the Virgin kneels and honors the cross, "for thou maiht thence & understande that she was the first that honored the cross as she was the first that honoured hir sone born" (Love, 186: lines 20-23). Again, as the mourning group returned to the city, "when thei comen there as thei miht no more see the cross, oure lady & all other kneled & honourede it wepying" (Love, 186: lines 25-26).

Prayers in the Books of Hours and Primers, especially the Hours of the Passion, brought frequent attention to Christ's suffering. A highly popular prayer called the "Fifteen O's" (see illustration in the essay "Private Prayer and Books of Hours," p. 80) was comprised of fifteen short prayers addressed directly to Christ all beginning with O – "O blessed Jhesu, O Jhesu endless swetnes of lovyng soules," and so forth. The worshipper asks Christ to reflect on his suffering for humankind and to have compassion on the devotee. At the beginning of the fourteenth prayer, for example, is the reflection, "and soo thou lostest thy bodely life with a grete cryeing and with a torne body and broken hert shewyng to us our raunson the bowellis of thy mercy" (White, 217-20).

Recusants such as Thomas Lusher continued to produce images associated with devotion to the Passion of Christ. Lusher, a pupil in 1593-94 at St. Omers, the English-speaking Jesuit school in the Spanish Netherlands, carved a shrine 2 1/2 inches in height (CATALOGUE). When open it allowed meditation on Christ's suffering and death by showing Instruments of the Passion (ladder, hammer, nails, crown of thorns, etc.). On the base is incised *Ora pro Tho Lusher qui fecit 1623 (pray for Thomas Lusher who made this in 1623)*. One may well wonder about the shrine's use; it was a dangerous object be found with. Its small size encourages the thought that Lusher might carry it as a pocket devotional object, especially if he were leading a public life in which he conducted daily business with persons of the majority religion. The devotion continued in later recusant use. Recusant chalices, for example often represented the Instruments of the Passion on the segments of the foot (Oman, 266-71, pls. 155-59). A chalice hallmarked 1637 in St. Ignatius College, South Tottenham, was made by the same maker as a chalice in

Shrine with Instruments of the Passion owned by Thomas Lusher, England, 1623, Stonyhurst College. Photo: Virginia Raguin

Wardour Castle (Wiltshire) (Oman, 269, pls. 158 and 159) and both are similar in form to the *Constable Chalice* from the Bar Convent, York (CATALOGUE). When in the seventeenth century the Shireburn family acquired images for their chapel at Stonyhurst, many were narratives of the Life of Christ (see in this catalogue, "Picture and Policy: Contested Control of the Image," pp. 37-41). In the group, was an image of Our Lady of Sorrows with seven swords piercing her breast under an image of the bloodied face of Christ as well as a separate image of Christ as Man of Sorrows.

Christ with Signs of the Passion, Book of Hours, Printed in Paris? 1530, Stonyhurst College, Lancashire, S.3/8, 52v

Our Lady of Sorrows with Instruments of the Passion, Antwerp? mid 17th century, formerly Shireburn chapel. Stonyhurst College, Lancashire. Photo: Virginia Raguin

TRUE CROSS

CATALOGUE

Arma Christi Roll
Tempera and ink on vellum, 74 ¼ x 4 ¾ in. (188.5 x 12 cm.)
England, ca. 1440 (poem late 14th century)
Stonyhurst College, Lancashire

Twenty-four illustrations colored in pink, green, red, blue, and gold in a naive style, are generally similar to those of the Arma Christi Roll in the British Library, London, Add. 22029.

1, the Vernicle with the face of Christ in the center of a large cloth, geometrically divided; 2, knife for the Circumcision; 3, pelican in its piety; 4, thirty pieces of silver; 5, lantern; 6, sword and stave; 7, rod; 8, cloth to blindfold Christ; 9, image of a hand with strands of Christ's hair and the hand that slapped him; 10, dice and the unseamed coat; 11, two scourges; 12, crown of thorns; 13, pillar

entwined with ropes; 14, standing Christ holding the cross; 15, three nails; 16, vessel; 17, rod with sponge; 18, spear; 19, ladder; 20, hammer; 21, pliers; 22, the face of Christ in the center with a Jew spitting at him from either side; 23, cross with a nail at each end; 24, sepulcher with Christ's body lying in it.

The text parallels the text of London, Brit. Lib., Add. 22029 (R. Morris, 171-93). The images and division of the text are similar to those of the Arma Christi Roll in the Huntington Library, Pasadena, California HM 26054. The Huntington Library

Pelican in its Piety, Arma Christi Roll, England, ca. 1440, Stonyhurst College

Sponge, spear, ladder, hammer, and pliers, Arma Christi Roll, England, ca. 1440, Stonyhurst College

manuscript was kept in a green silk bag with a drawstring. It was written in the second half of the fifteenth century and acquired by the Huntington Library at Sotheby's, 11 April 1961, lot 139 (Preston, 2-9).

The poem first appeared in Middle English before the end of the fourteenth century. More than 15 copies of the poem survive, testifying to its high popularity as an example of devotional literature. Eight copies of the poem are written on rolls, as is the Stonyhurst manuscript, most averaging 5 to 6 feet in length. No other religious text written in scroll form survives in more than one text, which indicates that the Arma Christi's function was clearly linked to the scroll's ability to present text and image in a continuous format. The evidence of comparative manuscripts strongly suggests that the roll was made for public use, to be "publicly displayed in churches to stimulate the devotion of the 'lewd' (ordinary) folk" (Robins, 417).

Morris, R. ed., *Legends of the Holy Rood; Symbols of the Passion and Cross-Poems.* Early English Text Society o.s. 46. London, 1871, 171-93.

Robbins, R. H. "The 'Arma Christi' Rolls," *Modern Language Review* 34 (1939): 415-21.

Preston, J. "Medieval Manuscripts at the Huntington: Supplement to De Ricci's Census," *Chronica: a Newsletter Published by the Medieval Association of the Pacific* 21 (1977): 2-9.

Prayer Card of the Holy Rood of Bromholm
Vellum, 1 15/16 x 1 7/16 in. (4.9 x 3.6 cm.)
England, late 15th century
Pasted in a Book of Hours, MS 57, fol. 174
Stonyhurst College, Lancashire

This Book of Hours associated with Cardinal Wolsey carries a pasted-in prayer card of The Holy Rood of Bromholm. The relic itself was shaped with two slanted transverse pieces, known as a patriarchal cross. It is depicted in the middle of the card and surrounded by a green wreath formed of two twisted elements very similar to representations of the Crown of Thorns. The wreath sprouts flowers intermingled with large tear-drop shaped

green leaves. The flowers and accompanying fronds are executed in outline, with gold circles at the heart of the four-petal flowers. Red ink delineates the halo and loin cloth of Christ and the decorative letter A which begins the prayer behind the cross: "Adesto nobis Domine Deus noster, et quos sancte cruces letari facis honore ejus quoque perpetuis defende subsidies. Per Christum Dominum nostrum tuum filium." (Come to us, Lord, our God, and may the holy cross which we praise with his (Jesus's) honor be forever our courage and aid. Through your son, Christ Our Lord, Amen.)

Shrine with Instruments of the Passion
Wood and paint, 2 ½ x 3 ½ in. (6.4 x 8.9 cm.) open
England, 1623
Inscription on base: Ora pro Tho. Lusher qui fecit 1623
Stonyhurst College, Lancashire

Thomas Lusher, a pupil in 1593-94 at St. Omers constructed this small shrine in 1623. Meditation on the Instruments of the Passion facilitated prayer. On the center of this tiny shrine is the cross with the ladder used to remove the body from the cross, the spear that pierced his side on the left and the sponge with vinegar on the staff on the right. The images are not presented in any chronological order, such as the taking of Christ in the Garden of Gethsemane, then the presentation before the High Priest, Peter's denial, presentation before Pilate, the crowning with thorns, crucifixion, and so on, as found in the Gospel accounts, such as Mark: 14-15. The objects that represent these events float in space. This gives the viewer a stimulating sense of freedom; it allows a worshipper from any time period to focus on the images in any order chosen as significant to their culture or to them personally. To the far left, the column with the cock of Peter's reminder and close to it three dice representing the men who cast lots for Christ's garments. On the right is the basin and ewer used as Pilate washed his hands, and immediately next to it the reed placed in Christ's hands as he was mocked, and off in a corner we find a column, reminding us of Christ's lashings.

Constable Chalice
Silver gilt with precious and semi-precious stones,
8 in. (20.3 cm.)
England, ca. 1630-40 and early 19th century
Inscriptions: 1 E S V S
Bar Convent, York, Inv. No. M/41

An eight-segmented foot rises from a shaped wire, terminating in a two layered, circular button set with pearls and gemstones. The stem is hexagonal and is interrupted by a circular knop with six canted projecting squares incised with the letters (left to right from center) I E S V S and an outline of the Sacred Heart. Between squares are jewel clusters consisting of a pearl flanked by two small gemstones. Above and below are gilt trefoils; those above have been used as the settings for larger gemstones; those below are blank. Closest to the stem, above and below the knop, are single rows of small gemstones. On the stem just under the cup,

on the segment aligned with the Crucifixion is an oval diamond cluster, probably from a ring or pin. The raised bowl sits on a disk.

A series of Instruments of the Passion is incised on the eight petals of the octofoil foot, clockwise from crucifixion:

1) crucifixion, Christ alone, INRI on cross, Jerusalem in background
2) ladder, pliers, hammer, lance, sponge on pole
3) cock
4) pillar, scourge, bound switches
5) lantern – birds(?) to left
5) crown of thorns, club, reed put in Christ's hand
7) two torches, shield, arrow, pike (Christ taken in Gethsemane)
8) 3 die (at bottom) robe

The chalice can be compared to recusant chalices of the 1630s and 1640s in what Oman categorizes as Group C.R. 2 (Oman, 266-69, pls. 155-57). The *Constable Chalice* is unusual because of its foot in eight segments, rather than the standard sexfoil foot. All the sections of the foot are outlined with a feather pattern, similar to the pattern used on a chalice with a maker's mark *WR below a bow*, hall-marked for 1633 (National Museum, Dublin: Oman, 267, pl. 155a). This maker, however, still unidentified, made a number of chalices during this era, working in a period of brief tolerance, for both Catholic and Anglican patrons. Oman connects the Bar Convent chalice with this group but "more squat than those made by WR," and closely allied it to a recusant chalice belonging to the Anglican

Constable chalice, England, about 1630-40 and early 19th century, Bar Convent, York, Inv. No. M/41. Photo: Virginia Raguin

Detail of foot of Constable chalice: crown of thorns, lantern, column and scourge, and cock. Photo: Virginia Raguin

parish at Ashow, Warwickshire (near Kenilworth). Its sexfoil foot, like the Bar Convent example is engraved with the instruments of the Passion and a view of Jerusalem behind the Crucifix (Oman, 268, pl. 157). Engraving to adorn the foot of a chalice was not unusual in pre-Reformation times. A lavish gold chalice hallmarked for 1507 was owned by Bishop Foxe and displays six saints engraved on each of the segments of the foot (Corpus Christi College, Oxford: Oman, 45-46, pls. 18, 32; Marks and Williamson, 242, No. 105).

The chalice was used and probably commissioned by the Constable family of Everingham for their private chapel in the seventeenth century. Upon completion of a new chapel at the Bar Convent in 1769, the chalice was given to the convent. Thus, the chalice could represent four or five generations of use before being transferred to the convent, increasing its value as a testimonial of recusant fidelity. The original notice of transfer is now lost but was copied in later inventories. The jewels embellishing the chalice were presumably added in the first half of the nineteenth century, at a time preceding the Pugin/Hardman "archaeological" Gothic Revival influence. The additions appear to be the work of a local vernacular metal-beater's or gem-setter's work.

THE SOCIETY OF JESUS: ITS EARLY HISTORY, SPIRITUALITY, AND MISSION TO ENGLAND

Robert E. Scully, S.J.

Although it was by no means the only religious order instrumental during penal times in England, the Society of Jesus exerted a profound influence. First, through the school of St. Omers in the Spanish Netherlands, now in northern France, it educated a majority of the English Catholic gentry, and through the foundation of the Maryland Colony, it was an early and lasting presence in the formative years of the United States (see "The Founding of Maryland and Catholics under British Colonial Policy"). The founder of the Society, Inigo de Loyola, who was born in the Basque country of northern Spain, went on, as Ignatius Loyola, to build a movement that played a particularly strong role in the Catholic Reformation. The turning point for Ignatius began with his own profound conversion in 1521. Wounded in a battle at Pamplona and recovering in the family castle at Loyola, Ignatius tried to relieve his pain and boredom through reading. With no novels of chivalry and romance available, he read a book on the life of Christ by Ludolf of Saxony and one on the lives of the saints. Slowly, this conventionally Christian, Basque nobleman began to undergo an inner transformation that commenced his own spiritual journey, one that would not only profoundly change his own spiritual life, but would also have a major impact on the lives of many others. Of particular importance was Ignatius's reflection on his progress, a practice which led him to additional insights concerning discernment of spirits and other knowledge contained in his *Spiritual Exercises*.

Portrait of Ignatius Loyola, from P. Pazmany, S.J. and N. Lancicius, S.J. *Vita Beati P. Ignatii Loiolae*. Rome 1609, frontispiece. The text is drawn from Joshua 22:5: *Be careful to observe the precepts and law which the servant of the Lord has enjoined upon you: follow him faithfully, and serve him with your whole heart and with your whole soul.*

With the sometimes excessive zeal of a convert, Ignatius over the next several years underwent intermittently long periods of prayer, fasting, and bodily mortification. After a vigil at the shrine of the Black Virgin at Montserrat, he settled for about a year at Manresa, living in a cave, praying intensely, experiencing great spiritual highs and lows (consolation and desolation), receiving some profound spiritual insights, and beginning to write his classic manual, *The Spiritual Exercises*. He then journeyed to the Holy Land, but, when his plans to remain there proved impossible, he decided to return to Spain to obtain a solid, classical education, the *sine qua non* of which was the study of Latin. He studied for periods in Barcelona, Alcala, and Salamanca, but also had some encounters with the Inquisition, which was troubled by a layman, uninstructed in theology,

The Battle of Pamplona, from P. Pazmany, S.J. and N. Lancicius, S.J. *Vita Beati P. Ignatii Loiolae*. Rome 1609, pl. 2. *Ignatius having followed a military career, he is badly wounded by a canon ball during the defense of the city of Pamplona. Leaving behind the military and secular, he thus turns to the divine.*

teaching others about spiritual realities. After being told that he must desist with his spiritual activities until he received the proper theological training, Ignatius set off for the pinnacle of philosophical and theological studies in that age: the University of Paris.

Ignatius arrived in Paris in 1528 and spent the next seven years imbibing what he thought was best of both the scholasticism of the Middle Ages and the humanism of the Renaissance. The form and substance of the *modus Parisiensis* would have a significant influence on Jesuit education. But Ignatius did not spend all of his time in Paris at his studies. He continued his practice of sharing his religious experiences and insights with others, including his roommates: the receptive shepherd from Savoy, Peter Faber, and the initially standoffish nobleman from Navarre, Francis Xavier. Eventually, these two and four additional students formed an affective and spiritual bond with Ignatius and with each other. On August 15, 1534 these seven companions took vows of poverty and chastity at Montmartre, the initial step toward a yet deeper union of minds and hearts.

Yet, in spite of the joy and inner peace of these "friends in the Lord," the world around them was swirling with religious turmoil and change. In the same year that they took their vows, France was shaken by the "affair of the placards," anti-Catholic sentiments that were posted in Paris and other cities. King Francis I reacted strongly by persecuting his Protestant subjects. Therefore, a number of French reformers fled their homeland, including John Calvin, who had converted to Protestantism earlier that year. Calvin eventually settled in Geneva, which became the center of international Calvinism, the "Protestant Rome." Similarly, Henry VIII broke with Rome in 1534. In that same year, Alessandro Farnese became Pope Paul III, in many ways exemplifying the Counter-Reformation during the fifteen years of his pontificate. A scion of one of the aristocratic Roman families, he could not resist the temptation of nepotism and appointed two of his teenage nephews as cardinals. On the other hand, he also appointed a number of reform-minded men to the College of Cardinals, including the Englishman Reginald Pole. Moreover, Paul III gave his approbation to the Jesuits as a new religious order and, through persistent efforts, finally convoked the Council of Trent (1545-1563). Over the course of three sessions, Trent addressed the more serious abuses in the Church, proposed a reform agenda, and clarified Catholic doctrine on essential issues such as salvation and the sacraments. Tridentine dogma and spirituality would continue to dominate the Catholic world throughout the early modern era and beyond (O'Malley 2000).

Ignatius received his Master of Arts degree in 1535 and returned for some months to his Basque homeland. Toward the end of the year he set off for Venice to join the other companions in their plan of becoming missionaries among the Muslims. By 1537 the initial seven friends from Paris had all arrived in Venice, but due to a war between the "Serene Republic" and the Turks, travel to the Holy Land was all but impossible. They then turned to various ministries to the sick, the poor, and the needy in Venice and other northern Italian cities. They agreed to place themselves at the service of the pope, reasoning

SOCIETY OF JESUS

that the pontiff knew best what and where would be the greatest needs of the Church. Developing focus through what Ignatius would call a process of discernment, they also agreed to take vows of obedience and form a religious order. This led to the drafting of the "Formula of the Institute," a blueprint for their new congregation. Ignatius was insistent that the order not be named after him, but rather be dedicated to the Lord himself, thus, the Society of Jesus. After giving verbal approval in 1539, Paul III gave his official imprimatur to the Society of Jesus on September 27, 1540 in the bull *Regimini Militantis Ecclesiae*.

There have been many myths surrounding the Jesuits, especially concerning their founding. Some have seen them primarily as a quasi-military religious order functioning as the shock troops of the "Church militant" at the vanguard of the Counter-Reformation. In fact, the initial focus of the first companions was on conversion of the Muslims in the Holy Land, not on Protestant confrontation in Wittenberg or Geneva. Prevented from travel to the east, they then focused on pastoral work in Italy. Thus, as the Jesuit Juan de Polanco wrote concerning ministries at Rome in 1543, his confreres were actively engaged in "the usual ministries proper to our Institute—preaching, administering the sacraments of confession and Communion, teaching catechism, giving the Spiritual Exercises, bringing peace to quarrelling factions, and carrying out other similar pious works . . ." (Polanco, 19).

The Jesuits were also not founded as a teaching order. Ignatius placed a great deal of emphasis on mobility, on the ideal that Jesuits should be readily available to be of service, to "help souls," wherever needed. This was summed up in the Jesuit motto: *Ad Majorem Dei Gloriam* (To the Greater Glory of God). Ignatius initially feared that institutional commitments would tie Jesuits to specific ministries and locales, and thus make them unavailable for greater needs and possibilities elsewhere. Mobility also encouraged the Jesuits not to pray the Divine Office in common, as was standard for other religious orders. Saying the office in common would have necessitated members coming together throughout the day, limiting the time available for ministry. Although official prayer may have been lessened, it was supplemented by what was essentially the prayer of living out the Gospel. Thus, the Jesuit ideal was to be a "contemplative in action." Ignatius's distrust of institutional commitments was also a major reason why he did not approve the development of a female branch, similar to most other orders. He feared that the obligations of Jesuit priests serving as spiritual directors and confessors and ministering the other sacraments to Jesuit nuns would similarly limit their availability for ministry out "in the world."

Although the Jesuits were particularly motivated by an "activist" spirituality, they were not alone in their shift away from the ideals of contemplative religious life practiced by the desert fathers in the early Church, and the Benedictines, Cistercians, and other orders of the Middle Ages. Traditional monastic life had already been modified with the rise of the friars, especially the Franciscans and Dominicans in the thirteenth century, who addressed the often unmet needs of people in the growing towns and cities. Yet, in the sixteenth century, in the context of the Renaissance, the Reformation, and the ever-increasing contact with Asia, Africa, and the Americas, many new and reformed religious orders, to various degrees, moved beyond other traditional boundaries of religious life. Reformation debates on the validity of monasticism, religious orders, and chastity may also have encouraged restructured vocations. In any event, orders of men and women in the early modern period tried to combine contemplation and action in ways that gave greater emphasis to the latter. Besides the Jesuits, examples can be found in the Capuchins, Oratorians, and Ursulines, as well as the Institute of Mary Ward, discussed in this catalogue (DeMolen).

Based on their rapid rate of growth, and on the novelty and range of a number of their ministries, the Jesuits almost certainly had the greatest impact on the religious and intellectual culture of the time. A year after their founding, Ignatius was elected as the first superior general in 1541. As this is a post held for life, Ignatius guided this fledgling order until his death in Rome in 1556. In 1541, Francis Xavier, one of Ignatius's original six companions, left Portugal for Asia, launching the Jesuits on their centuries-long involvement in overseas missions. Over the course of his ten years in Asia, Xavier logged thousands of miles as he traveled throughout the Far East trying to spread the faith, especially in India, the Spice

Cum Anglis toto terrarum orbe unicum templum Catholicum relictum sit, idq̃ Romæ
S.me Trinitati Sacrum, cuius in Summa ara hæc tabula conspicitur; meritò in illo
suorum cum priscæ, tum huius ætatis martyrum certamina exprimi curarunt: ut
alios ad laudes, preces̃q, se uerò etiam ad parem animi constantiam, maiorum et
sociorum exemplis, excitarent.

2

The Trinity as Throne of Mercy, , from *Ecclesiae Anglicana Trophaea*, 1584, pl. 36 (Stonyhurst College)

Islands, and Japan. He came almost within reach of his great desire to preach the Gospel in China, dying on an island just off the coast of the mainland in 1552 while awaiting permission to enter.

In Europe, two events of 1548 established traditions which would dominate Jesuit ministries throughout the Society's history. One was the confirmation of activities already becoming normative in Jesuit ministrations, while the other was a new beginning that would transform both the Society and early modern culture. Ever since 1521 and Ignatius's process of conversion at Loyola and Manresa, the founder had systematized his insights into a program of spiritual exercises. In their complete format, they are designed to run for about thirty days, during which time an individual withdraws to a quiet place or "retreat" and prays intensely, assisted by a spiritual director. The manual of *The Spiritual Exercises* is really designed as a guidebook for the director more than a text for the directee or exercitant. They follow a progression of "Four Weeks," though the First and Second Weeks often go longer than a strict seven-day period. In the First Week, exercitants immerse themselves in the reality of God's unconditional love for them and then, in that context, consider their lifelong response to the Creator's loving initiative, which almost always requires confronting the pervasiveness of sin in one's life. The goal is to experience God's forgiving and healing love in order to be freed of the harmful effects of sin and selfishness, and seek only God's will, not one's own. All of this flows from the First Principle and Foundation: "Human being are created to praise, reverence, and serve God our Lord, and by means of doing this to save their souls. The other things on the face of the earth are created for the human beings, to help them in the pursuit of the end for which they are created. From this it follows that we ought to use these things to the extent that they help us toward our end, and free ourselves from them to the extent that they hinder us from it" (*Spiritual Exercises*, 32, no. 23).

Building on this foundation, in the Second Week exercitants pray by focusing on the major events in Christ's life from the Incarnation to Palm Sunday. The goal is to identify intimately with Jesus himself though contemplation of his activities, healings, and teachings. At the end of the Second Week one is encouraged to make an election of a way of life. If one has already made a commitment, such as to marriage or the religious life, one prays for the grace to live out that life faithfully. If no such commitment has been made, the individual prays for "indifference," i.e., a complete openness to discern God's plan for one's life. In the Third Week one focuses on "Holy Week," the events surrounding Christ's Passion and Death, through which the exercitant realizes that Christ suffered and died personally for him or her. In the Fourth Week the theme is Christ's Resurrection, which includes Ignatius's belief, common to that era, that the Lord first appeared to his mother. After contemplating the graces of resurrection and new life offered to all, the exercitant concludes the retreat with the Contemplation to Attain Love. In this final prayer the reality of God's love is reinforced and all are encouraged to devote their lives to the One from whom all life and love emanates. Although the text of *The Spiritual Exercises* is certainly no literary masterpiece, Ignatius does prove himself in these pages to be something of a spiritual and psychological genius, sharing his own personal experiences which were refined through years of reflection and prayerful discernment. Pope Paul III declared that the *Exercises* were a great gift to the Church and in 1548 formally approved their use among the faithful.

The year 1548 also proved to be a watershed in terms of Jesuit identity through the opening of the Society's first school for the laity. Some schools for the training of its new, younger recruits had been in existence, but Ignatius was initially adverse to a broader educational mission, fearing that Jesuit availability and mobility—hallmarks of the Society—would be compromised. Officials of the city of Messina, Sicily, however, entreated him to educate their sons. After some experimentation elsewhere, involving the teaching of students at a school/seminary at Goa in India, as well as a school for both Jesuit and secular students at Gandia in Spain, Ignatius agreed to send a group of ten Jesuits to Messina. Perhaps already discerning the great potential in such a step, he selected some of the most talented men of the first generation, including Jerome Nadal and Peter Canisius. The school's success and the pressing need for both secular and religious education caused Jesuit schools to multiply rapidly. The crown jewel in

A. Gregorius XIII.Pont.Max.huius Anglorum Collegij fundator, ac parens
optimus Alumnos suos Christo commendat: ut, quos in Angliam ad fidei
defensionem mittit, aduersus hostium insidias, atq; tormenta diuina uirtute
confirmet: qua freti iam aliquot pro Catholica Romana ecclesia
fortiter occubuerunt.

B. Philippus Boncompagnus S.R.E.presb. Card.tit S. Sixti eiusdem
Pont. Fr. Fil. Collegij Protector, et Benefactor munificentiss.idé à Deo precatur.

36

Pope Gregory XIII, founder of the English College in Rome, and English students, from *Ecclesiae Anglicana Trophaea*, 1584, pl. 36
(Stonyhurst College)

terms of the quality of its professors and students (and its pride of place in the heart of Ignatius) was the Roman College, which opened in 1551 and eventually became the Gregorian University. Most of the Jesuit "colleges" were analogous to American high schools, but, in a population that was largely illiterate, their graduates were exceptionally well educated. About forty colleges opened within a decade of Messina and hundreds more would follow in the next century and beyond.

As the nascent Society of Jesus was growing in size, in its geographic spread, and in the increasing breadth of its ministries, Ignatius and others realized that it was vital to systematize the initial rationales and charisms that had brought the first companions together. The founder was convinced of the role of Divine Providence in the formation of the Society, at the heart of which was "helping souls" through loving service, propelled by the indispensable grace of God. The initial draft of the Jesuit *raison d'être*, the "Formula of the Institute," had been approved by Pope Paul III in 1540, and Pope Julius III gave his approval to the second version in 1550 which incorporated the fruits of a decade of experimentation and reflection. With these brief texts as a foundation, Ignatius (along with the assistance of his secretary, Juan de Polanco, S.J.) completed the first draft of the Jesuit *Constitutions* in 1550-1551. He continued to amend this seminal document until his death in 1556. Even then, the *Constitutions* were not quite

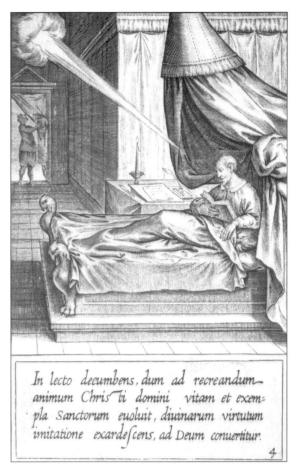

In lecto decumbens, dum ad recreandum animum Christi domini vitam et exempla Sanctorum euoluit, diuinarum virtutum imitatione exardescens, ad Deum conuertitur.

Ignatius reading spiritual literature during his convalescence, from P. Pazmany, S.J. and N. Lancicius, S.J. *Vita Beati P. Ignatii Loiolae.* Rome 1609, pl. 4. *While confined to bed, in order to occupy his mind, he peruses the life of Christ the Lord and the lives of the saints. Inflamed by the desire of imitating these virtues, he is converted to God.*

completed. This seems to have been a deliberate choice, so as not to foreclose the ways in which the grace of God and the needs of humanity might point the Society in yet new directions. It is also important to note that Ignatius probably devoted as much or more time to the writing and revising of the *Constitutions* as he did to that of *The Spiritual Exercises*. He considered both of these documents to be essential to Jesuit self-understanding and ministry, and he saw the *Constitutions* not only as a juridical document but also as a spiritual guide. With some minor changes, the First General Congregation of the Society approved a Latin translation of the founder's text in 1558. With a few other variants, the Fifth General Congregation gave its approbation to a Spanish text in 1590.

Jesuit ministry and missions in Europe largely followed the contours of the religious landscape as reconfigured by the Reformation. Although in general southern Europe remained Catholic while most of northern Europe became Protestant, a more precise analysis for the sixteenth century could describe three horizontal bands of religious differentiation. Southernmost Europe was the Catholic heartland, centered on Italy, Spain and Portugal. Jesuit churches, schools, and other apostolates proliferated throughout these countries and throughout much of the Spanish and Portuguese empires. The middle band included many of the countries and areas in religious flux during this period, making them the primary battlegrounds of the Reformation, often involving a volatile mixture of political, religious, and other issues. This band encompassed France, the Low Countries (Spanish Netherlands), the Holy Roman Empire, and large areas of Austria, Hungary, and Poland. The Catholic or Counter-Reformation probably had its greatest

long-term successes in this middle swath of Europe, much of which was tending to Protestant allegiances during the sixteenth century but returned to the Catholic fold by the seventeenth. In addition to the revitalized papacy, and the reforms and spiritual renewal associated with Tridentine Catholicism, the new and reformed religious orders played a significant role. The Society of Jesus was particularly successful as it was "international in its early backgrounds, supranational in its thinking and in its objectives" (Dickens, 74).

Northern Europe was to prove a far more difficult region for Catholic missionaries. The Protestant Reformation had begun in northern Germany with Martin Luther, and Lutheranism triumphed in the Scandinavian countries and much of the northern Holy Roman Empire. Calvinism became the dominant religion in the northern Netherlands (Dutch Republic), Scotland, and many cantons in Switzerland, but it also had many adherents in parts of France, the Holy Roman Empire, Hungary, and Poland. Anglicanism became the established church in England and Wales. There was also an attempt by successive English monarchs and dynasties to impose an Anglican establishment on Ireland, but a majority of their Irish "subjects" remained Catholic, making Ireland the only country in Europe after the Reformation where the monarch adhered to one religion and the majority of the people to another.

Non longe ab Vrbe templum defertum ingreſſo inter orandum ſe Deus Pater oſtendens illum filio ſuo crucem geſtanti ſocium attribuit; filius item placidiſſima illa verba pronuntians EGO VObIS ROMÆ PROPITIVS ERÓ illū recipit in ſocium Vnde Ignatio lux oborta ſocietatis IESV nominandæ.
53

Ignatius's vision of Christ at La Storta, from P. Pazmany, S.J. and N. Lancicius, S.J. *Vita Beati P. Ignatii Loiolae.* Rome 1609, pl. 53. In 1537, Ignatius traveled to Rome, taking the road from Sienna, and stopping at La Storta. He is shown as a pilgrim, with staff, sack and hat, before one of the most well-known miraculous events of his life. *Not far from the city, he enters a deserted chapel; in the midst of his prayer God the Father shows himself, presenting as a companion (Latin* socium*), his Son who is carrying his cross. The Son, pronouncing the comforting words, "I will be propitious to you in Rome," brings him (Ignatius) into his society. Hence Ignatius receives the illumination for the naming of the Society of Jesus.*

The pope had formally excommunicated Elizabeth I in 1570, spurred on by the idea that this would facilitate the overthrow of the Protestant queen and the restoration of the Catholic faith. In fact, this played into the hands of the Elizabethan regime because Catholics could now be portrayed as not only religiously aberrant but politically treasonous. There followed the growing realization on the part of certain English Catholic leaders that they had entered a new religious reality in which Protestantism was (or was fast becoming) the norm, and Catholicism was increasingly viewed as a foreign, "papist" religion. Even more ominous, at least in the minds of many English Protestants, was the fear that Catholicism might be forcibly re-imposed on the nation by Spain, France, or a coalition of Catholic powers. Since the old faith was now illegal, and because the government viewed it as a serious threat, new strategies would have to be devised if English Catholics had any hope of retaining, much less officially restoring, their religion.

The seminal figure in this new and troubled religious landscape was William Allen, a priest who became the leader of the English Catholics, and who, in 1587, was named a cardinal. He realized that an essential part of keeping the Catholic faith alive in England was the necessity of supplying a steady stream of priests. In 1568 he established a seminary at Douai in the Spanish Netherlands where students could study in relative safety, and from which they could return to their native land to revitalize the faith. The first of these seminary priests began to arrive in England in 1574 and they achieved some successes, though at an increasingly great cost. Cuthbert Maine, in 1578, was the first of the seminary priests to be executed. The Elizabethan government went to great lengths to argue that Catholics went to their deaths not because of their religious convictions but because of their political disloyalty. In other words, their true crime was treason, not heresy. Catholics for the most part insisted that they recognized Elizabeth as the rightful queen (despite the papal stance), but could not in good conscience accept her as the head of the Church.

Despite the heroic efforts of the seminary priests, Allen realized that further help was needed. Together with the Jesuit Robert Persons, and eventually supported by Pope Gregory XIII, he exerted great efforts to bring the Society of Jesus into the fray. Initially reluctant, perhaps because he intuited the significant human cost, Father General Everard Mercurian finally acquiesced and in 1580 the Jesuit mission to England was launched with Persons as the superior, accompanied by Father Edmund Campion and Brother Ralph Emerson. The three Jesuits arrived in their homeland in disguise to reinvigorate the faith among the somewhat demoralized but spiritually hungry Catholic population. Through their preaching, sacramental ministry, spiritual direction, writing, and other activities, Campion and Persons had a significant impact. They strengthened individuals who were wavering in their faith and even made Protestant converts. In addition, they tried to better coordinate the efforts of the Catholic clergy, including the secular priests, who were to continue to outnumber the Jesuits by far over the course of the mission.

While there were many instances of cooperation, there was disarray among the Catholic clergy as a whole. Some clergy retained a "restorationist" mentality, believing that England was at heart a Catholic country which could still be won back to the old faith. Others acknowledged the Protestant status quo and saw England as

A. Edmundus Campianus societatis Iesu sub patibulo concionatur, statimq̃ cum Alexandro Brianto Rhemensis, et Rodulpho-Sheruiño huius Collegij alumno suspenditur.

B. Illis adhuc tepentibus cor et uiscera extrahuntur, et in ignem proijciuntur.

C. Eorundem membra feruenti aqua elixantur, tum ad urbis turres et portas appenduntur, regnante Elizabetha Anno M.D.LXXXI. die prima Decēbris. Horum constanti morte aliquot hominum millia ad Romanam Ecclesiam conuersa sunt.

33

Edmund Campion and his companions Alexander Briant and Ralph Sherwin hanged, drawn, and quartered at Tyburn, from *Ecclesiae Anglicana Trophaea*, 1584, fig. 33 (Stonyhurst College)

a "mission." Although there were areas, especially in the far north and west of England, and parts of Wales, where Catholics maintained significant numbers, the Church of England dominated the more populous and wealthy south and east, including London and much of the Thames Valley. The Jesuits and a significant percentage of the secular priests acknowledged the bitter truth of Protestant ascendancy and focused their efforts on sustaining the faith among the Catholic minority. A contentious divide also surfaced over governance. In 1598 Pope Clement VIII established the novel office of "archpriest" (i.e., superior of the secular clergy) and named George Blackwell to that position. The archpriest was obliged to consult with the Jesuit superior on issues central to the mission, presumably to bring about better coordination and cooperation. This arrangement, however, sometimes had the opposite effect; a number of seculars resented what they viewed as a Jesuit attempt to dominate the mission, if not the Church itself, in England. This led to a bitter war of words, known as the Appellant Controversy, which raged until both sides were chastised by Rome and a new archpriest was made independent of the Jesuit superior in 1602.

The initial burst of Jesuit activity turned tragic as Campion was captured, tortured, and eventually hanged, drawn, and quartered on December 1, 1581. Persons, now on the Elizabethan secret service's "most wanted" list, had little choice but to flee to the Continent. Although he may have hoped to return to England, he became instead the prefect of the English mission, directing its work through his efforts at recruiting, fundraising, establishing new seminaries, and producing prolific letters and tracts. Among the Jesuits who worked on the Elizabethan mission, John Gerard and William Weston were men of quite differing personalities, but remarkable in their mutual efforts and sacrifices. Weston spent many years in various prisons and yet still managed to engage in a host of spiritual ministries before he was finally banished in 1603. Gerard suffered imprisonment and torture in the Tower of London, from which he made a daring escape; remarkably, he remained for many more years ministering in England before finally going into exile in 1605. Fortuitously, both Gerard and Weston wrote autobiographies, which are invaluable sources on the Elizabethan Jesuit mission.

Like Edmund Campion, three other Jesuits were also executed by the Elizabethan regime and went on to receive their Church's highest accolade: canonization. Alexander Briant was a secular priest who requested and received admission into the Society while in prison awaiting his sentence. Along with Campion, he died a gruesome death at Tyburn on December 1, 1581. Robert Southwell, who arrived on the mission with his friend and superior of the mission, Henry Garnet, in 1586, engaged in a wide-ranging spiritual and literary apostolate until his arrest in 1592. After three years of imprisonment and torture, Southwell, one of the great poets of the Elizabethan age, went to his death in 1595. In that same year, Henry Walpole also made the ultimate sacrifice for his faith. Like Southwell, he had exchanged his worldly status and aristocratic life for the vows of the religious life, and also used his literary talents to express through poetry some of his deepest spiritual emotions and insights.

There were many other examples of heroism and accomplishment on the English mission, both during the reign of Elizabeth and during those of her Stuart successors in the seventeenth century. As a tribute to some of the outstanding figures of that struggle, in 1970 Pope Paul VI canonized forty of the martyrs of England and Wales who lived and died for their faith in the Tudor and Stuart eras. Ten of these martyr-saints were Jesuits: nine priests and one brother, Nicholas Owen, the ingenious designer and builder of many of the "priest holes," the hiding places that undoubtedly saved the lives of many of his fellow Jesuits and other co-religionists. Collectively, theirs is a legacy of remarkable sacrifice and suffering, but also of persistent effort and no small measure of achievement in sustaining the Catholic faith among at least a portion of the people of England and Wales.

CATALOGUE

Agnus Dei
Wax medallion in metal oval frame - glass cover, 5 in. (12.7 cm.)
Rome, 1578
Jesuit Community, Campion Hall, Oxford

An Agnus Dei is a small wax disc of round or oval shape impressed with the image of the Agnus Dei (Lamb of God) on one side and other religious scenes on the other. Papal gifts of great distinction, they are sometimes worn as medallions. The tradition of the Agnus Dei may date to earlier times, but by the ninth century it was an accepted pious custom. A pope consecrated the images during the first year of his pontificate and repeated the act at seven year intervals. The blessed discs were distributed Saturday of Easter week after the "Agnus Dei" was said at Mass. The distribution of such an object generally attested to high esteem for the recipient; for example, Urban I sent an Agnus Dei to the Byzantine Emperor John Palaeologus in 1366.

This disc shows the lamb holding a cross banner, symbolic of the resurrection, and resting on Sacred Scripture. Around the edges is the Latin text of the prayer at Mass ECCE A(gnus) DEI QUI TOLLIT P(ecatta) M(undi): Behold the Lamb of God who takes away the sins of the world. On the reverse is the Transfiguration of Christ. The Agnus Dei also bears the seal of Pope Gregory XIII (reigned 1572-1585) an ardent proponent of efforts to regain Protestant lands for the Catholic cause. It is marked with the year VII, the seventh year of Gregory's pontificate, 1578. Gregory had founded the English college in 1579 where, in December of the same year, Robert Persons and others planned the Jesuit mission to England. This Agnus Dei was a possession of Edmund Campion and hidden in rafters of Lyford Grange, near Wantage in Berkshire, when Edmund Campion was arrested on July 17,1581. It was only discovered in 1959 when the roof of the grange was restored. Elizabethan Reforms explicitly mentioned Agnus Deis as "popish trumperies" and forbade their importation. It is all the more significant then that Campion had one in his possession, and that he kept it on his person, when fleeing the agents who eventually tracked him down at Lyford Grange.

Agnus Dei, a papal gift, owned by Edmund Campion, 1578, Jesuit Community, Campion Hall, Oxford. Photo: Virginia Raguin

Jesuit and Early Modern History

Bangert, William V., S.J. *A History of the Society of Jesus*. 2nd ed. St. Louis: Institute of Jesuit Sources, 1986.

Bray, Gerald, ed. *Documents of the English Reformation*. Minneapolis: James Clarke Company, 1994.

Cameron, Euan. *The European Reformation*. Oxford: Oxford University Press, 1991.

DeMolen, Richard L. ed. *Religious Orders of the Catholic Reformation*. New York: Fordham University Press, 1994.

Dickens, Arthur. G. *The Counter Reformation*. London: W.W. Norton & Co., 1969.

Donnelly, John Patrick. *Ignatius of Loyola: Founder of the Jesuits* . New York: Longman, 2004.

Evennett, H. Outram. *The Spirit of the Counter-Reformation*. Notre Dame, Ind.: University of Notre Dame Press, 1968.

Gregory, Brad S. *Salvation at Stake: Christian Martyrdom in Early Modern Europe*. Cambridge, Mass.: Harvard University Press, 1999.

Hsia, R. Po-chia. *The World of Catholic Renewal, 1540-1770*. Cambridge, U.K.: Cambridge University Press, 1998.

Ignatius of Loyola. *St. Ignatius' Own Story: As Told to Luis Gonzalez de Camara*, trans. William J. Young, S.J. Chicago: Loyola Press, (1956) 1998.

Lacouture, Jean. *Jesuits: A Multibiography*. Washington, D.C: Counterpoint Press, 1995.

O'Malley, John W. *Trent and All That: Renaming Catholicism in the Early Modern Era*. Cambridge, Mass.: Harvard University Press, 2000.

O'Malley, John W. *The First Jesuits*. Cambridge, Mass.: Harvard University Press, 1993.

Polanco, Juan de, S.J. *Year by Year with the Early Jesuits (1537-1556): Selections from the* Chronicon *of Juan de Polanco, S.J.* trans. John Patrick Donnelly, S.J. St. Louis: Institute of Jesuit Sources, 2004.

Wright, Jonathan. *God's Soldiers: Adventure, Politics, Intrigue, and Power—A History of the Jesuits*. New York: Doubleday, 2004.

Jesuit Spirituality

Conwell, Joseph, S.J., *Impelling Spirit: Revisiting a Founding Experience*. Chicago: Loyola Press, 1997.

de Jaer, S.J., Andre. *Together for Mission: A Spiritual Commentary on the Constitutions of the Society of Jesus*. St. Louis: Institute of Jesuit Sources., 2001.

Ignatius of Loyola, *The Spiritual Exercises of Saint Ignatius*. trans. George E. Ganss, S.J. St. Louis: Institute of Jesuit Sources, 1992.

Ignatius of Loyola, *The Constitutions of the Society of Jesus and Their Complementary Norms*. St. Louis: Institute of Jesuit Sources, 1996.

Ravier, Andre. *Ignatius of Loyola and the Founding of the Society of Jesus*. San Francisco: Ignatius Press, 1987.

The English Mission

Allison, Antony F. and David M. Rogers. *The Contemporary Printed Literature of the English Counter-Reformation between 1558 and 1640*. 2 vols. Aldershot: Scolar Press, 1989 and 1994.

Caraman, Philip, S.J. *A Study in Friendship: Saint Robert Southwell and Henry Garnet*. St. Louis: Institute of Jesuit Sources, 1995.

Edwards, Francis, S.J. *Robert Persons: The Biography of an Elizabethan Jesuit, 1546-1610*. St. Louis: Institute of Jesuit Sources, 1995.

Foley, Henry, S.J. *Records of the English Province of the Society of Jesus*. 7 vols. in 8. London: Burns and Oates, 1877-1884.

Gerard, John. *The Autobiography of a Hunted Priest*. New York: Collins, 1952.

McCoog, Thomas M., S.J. *The Society of Jesus in Ireland, Scotland, and England, 1541-1588: "Our Way of Proceeding?"* Leiden: Brill Academic Publishers, 1996.

Weston, William. *The Autobiography of an Elizabethan*. London: Longmans, Green, 1955.

THE BATTLE OF THE BOOKS: POLEMICAL AND MARTYROLOGICAL WRITINGS OF CAMPION, PERSONS, AND OTHER ENGLISH CATHOLICS

Robert E. Scully, S.J.

The Elizabethan Settlement of 1559 overturned Queen Mary's brief restoration of Catholicism and revived in a slightly modified form the Church of England that had evolved under the regime of Edward VI. Queen Elizabeth became the "Supreme Governor" of the Anglican Church, which, although it retained some Catholic aspects such as bishops and a few ritual elements, was essentially Protestant in its theology and most of its practices. To deflect Catholic opposition, both at home and abroad, and to build up support for this nascent, national church, a number of English Protestant writers took up the pen to show that there were solid theological and historical foundations for the "church by law established."

One of the earliest and most famous of these writers was John Foxe (1516-1587). He was one of an influential group of "Marian exiles" who had fled to the Continent during the reign of the Catholic queen and returned upon the accession of the Protestant queen, imbued with the zeal of the major Continental Reformers. Building upon a Latin history of the English Protestant church and martyrs that he had produced overseas, Foxe expanded this prototype and published it in 1563 in an English edition entitled *Acts and Monuments of These Latter and Perilous Days*. He wanted to prove that the Anglican Church could trace its roots through the centuries to the era of Christ. His words and illustrations were also an appeal to the heart, for Foxe was determined to show that his church was built on the blood of martyrs, especially the men and women who had suffered death during the reign of "Bloody Mary." Foxe's work became popularly known as the "Book of Martyrs" and was probably the most widely read tome in Elizabethan England. He continued revising and expanding it, and although he produced his last edition in 1583, other editions and versions appeared over the next century, leaving an indelible mark on the English Protestant consciousness.

Many other Protestant writers contributed to the effort to shore up the historical and theological underpinnings of Anglicanism. John Jewel (1522-1571) was of particular importance. His *Apologia Ecclesiae Anglicanae* (1562) was the first major attempt to produce an Anglican systematic theology. In this work, Jewel not only defended the Anglican Church; he also tried to turn the tables by accusing the Catholic Church of innovation. As these and numerous other books poured off the presses in England, the Catholic community was at a seemingly ever greater disadvantage. In this crucial area of religious persuasion, the burgeoning medium of publishing played a major role —the battle of the books.

Initially the Catholic mission to England, begun in 1574 with the arrival of the first of the seminary priests, was concerned primarily with attending to the immediate spiritual needs of the Catholic population. This included celebrating Mass, preaching, offering the sacraments,

Jesuit Emblem from title page of *Decem Rationes*, Stonor Park (Oxfordshire), 1581, (Campion Hall, Oxford)

providing spiritual counsel, and other pastoral activities. There was precious little time available for the polemics of publishing. That began to change with the launching of the Jesuit mission in 1580. The Jesuits were never as numerous as the seminary priests, to whom they were indebted in many ways. Yet, although the Jesuits were usually few in number, they had certain advantages that many of their fellow priests—as well as many of their Protestant adversaries—did not have. These included years of solid philosophical and theological education, intensive spiritual development, and connections to an international religious order that, although relatively young, was already making quite an impact, not only in Europe but across the world.

The two Jesuit priests who landed in England in June 1580—Edmund Campion (1540-1581) and Robert Persons (1546-1610)—had a particularly dramatic impact on the English Catholic mission. Not only were they active on the missionary circuit as gifted preachers and dispensers of the sacraments, but they also realized that in order to maintain and expand Catholic support, perhaps especially among the literate gentry, they would have to engage in the apostolate of the pen. Although this included some works of spiritual devotion, such as Person's influential *Christian Directory*, many of their works were of a polemical nature, which responded to Protestant attacks and also affirmatively set forth the truth of Catholic doctrine and praxis. Just as Foxe, Jewel, and other polemicists were writing in support of Protestantism, Campion, Persons, and additional apologists were determined to show that Catholicism had history and theology on its side, not to mention the witness of the martyrs from the first century to their own time.

Robert Persons S.J., copied by Charles Weld in 1810 from a contemporary portrait at the English College, Rome. Photo: Courtesy Stonyhurst College

They realized that they might well become actors in the spiritual drama that was playing out before them, indeed at the very center, which could mean imprisonment, torture, exile, or death. In a very real sense, they were writing for their lives—and for the survival of English Catholicism itself. In this essay we will focus on several of the more important polemical and martyrological works that Campion, Persons, and others in the Catholic community produced in the late sixteenth and early seventeenth centuries.

Perhaps the most famous and influential of Edmund Campion's tracts was *Decem Rationes* (usually translated as *Ten Reasons for Being a Catholic*). The copy exhibited is from the first printing of 1581 and is one of five copies surviving of the original edition. The book is of small size, only 6 by 4 inches, and was produced in secret at the Jesuit Press, located at Stonor Park near Henley-on-the Thames run by Stephen Brinkley. Four hundred copies were smuggled into the University Church, St. Mary the Virgin, Oxford on Commemoration Day, June 27, 1581. It was a direct and highly inflammatory challenge to the control of the university by the Church of England. Under Queen

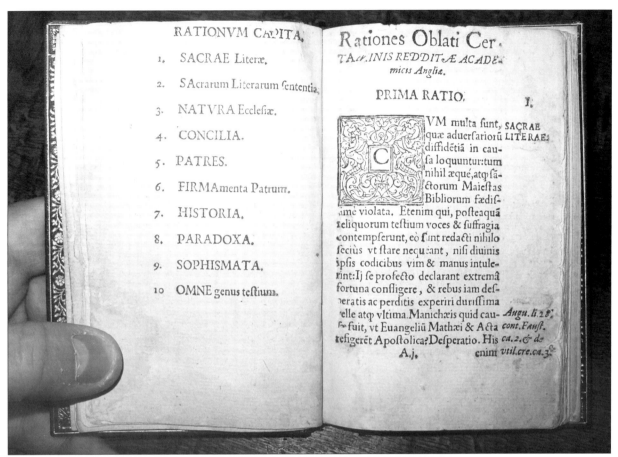

Edmund Campion, *Decem Rationes*, Stonor Park (Oxfordshire), 1581 (Campion Hall, Oxford)

Mary, St. Mary the Virgin at Oxford had borne witness to Thomas Cranmer's repudiation of Catholicism and subsequent death at the stake. Campion was captured a few weeks later on July 16, and shortly afterwards Brinkley and his printers were apprehended. Brinkley suffered torture but was discharged after two years in prison, June, 1583. He accompanied Persons to Rome and then to Rouen, continuing to operate presses in service of the Catholic "battle of the books."

The *Ten Reasons* was evidently meant to be a prelude to an academic disputation and, therefore, laid out what were essentially ten theses for further debate. The first two reasons focused on sacred Scripture, probably to confront at once the Protestant rallying cry of "*sola Scriptura*." Campion argued, first, that Protestants had "emasculated" Scripture by omitting or discounting books that went against their beliefs, such as the Epistle of James. Secondly, the Protestant reformers were misinterpreting the true sense of Scripture, going back to the church fathers, and they were disputing its meaning even among themselves, as dramatically exemplified in the debate between Luther and Zwingli over the proper understanding of the Lord's Supper (*Ten Reasons*, 92-100).

The third reason dealt with ecclesiology, including the church's visibility and authority. This section was arguably one of Campion's weaker ones, particularly as he engaged (as did many other Catholic and Protestant polemicists of the Reformation) in personal attacks, here directed against Luther, Calvin, and others. Campion expanded on the issue of authority in his next several reasons. The fourth one addressed the status and authority of ecumenical councils, not only the first "four Ecumenical Councils of the ancients, the doctrine whereof was so well established," and which were generally accepted by Protestants, but all the major councils since then, including the recently concluded Council of Trent (*Ten Reasons*, 100-108).

St. Helena discovers the True Cross in Jerusalem, from *Ecclesiae Anglicana Trophaea*, 1584, pl. 8 (Stonyhurst College)

In his fifth reason, Campion discussed at some length the importance and authority of the church fathers, "who had flourished within the first six hundred years of Christianity." These included great theologians, many of whom were also saints, ranging from Ignatius of Antioch to Augustine. Their writings, said Campion, supported traditional Catholic beliefs, as opposed to the "new-fangled fancies" of Protestant theologians such as John Jewel, "a foremost champion of the Calvinists in England," in spite of Jewel's and others' failed attempts to provide patristic support for their side. According to Campion's sixth reason, the church fathers grounded their arguments in the Bible. Moreover, they agreed in general with each other's interpretations. The seventh reason, also based on authority, was the argument from history. Campion contended that more than fifteen hundred years of history supported Rome and the Catholic faith. Therefore, "the adversary's raids upon history are utterly without point" (*Ten Reasons*, 109-21).

Campion's eighth reason was based on what he saw as the contradictions of the various Protestant reformers. These included such issues as Christology, soteriology, the sacraments, and divergences concerning Christian life and morals. The ninth reason focused on the four supposed sophisms of the Protestants, the first three of which were their attacks on celibacy and vowed chastity, the Mass and purgatory, and Holy Orders and the priesthood. The fourth was what he called their "vicious Circle," i.e., insisting that all doctrine had to be grounded in Scripture, and then rejecting fifteen centuries of Christian consensus concerning Scripture and its interpretation (*Ten Reasons*, 121-32).

In his last reason, Campion concluded with "all manner of witness." He spoke of the witness of the martyrs, as well as the witness of "the Roman Succession," namely, the long line of popes in which "the Primacy of the Apostolic Chair has ever flourished." He also called as witnesses "the Pastors of the nations" (i.e., great religious leaders), as well as "Kings . . . and their Commonwealths" of many times and places, who were dedicated to the Catholic Church. He prayed, fervently, that England and its queen would come to see the light: "There will come, Elizabeth, . . . that day which will show thee clearly which have loved thee, the Society of Jesus or the offspring of Luther." He concluded by presenting to the "Gentlemen of the University, this little present, put together by the labor of such leisure as I could snatch on the road" (*Ten Reasons*, 132-45).

Brief mention should also be made of Campion's earlier manifesto of 1580, "To the Right Honorable, the Lords of Her Majesty's Privy Council," generally known as his "Brag." He stated that he had come into "this noble realm, my dear Country, for the glory of God and benefit of souls. . . ." He went on to say: "My charge is, of free cost to preach the Gospel, to minister the Sacraments, to instruct the simple, to reform sinners, to confute errors—in brief, to cry alarm spiritual against foul vice and proud ignorance, wherewith many [of] my dear Countrymen are abused." Contrary to false charges, "I never had mind, and am strictly forbidden by our Father that sent me, to deal in any respect with matter of State or Policy of this realm, as things which appertain not to my vocation, and from which I do gladly restrain and sequester my thoughts" ("Brag" in *Ten Reasons*, 7-8).

Like Persons had done, Campion requested an audience before public authorities to present his case. He asked this humbly, since "I would be loath to speak anything that might sound of any insolent brag or challenge," ironic words in light of how his adversaries would use them. He spoke well of the queen, yet he realized that many government officials longed for his destruction and that of his companions. Still, in spite of these very real dangers, he bravely proclaimed that the Jesuits and missionary priests were

A. S. Edmundus Estanglorum rex ultimus a Danis telis configitur.
B. Eidem caput præciditur, quod procul abiectum dum a suis quæritur ter respondit Hic.
C. Eius corpus cum deinde transferretur capiti iunctum reperitur rubra cicatrice uulnus indicante.
D. S. Humbertus Episcopus Halmensis iuxta regem obtruncatur.

Martyrdom of St. Edmund, king of England by the Danes, from *Ecclesiae Anglicana Trophaea*, 1584, pl. 19 (Stonyhurst College)

more than willing "to carry the cross you shall lay upon us, and never to despair your recovery, while we have a man left to enjoy your Tyburn, or to be racked with your torments, or consumed with your prisons. The expense is reckoned, the enterprise is begun; it is of God, it cannot be withstood. So the faith was planted: so it must be restored." After these heartfelt but provocative words, Campion concluded with ones far more conciliatory, hoping that, in the end, "we may at last be friends in heaven, when all injuries shall be forgotten" ("Brag" in *Ten Reasons*, 8-11).

Persons wrote two works in support of Campion's *Brag*, which two Protestant writers - William Charke in 1580 and Meredith Hanmer in 1581 - had attacked vociferously. The first of Persons' responses, *A Brief Censure yppon two bookes written in answere to M. Edmonde Campion's offer of disputation*, was published in 1581. This was followed up by *A Defense of the Censure, gyuen vpon two bookes of William Charke and Meredith Hanmer mynysters, which they wrote against M. Edmonde Campion* (1582). In his preliminary Epistle and Answer to Charke, Persons raised several of the classic issues of contention between Catholics and Protestants. These included the latter's reliance on Scripture as the sole source of religious revelation and certitude, as well as the Catholic belief in the Real Presence of Christ in the Eucharist, which they based on both Scripture and Patristics. Persons also contended that many Protestant doctrines were in accord, not with the Bible, but with ancient and long-condemned heresies (*Defense of the Censure*, A 1-37).

In the main body of the text Persons engaged in both defense and offense. In response to the Protestants' attack on monastic and religious life and vows, he defended the three vows (poverty, chastity and obedience) and stated that the religious life of his time was one in substance with that of the primitive church. Moreover, he argued, the essence of the religious state such as voluntary poverty could be traced back to the ancient fathers, John the Baptist, and Christ himself. As to his own order, the Jesuits, he stated that they were not, as their adversaries charged, a sect, but rather "a Society dedicated peculiarly to the honoring of the name of Jesus, by preaching the same in all places of the world, without any reward, and with what danger bodily soever" (*Defense of the Censure*, 18-40, esp. 19).

Persons proceeded to discredit the major Reformers, in their personal lives and in their doctrine. He focused especially on Luther and Calvin, but also disparaged Beza, Corolostadius, Oecolampadius, Zwingli, and Bucer. Persons discussed a range of doctrinal differences, including human nature and sinfulness, the proper division of the Ten Commandments, the role and weight of Scripture versus Tradition, and what could be called the fight over the fathers, i.e., what were the true doctrinal beliefs and teachings of the church fathers, and how much deference should be given to them? (*Defense of the Censure*, 44 ff.).

These works provided proof of Persons' speed and skill as a controversialist. One clear indication of this, especially Persons' skill and impact, is found in the frontispiece of the copy of the *Defense of the Censure* in the Stonyhurst collection. There it states that this "seems to be a dangerous book, for it converted Fr. Walsingham, in a manner unusual and very extraordinary, as related by him in his *Epistle to the Reader . . . His Search into Matters of Religion*." This refers to Francis Walsingham (1576-1647), who had been a deacon of the Anglican Church before he became a Catholic and eventually a Jesuit.

It is not surprising that Persons published these two books anonymously, though some years later he acknowledged his authorship. As he wrote at the beginning of the second of these works: "In general, every one can imagine . . . how difficult a thing it is in England at this day, for a Catholic man to write any book: where neither liberty, nor rest, nor library, nor conference, nor being is permitted him" (*Defense of the Censure*, A 1). Another work that Persons wrote in that same period was also published anonymously, both the initial work and a subsequent edition: *De Persecutione Anglicana Epistola* (1581) was soon followed by *De Persecutione Anglicana Libellus* (1582) (exhibited). These were written in Latin so that they could reach a European-wide audience and thereby publicize the extent of the persecution and suffering of the Catholics in England. The 1582 edition is particularly noteworthy for its final leaves entitled "Praesentis Ecclesiae Anglicanae Typus," which highlights six engravings of the sufferings of the English

A. S. *Thomas* Archiep̃us Cantuariensis ab Henrico II. Angliæ rege inique damnatus ad Pont. Max. appellat, fugamq̃ init.

B. Coram Alexandro III. ſumo Pontifice Senone in Gallia cauſã ſuã agit.

C. A regijs ſatellitibus pro ecclesiaſtica libertate occiditur anno ii7i.

D. Eius ſanguis ac cerebrum in templi angulo proiecta, fontem aquæ producunt; qui ſemel in lac, quater in cruorem uerſus eſt.

25

Martyrdom of St. Thomas Becket, from *Ecclesiae Anglicana Trophaea*, 1584, pl. 35 (Stonyhurst College)

Catholics, especially the missionary priests. These were copied from woodcuts in a broadsheet produced by Richard Verstegan, who was one of the most active and devoted of the English recusant writers and lay assistants.

With regard to the six engravings of 1582, the first three illustrate the arrest, imprisonment, public parading, abuse, and trial of one or more of the missioners. The fourth plate shows the harsh interrogation and torture of one prisoner—on the dreaded rack—while three others await a similar fate if they do not confess and divulge the information demanded from them. The fifth plate reveals a prisoner being dragged to his place of execution while the executioners await with their deadly devices in hand. In the final plate, the prisoner-martyr suffers the horrendous fate of being hung, drawn, and quartered, during most of which he is still alive and undoubtedly in great agony (see preceding essay, "The Society of Jesus").

A major controversy between Protestants and Catholics was the compound question of when England first became Christian, and where the missionary impulse originated from. Some Protestant apologists argued that English Christianity derived in its origin not from Rome but from the apostolic church of the East. To counter these contentions, Persons wrote an extensive work entitled *A Treatise of Three Conversions of England from Paganisme to Christian Religion* (*The Conversion of England*, 1603). The extended titled laid out what Persons believed these three successive conversions were: "The first under the Apostles, in the first age after Christ: The second under Pope Eleutherius and K. Lucius, in the second age. The third, under Pope Gregory the Great, and K. Ethelbert in the sixth age. . . ." Thus, Persons contended, from the first through the sixth centuries there were three attempts to implant Christianity in England. His goal in this work was to show that "all these . . . have been from Rome, and to the Roman Catholic faith, and that the same faith has continued in England ever since throughout all ages to this day. . ." (*Three Conversions*, Introduction).

Persons dedicated this book "to the Catholics of England," and although he began the first part of it in answer to the writings of one Protestant author, Sir Francis Hastings, he continued "and enlarged [it] against John Fox his false Acts and Monuments." In a similar vein, Persons' design in the second part of the work was to search out "the beginning, state and progress of protestant Religion from age to age, and is against the whole course of John Fox his said Acts and Monuments from Christ's time to this, especially against the former part thereof, from the primitive Church doctors to the time of K. Henry the 8th" (*Three Conversions*, Introduction). This is proof positive that one of the most hotly contested subjects in the battle of the books was church history, especially the early church. Each side tried to demonstrate as conclusively as possible that previous church history, especially the primitive or apostolic church up through the major church fathers (i.e., the first through the fifth or sixth centuries), supported their version—the true version—of Christianity.

Another major source of contention was the debate over the nature of (and implicitly the requirements for) true martyrdom. Therefore, in the third part of his work, Persons set out to examine "more particularly the second volume of Fox his Acts and Monuments wherein he treateth of new martyrs, and Confessors of his Church, placed by him in an Ecclesiastical Calendar in the beginning thereof; which calendar is discussed, and compared with the Catholic Calendar. . ." (*Three Conversions*, Introduction). As extensive as the first two parts of this opus were, the third part grew even longer and so was printed separately and published in 1604. Persons and other Catholic apologists, like Foxe and other Protestant apologists, argued that in order to be a true martyr, one needed to believe in and die for the true church. Thus, each side trumpeted its own martyrs and disparaged the sufferings of their opponents, arguing that the latter's heretical beliefs and practices placed them outside the true church and prevented them from claiming the genuine mantle of martyrdom (Gregory).

Persons' ongoing debate with another author, Thomas Morton, resulted in *A Quiet and Sober Reckoning* (1609). This particular war of words began with Thomas Morton's *An Exact Discoverie* (1605) and *A Full Satisfaction* (1606). The thrust of these works, and Persons' overriding objections to them, are made clear

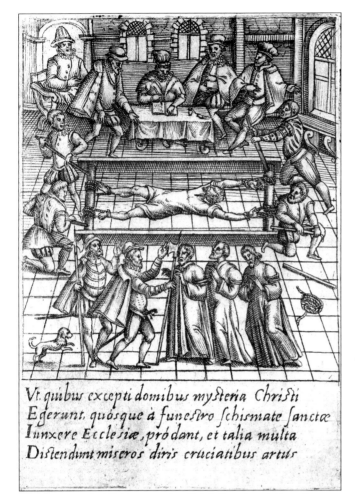

Campion tortured while his companions Ralph Sherwin and Alexander Briant stand bound and await a similar fate, from *De Persecutione Anglicana Libellus*, 1582 (Stonyhurst College)

in the extended title of his response: *A treatise tending to mitigation towardes Catholicke-subjectes in England. Wherein is declared, that it is not impossible for subjects of different religion . . . to live together in dutifull obedience . . . against the seditious wrytings of Thomas Morton* (1608). Morton fired back in *A preamble unto an Incounter with P. R.* [i.e., Robert Persons] (1608), leading in turn to the treatise under consideration here: *A quiet and sober reckoning with M. Thomas Morton somewhat set in choler by his adversary P. R.*

In addition to defending his work of the year before (*Mitigation*), Persons rejected Morton's charges regarding alleged Catholic rebellion and equivocation. He also refuted what he said were falsities leveled against Cardinal Bellarmine, who was probably a major target of Protestant invective not only because he was one of the leading Catholic scholars and theologians of the time, but also because he was a Jesuit (*Quiet and Sober Reckoning*, chs. 2 and 3). Among his other responses, Persons strongly criticized the views of Sir Edward Coke, Lord Chief Justice, who was among the most prominent legal scholars of the Elizabethan and Jacobean eras, and a defender of what Persons considered to be the government's unjust treatment and persecution of its Catholic subjects (*Quiet and Sober Reckoning*, chs. 7 and 8).

A major tribute to the long pedigree of English Catholicism, its sufferings, and its ties to Rome, are presented in *Ecclesiae Anglicana Trophaea* (1584) (exhibited). The pages reproduce the images in the fresco cycle by Niccolò Circignani in the English College in Rome, destroyed in 1866. The cycle was paid for by George Gilbert, noted for piety, who financed printing and missionary work to England. A lay pensioner at the College who became a Jesuit at the end of his life, Gilbert's funding enabled Circignani to complete the first half showing saints from the time of the Apostles to the reign of Elizabeth in 1582. In 1583 Circignani was called back to paint the story of the Jesuit martyrs based on Persons's *De Persecutione Anglicana Libellus* of 1582. The prints by Giovanni Battista Cavallieri show 35 of the 63 images of English martyrs that embellished the walls of the chapel of S. Tommaso di Canterbury (Bailey, 156-65, figs. 67-71). The publication is attributed to William Good, S.J., who was probably an advisor on these subjects for the Circignani frescoes (Allison and Rogers, 1: 131-32, Nos. 944-46). The early plates highlight important themes: Christian (the Trinity, pl. 2); Catholic (St. Peter, apostle and pope, pl. 3); and English (St. Alban, the first English martyr, pl. 5, and St. Edmund, the English king killed by the Danes, pl. 19). The ancient and ongoing connection between Rome and England are stressed by references to the English origins of St. Helena, the mother of the Emperor Constantine (pl. 8), and to the examples of St. Gregory the Great and St. Augustine of Canterbury in the sixth century (pl. 10), and St. Thomas Becket in the twelfth century (pl. 25). The last ten or so of the plates present in sometimes graphic detail

Viri plurimi in Anglia pro fide Catholica retinenda hoc qui expresfus
est modo coucq, cruciantur donec uniuersi corporis artus singulatim
luxentur. Sic Edmundus Campianus Societatis Iesu religiosus,
Rodulphus Sheruinus, Alexander Briantus, alijq, Sacerdotes summi
Pontificis Alumni accrbissimè torti fuere. Anno Dñi 15 81.15 8 2.et.15 83.

3 1

Campion tortured while his companions Ralph Sherwin and Alexander Briant
stand bound and await a similar fate, from *Ecclesiae Anglicana Trophaea*, 1584, fig. 31
(Stonyhurst College)

the persecution and martyrdom of many Catholics during the course of the English Reformation in the sixteenth century. These sufferings commenced under Henry VIII and included John Fisher and Thomas More, the London Carthusians, and a number of others whose consciences refused to allow them to recognize the king's spiritual supremacy (pls. 27-29).

From the 1570s onward, the Elizabethan regime resorted to harsher persecution of English Catholics, reacting in part to Pius V's excommunication of the queen in 1570, which allowed the government to argue that it was not imprisoning and executing Catholics for heresy but rather for treason. This charge was often hypocritical since most English Catholics maintained (and evidently believed) that they could be and were politically loyal to the queen and England, while also being spiritually loyal to the pope and Catholicism (pl. 30). Much attention is given to the suffering and martyrdom of Edmund Campion and his companions, Ralph Sherwin and Alexander Briant. Campion is shown being interrogated and racked, while the others stand bound nearby and await a similar fate (pl. 31). Next all three are dragged on hurdles to their place of execution as large crowds await the spectacle (pl. 32). Finally, the three missionary priests suffer the excruciating death of being hanged, drawn, and quartered, and their heads and limbs are prominently displayed throughout the city as a warning to others (pl. 33). Further scenes reveal the range of sufferings of other Catholic martyrs (pls. 34-35). The last etching features Pope Gregory XIII, the founder of the English College and a great benefactor of the English mission, and thereby reemphasizes the ties of faith and blood between the papacy and England from time immemorial (pl. 36).

Martyr Angliae provides yet another record of the English Catholic martyrs of the Reformation (Stonyhurst MS A, V. 21). This is a manuscript, probably written primarily in the early seventeenth century and added to later, that includes a list and a further description of martyrs in the Tudor and Stuart periods, from 1534 to 1681. After an alphabetical listings of martyrs (no pp.), the manuscript gives a more or less chronological description of martyrs, though a number of individuals are also discussed at later points in the chronicle. There would undoubtedly be some disagreement as to whether or not some of those listed were truly martyrs, however unfortunate their situation, such as Elizabeth Barton, the Maid of Kent (1534), and Queen Catherine of Aragon (1536). On the other hand, it is not at all surprising that John Fisher and Thomas More (1535) are given their due weight.

A considerable amount of space is devoted to the Elizabethan martyrs. Thomas Woodhouse became the first Jesuit martyr in England in 1573 (before the official Jesuit mission had begun). Cuthbert Maine was the proto-martyr of the seminary priests, suffering a grisly death in 1577. A trio of Catholic

In crate uiminea positi, lorisque ligati,
Per saxa, ad furcas, et per loca fœda trahutur
Carnifices laqueos, cultrosque, ignesque parant
Expediunt, priusæque attendunt tempora mortis

Campion, Sherwin, and Briant dragged on hurdles to their execution
from *De Persecutione Anglicana Libellus*, 1582 (Stonyhurst College)

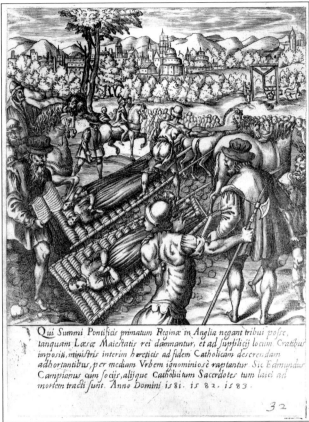

Qui Summi Pontificis primatum Reginæ in Anglia negant tribui posse,
tanquam Læsæ Maiestatis rei damnantur, et ad supplicij locum Cratibus
impositi, ministris interim hæreticis ad fidem Catholicam deserendam
adhortantibus, per mediam Vrbem ignominiose raptantur Sic Edmundus
Campianus cum socijs, alijque Catholici tum Sacerdotes tum laici ad
mortem tracti sunt. Anno Domini 1581. 1582. 1583.

32

Campion, Sherwin, and Briant dragged on hurdles to their execution
from *Ecclesiae Anglicana Trophaea*, 1584, fig. 32 (Stonyhurst College)

heroes—Edmund Campion, Ralph Sherwin, and Alexander Briant—as discussed in the previous essay, went to their deaths in 1581. Margaret Clitheroe, in 1586, was the first of three women (four if one counts Mary, Queen of Scots, as this manuscript does) to be martyred during Elizabeth's reign, suffering the terrible fate of being pressed to death because she refused to plead, so as not to implicate any of her family or friends. Dozens of others, about two-thirds of whom were priests, were executed in the later Elizabethan era. The number of Catholic martyrs declined dramatically during the Stuart era, though there were a few spikes during periods of crisis, especially the Gunpowder Plot (1605-1606), or at times of manufactured hysteria, particularly during the Popish Plot and its aftermath (1678-1681). Oliver Plunkett, the Catholic primate of Ireland and the last of the innocent victims of the Popish Plot, went to his death in 1681 and his is the last name recorded in the *Martyr Angliae*.

Bibliography

Primary Sources

Campion, Edmund. *Decem Rationes.* Stonor Park (Oxfordshire), 1581 (exhibited: Campion Hall, Oxford)

Campion, Edmund. *Ten Reasons Proposed to his Adversaries for Disputation in the Name of the Faith and Presented to the Illustrious Members of our Universities.* St. Louis: B. Herder, 1914.

Foxe, John. *Foxe's Book of Martyrs,* ed. William Byron Forbush. Grand Rapids, Mich.: Baker, 1978.

More, Henry. *Historia Missionis Anglicanae Societatis Jesu* (1660) ed. and trans., Francis Edwards, *The Elizabethan Jesuits.* London: Phillimore, 1981.

Persons, Robert and William Allen. *De Persecutione Anglicana Libellus.* Rome, 1582 (exhibited: Stonyhurst College)

Persons, Robert. *The Defense of the Censure of Two Books.* 1582.

Persons, Robert. *The Conversion of England.* St. Omers, 1603.

Persons, Robert. *A Quiet and Sober Reckoning.* St. Omers, 1609.

Ecclesiae Anglicana Trophaea. . .Romae in Collegio Anglico per Nicolaum Circinianum depictae. Rome, 1584 (exhibited: Stonyhurst College)

Martyr Angliae (MS A, V.21, Stonyhurst College Archives)

Secondary Sources

Allison Antony F. and David M. Rogers. *The Contemporary Printed Literature of the English Counter-Reformation between 1558 and 1640. Volume I: Works in Languages other than English. Volume II: Works in English.* Aldershot: Scolar Press, 1989, 1994.

Bailey, Gauvin. *Between Renaissance and Baroque: Jesuit Art in Rome, 1565-1610.* Toronto: University of Toronto Press, 2003.

Bellenger, Dom Aidan, ed. *English and Welsh Priests, 1558-1800.* Bath, England: Downside Abbey, 1984.

Carrafiello, Michael L. *Robert Persons and English Catholicism, 1580-1610.* London: Associated University Presses, 1998.

Edwards, Francis. *Robert Persons: The Biography of an Elizabethan Jesuit, 1546-1610.* St. Louis: Institute of Jesuit Sources, 1995.

Gregory, Brad S. *Salvation at Stake: Christian Martyrdom in Early Modern Europe.* Cambridge, Mass.: Harvard University Press, 1999.

Hayner, Alan. *Invisible Power: The Elizabethan Secret Services, 1570-1603.* New York: St. Martin's Press, 1992.

Reynolds, Ernest E. *Campion and Persons: The Jesuit Mission of 1580-1.* London: Sheed and Ward, 1980.

Southern, Alfred C. *Elizabethan Recusant Prose, 1559-1582.* London: Sands, 1950.

Mary Ward and her Institute in Recusant England

Virginia C. Raguin

The history of Mary Ward (1585–1645) and her Institute, known today as the Congregation of Jesus and the Institute of the Blessed Virgin Mary, profiles not only a specific organization of women, but more broadly the changing perspectives on the role of women in the Roman Catholic Church from the Counter-Reformation to the present. Mary Ward's clear determination was to move women's agency out of the confines of medieval monastic structure into the wider community. She took as her example the principles and structure of the Society of Jesus, recently authorized in 1534, which developed an organization independent of local ecclesiastical jurisdiction. Members prayed individually, not in the communal daily practice that had been the custom of religious orders since the fifth century. This gave them much greater mobility and freed them to work away from their residences. To understand how radical – and how contested – Mary Ward's position was in adapting these practices for an order of women, we need to look back at her life as lived under English recusancy.

The Early Life

She was born in 1585 in the Manor House of Mulwith, near Ripon, Yorkshire, the eldest daughter of Marmaduke Ward and Ursula Wright, both Catholics. Yorkshire, like the other northern English counties of Northumberland, Durham, and Lancashire, possessed a considerable and still identifiable Catholic population: in 1641–2, 11–20 percent of the households of Yorkshire were still Catholic (Bossy, 404–405). During Elizabeth I's reign, however, Catholicism was a highly dangerous confession. In 1586, the year following Mary's birth, Margaret Clitherow, the thirty-two-year-old wife of a butcher in York, was accused of harboring priests in her house. Her punishment was death by being crushed, laid on the ground under a plank on which weights were placed. Twenty other Catholics in York met their deaths in the same decade. This was not a time when the practice of a banned religion, despite support of selected neighbors and family, could be anything other than tenuous.

Ward was early under the influence of matriarchs, spending the years between the ages of five and ten at Ploughland near Spurn Point with her grandmother Ursula Wright (Chambers I, 12–22; Peters, 34–37). Wright had earlier been imprisoned for recusacy for fourteen years. Ward recalls that her grandparents "for holy respect . . . lodged in separate chambers, and so great a prayer was she that I do not remember in the five years that I ever saw her asleep, nor did I ever wake when I did not perceived her to be at her prayers" (Orchard, 6). Ward's adolescence began when at the age of fifteen she went to live with Lady Grace Babthorpe, related to her mother's

Mary Ward at Osgodby: Painted Life of Mary Ward, no. 9, 17th century, Institute of the IBVM Augsburg, courtesy of the Congregation of Jesus (formerly IBVM)

family, in Osgodby, twelve kilometers south of York (Chambers I, 39–47; Peters, 43– 49). Devotion to the Virgin was an important part of recusant spirituality and the altar in the Osgodby scene from the *Painted Life of Mary Ward* shows an image of the Virgin (*Painted Life*, no. 9, seventeenth century, Institute of the BVM Augsburg: Littlehales, fig. 6; Peters, opp. p. 308). Evidently the example of strong family leadership by a woman and exposure to stories of women religious motivated her decision to enter the religious life. It was also in Osgodby that she read *The Spiritual Combat* by Lorenzo Scupoli, a sixteenth-century Theatine priest. Ward wrote with enthusiasm about the book as the "best master and instructor that I have had in spiritual exercises for many years" (Chambers I, 53; Peters, 48; Orchard 10). She must have read the English edition prepared and printed in 1598 by John Gerard, S. J. director of the Jesuits in East Anglia.

Convent Life and the Formulation of the Institute

In 1606 she obtained permission from her family to leave England for Saint-Omer, a city in the Spanish Netherlands that harbored a substantial English Catholic community. On the advice of the English Jesuits whose seminary was there, she entered the Franciscan foundation of Poor Clares as a lay-sister. She left after only a year to establish a new convent, one specifically designed for English recusants, at Gravelines (Peters, 84–93). This foundation would eventually move from Gravelines to Darlington, county Durham, after the French Revolution. Although established as part of the order founded in the thirteenth century by St. Clare, a follower of St. Francis, Ward's convent was directed by Jesuits, and membership was initiated with the Jesuit practice of the Thirty Days' Spiritual Exercises (Littlehales, 45–51; Peters, 95–98). After its founding, however, Ward's letters speak of her experiencing an "intellectual vision" that convinced her that her vocation was not as a Poor Clare in a cloistered community. Leaving the convent, she spent several months in London during 1609 and then with a small group of companions returned to Saint-Omer, and for seven years lived a religious life, but independent from any specific religious order. In 1611 she received another revelation, hearing "not by the sound of voice but intellectually [understanding] (the words), Take the same [religious structure] of the Society," convincing her to establish a new Institute modeled on the Society of Jesus (Chambers II, 283–84; Peters, 114–19).

Mary Ward, 17th century engraving, courtesy of the Congregation of Jesus (formerly IBVM)

Unlike women religious at other times, Mary Ward had matured in a world where traditional cloistered monastic life had been suppressed for over two to three generations. Furthermore, she was accustomed to women's active roles in early leadership of recusant life. "On few points in the early history of English Catholicism is there such a unanimous convergence of evidence as on the importance of the part played in it by women" (Bossy, 152–160, quote p. 153). Records from the 1580s present the legal problem of the conforming husband – who attends church and takes the oath acknowledging the English monarch as head of the Church, thus safeguarding his property – and the recusant wife. The state was perplexed because a wife's property had been vested in her husband at the time of her marriage and so she could not be fined. At the same time, a husband was independent of a wife's "corporal acts" and thus could not be held responsible for her recusancy. As complicit strategy or as genuine religious disagreement, such publicly divided English households were not uncommon.

Ward also had the example of her kin, whose Yorkshire homes were deeply pious, a piety that Lady Grace Babthorpe advocated for resident, visitor, and servant alike. Further, Ward's primary experience of the clergy had been with missionary priests, particularly Jesuit fathers. All of these forces combined to make her an anomaly on the Continent. From having witnessed the efficacy both of a new independence in religious rule and of women's agency among the laity, she saw a combination of the two as consistent with God' will.

Ward described the structure she wished approved for the Institute in 1616:

> 5) Our end then is to work constantly at the perfection of our own souls under the Standard of the Cross [an Ignatian phrase found in the *Spiritual Exercises* and *Formula of the Institute*].
>
> 6) Besides attending to our own perfection, we desire, in the second place, to devote ourselves with all diligence and prudent zeal to promote or procure the salvation of our neighbor by means of the education of girls, or by any other means that are congruous to the times. . . .
>
> 7) In order to attain our end, it is moreover necessary . . . that this our least and most unworthy Congregation [another Ignatian phrase] should be allowed. . . . to begin and exercise its duties without enclosure as otherwise our Institute and method of life can neither be observed or practiced with any hope of obtaining the fruit that we propose to draw from it.
>
> 8) But our . . . style of dress should, for the most part, be conformed to that generally worn by virtuous ladies in those countries or province where ours happen to live or reside.
>
> 10) Although as regards external mortifications, our manner of life may appear only ordinary, since no one is, by the Institute, obliged to observe strict enclosure, or wear a determined religious habit, or to perform external penances and austerities, nevertheless there will be a provision or clause in our constitutions [that teaches spiritual exercises]. . . .
>
> 25) . . .and we hope and humbly beg that neither the Bishop nor anyone appointed . . . may neither change nor add anything [to the rules and the Institute] either with regard to our end or to the means by which it is to be attained.
>
> (Orchard, 44–45)

This summary, which still contained monastic elements, was superseded by the use of 85% of Ignatius' *Formula of the Institute* itself, which Mary Ward took to Rome in 1621 and presented to Pope Gregory XV (Orchard, 63–65; Peters, 325 and 615-20).

OPPOSITION AND CONTINUATION

Opposition to Ward was widespread and sustained (Peters, 246–71). Contemporary ecclesiastical records reveal strong resistance to conceiving of women religious as anything other than enclosed. Dr. Matthew Kellison, president of the English seminary at Douai from 1614 to 1642, complained that Institute members "introduce the Jesuits into houses of the nobility and despise secular and religious priests. They pray only in private and have no office in choir. They travel about from Belgium to England on their affairs." Fr. Harrison, Archpriest of England 1614–1621, railed, "They have set the conversion of England as their goal and work for it like priests" (Orchard, 49). Though today's reader might regard such activities as not incompatible with a religious vocation, they were shocking in their time.

Houses of the Institute were established in Belgium, Bavaria, Austria, and Italy, and with the support of Archduchess Isabella, the Elector of Bavaria Maximilian I, and the Emperor Ferdinand II, Ward applied in 1624 to Pope Urban VIII for formal approbation. The response was disappointing. Given the sisters' refusal to renounce the freedom from enclosure that allowed them to travel and teach, the congregation was suppressed by a papal bull of January 31, 1631. A week later in Munich, Mary Ward was arrested and confined under onerous conditions in the Anger Convent of Poor Clares for nine weeks (Littlehales, 205–212). The year following her release, she was allowed to travel to Rome where Urban VIII received her warmly and exonerated her from any charge of heresy. Most of the Institute's members entered other religious orders or left the religious life, but a substantial number were protected in Munich by the Elector of Bavaria, Maximilian I. The Institute subsequently regrouped, operating with papal toleration but without approbation. Given the need for girl's schools, the "English Ladies," as they were known in German-speaking lands, soon found additional support, especially in Germany and Austria, and during the seventeenth and eighteenth centuries grew considerably.

Bar Convent, York, Georgian façade 1787, additional wing with four giant pilasters, 1844 by the architect G. T. Andrews. Photo: Virginia Raguin

The success of the Institute's foundations in England has a great deal to do with the fortunes of the English Catholic gentry, particularly under the Catholic queens (see *Timeline*). In 1639, with letters of introduction from Urban VIII to Henrietta Maria, French wife of Charles I, Mary Ward returned to England and settled in London (Chambers II, 456). She returned to the north in 1642, to the small village of Heworth just outside York across the river Ouse, and died in 1645 (Cambers II, 473–502). Five years later, the community at Heworth removed to Paris. When Charles II returned to take the throne after the civil wars, his Catholic queen, Catherine of Braganza, welcomed Frances Bedingfield (1616–1704) from the Paris house. Bedingfield had been a member of the group with Mary Ward at her death and knew the Yorkshire area. In 1667 she established a community of the Institute first in St. Martin's Lane, London, and afterwards at Hammersmith, about fives miles from the center of London on the Thames. Bedingfield then sent a colony north to Heworth, which moved in 1686 to the site of the present location of the Institute, outside the Micklegate Bar (Gate), York. Bedingfield herself came north and, using her alias of Frances Long, purchased the house that perseveres as a convent to this day (Kirkus 2001, 444–46).

SPIRITUALITY AND CECILY CORNWALLIS

The Institute mirrored the Society of Jesus both intellectually and socially, one aspect encouraging the other (see in this catalogue, "The Society of Jesus: Its Early History, Spirituality, and Mission to England"). The Jesuits early attracted a distinguished group of adherents and gained reputations as exceptional schoolmasters. They soon became an elite corps, insinuating themselves among the rich and powerful, who had means and political influence to further their missions. The companions of Mary Ward were also largely of the elite class, in England most being daughters of the gentry who constituted the life-blood of English recusancy. They were attracted not only by the Institute's Jesuit-style Constitutions and manner of life, with its apostolic ideal, mobility and self-government, but also by the spiritual appeal of the *Exercises*. Ignatius's series of twenty-one meditations structured a progression from confession to contemplation to transcendence and a more intimate discourse with the divine. Ignatius's writing further encouraged each exercitant to endeavor to achieve a sense of personal understanding about the state of life she should follow. The members of Mary Ward's Institute frequently found their vocational state to be teachers for daughters of the wealthy and cultivated, thus necessitating considerable learning on the part of the teacher. At the same time Mary Ward, and her companions after her, routinely founded schools for the poor alongside schools for the better-off.

One of the more intellectually distinguished members was Cecily Cornwallis (ca. 1653–1723), who owned and possibly commissioned the Spiritual Dial in the present exhibition (CATALOGUE). Her father, Francis Cornwallis, had an estate in Beeston, Suffolk, and her mother was the daughter of Lord Arundel of Wardour. She entered the Institute in Hammersmith about 1669 when she was sixteen, apparently already well educated. Records describe her as "much admired for her extraordinary learning beyond her sex and age, excellently well-versed in Latin, Greek, and several modern languages, being also very read in most parts of Philosophy and Mathematicks" (Kirkus, "Cecily Cornwallis"). This education was furthered by lessons in Latin, Greek, and Hebrew given by the Jesuit Chaplain Jeremiah Pracid. This rhythm of life continued until 1678 when Frances Bedingfield, the superior, sent her north to Yorkshire in association with the establishment of another house of the Institute (Kirkus 2001).

Cecily Cornwallis, artist unknown, late 17th century, Bar Convent, York, courtesy of the Congregation of Jesus (formerly IBVM)

This house had been established in 1677 with the support of Sir Thomas Gascoigne,who was determined to bring the Institute to Yorkshire and provided funding and a home in Dolebank northeast of York, three miles from Fountains Abbey. The plan was interrupted by the rumor of the so-called "Popish Plot" against the government whipped up by Titus Oates. Titus Oates was a failing Anglican clergyman who converted to Catholicism, but was twice expelled from his studies for the priesthood and became an anti-Catholic informer. The "Popish Plot" developed into national hysteria and the worst persecution of Catholics since Elizabeth's reign (CATALOGUE). Not until after the arrest of about a hundred clergy, the execution of seventeen, and the deaths of twenty-three in prison did Charles II regain the initiative in favor of the succession of his Catholic brother James (1685–1688).

The supposed parallel Yorkshire plot was instigated by a man called Robert Boldron and it implicated Gascoigne and the Institute. Cornwallis was imprisoned in York Castle with four other members of the community and the chaplain Fr. Pracid. The setting was unhealthy and one of the sisters, Margaret More, a descendant of Thomas More, died there in 1679. Cornwallis was imprisoned for eight years until James II came to the throne. Upon her release in 1685, she returned to Hammersmith and the following year became the second superior of the House, releasing Frances Bedingfield for work in York. The reign of a Catholic king, however, lasted but three years, and with the Glorious Revolution of 1688, James was deposed. The reign of his son-in-law and daughter, William (of Orange) and Mary, saw continued hostility towards Catholics, now identified as "Jacobite" supporters, and witnessed attempted invasions by a Catholic force led by the deposed King and his successors.

From the evidence of her contemporaries, corroborated by her own behavior, Cecily Cornwallis was apparently a highly sensitive, intelligent woman, with a deep personal piety and capacity for meditative prayer. No object comparable to the spiritual structure of the Dial has surfaced from this time, an indication that it probably was commissioned at her directive. Her inwardness, however, proved her

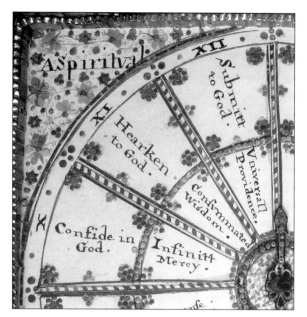

A Spiritual Dial, detail, England (London?), 1700–10, Bar Convent, York. Photo: Virginia Raguin

undoing as a superior in a time of considerable political and domestic stress. At the time, the Institute still was not approved by the Holy See, although it was protected by local religious authorities and had strong approval from the laity who sent their daughters to the Institute's five schools in Munich, Augsburg, Burghausen, Hammersmith, and York. Only in 1703 did Clement XI recognize the efficacy of the Institute and give a measure of papal approval, swayed perhaps by the petition of influential individuals including the Elector Maximilian Emanuel of Bavaria and the exiled Queen of James II, Mary of Modena. Apparently deeply anxious about female authority, particularly her own abilities, Cecily Cornwallis had the same year allowed Bonaventure Giffard, Vicar Apostolic of the London District, to assume Episcopal authority over the House, which Giffard interpreted as lasting in perpetuity. The rule of Vicars Apostolic, begun in 1685, was one of the few Catholic achievements to survive the deposition of James II. Supervision by a bishop was one of the principles Mary Ward had clearly rejected and this "secession" of Hammersmith caused great distress.

Vigorous correspondence ensued from the Chief Superior in Rome, Anna Barbara Babthorpe, followed by letters from her sister and successor Agnes Babthorpe. In 1713 Agnes sent an emissary to attempt to win back the community, an effort which utterly failed, after which Cecily Cornwallis resigned her office and retired to the Bar Convent in York in 1715. Under the Bishop's authority, Hammersmith declined, and in 1795 the few remaining nuns opened their house to exiled English Benedictine nuns from Dunkirk fleeing the French Revolution. The last IBVM nun at Hammersmith died in 1822 and the house became Benedictine (Kirkus 2001, 444–46).

Bar Convent, York, Georgian chapel in Neo-classical style, completed in 1769. Photo: Virginia Raguin

"CATHOLIC RELIEF" IN ENGLAND AND BEYOND

The eighteenth century saw a gradual relaxation of strictures against Catholics, and the sisters of the Bar Convent felt empowered to expand and to construct a chapel, discreetly located on the interior of the building. The chapel was the cherished dream of Ann Aspinal (1710–1789), who became Superior in 1760. The York Catholic Thomas Atkinson was selected as architect, but apparently it was Mother Aspinal who determined the choice of plan. She had acquired details of a church "outside of Rome," probably Santa Constanza, and the resultant chapel completed in 1769 was a rotunda in the neo-classical style. The chapel is an eloquent architectural space consisting of a domed area over the altar supported by eight Ionic columns, clearly an homage to the circular structure of the fourth-century Roman model (Krautheimer, 68–69). Aspinal continued building, and the resultant brick Georgian façade and the rooms behind it were erected in 1787. A wing fronting the street with four giant pilasters was added in 1844 by the architect G. T. Andrews.

For the dedication of the chapel, a chalice was given by the Constable family of Everingham (see in this catalogue "Veneration of the True Cross, the Holy Rood of Bromholm, and Passion of Christ," pp. 135-36). It was apparently an article the family used in their private chapel before giving it over to the sisters. In the early years of the nineteenth century it was embellished, presumably by a local metalworker, with what appears to be a heterogeneous series of jewels, very probably the personal jewels of a sister who entered the convent. Most noticeable is an oval diamond cluster, probably from a ring or pin, on the stem just under the cup. The chalice thus represents a recusant tradition of deep commitment to the tangible articles of faith that had sustained communities over time, and their renewal though reworking and rededication. The Blairs Museum, Aberdeen, Scotland, contains a recusant chalice whose

Constable chalice, England, ca. 1630-40 and early 19th century, Bar Convent, York. Photo: Virginia Raguin

Latin inscription proclaims a similar process of retention and embellishment: "Pray for the wellbeing of Lady Harriet Wentworth and her family who devoutly restored me after many years in exile to sacred purposes, 1888" (Inv. 6138 BLRBM).

Wentworth Chalice, 17th century?
The Blairs Museum, Aberdeen,
Scotland. Photo: Virginia Raguin

The subsequent history of the Institute, as well as its development on the Continent before the nineteenth century, cannot be covered here. It grew globally, with many branches, in Ireland, Spain, Hungary, Romania, Czech Republic, Slovakia, Korea, Mauritius, Gibraltar, India, Africa, Australia, Canada, and the United States, as well as England, Germany, Austria, and Italy. One of the best known former members of the order is Mother Theresa, who dedicated her life to relieving the suffering of the poorest of the poor in Calcutta. The Institute received full approbation by Pius IX in 1877 and in 1979 was allowed to adopt formally a selection from the Jesuit Constitutions. In 2004, the Institute actually received permission to adopt the full Jesuit Constitutions and to use a name similar to that requested by its founder, the "Congregation of Jesus" (Simmonds).

A Spiritual Dial, England (London?), 1700–10, Bar Convent, York. Photo: Virginia Raguin

CATALOG

A Spiritual Dial
Wood, paper, straw work, metal gilt, mica, ink and
tempera 7 x 7 x 3/4 in. (17.8 x 17.8 x 1.9 cm.)
England, (London?) 1700–10
The Bar Convent, York

Inscriptions:
A Spiritval Dyall Leading To a Bd Eternity
I. Run to God: Inexhaustible Treasure
II. Delight in God: Incomprehensible Sweetness
III. Repose in God; Immutable Peace
IV. Feare God: Incorruptible Justice
V. Expect God: Eternal Beatitude
VI. Adore God: Inaccessible Greatness
VII. Praise God: Incomparable Beauty
VIII. Love God: Ineffable Goodness
IX. Thank God: Immediate Liberality
X. Confide in God: Infinite Mercy
XI. Hearken to God: Consummate Wisdom
XII. Submit to God: Universal Providence

Written on the back of the dial (on brown wood)
is an inked inscription: "This dyall I leave to Mrs
Barnard at Hammersmith when I dy, witness my
hand this 25 of Jully 1720. M Cornwallis."
Cicely Cornwallis (ca. 1653–1723) was well
educated. At the age of 16, she entered the
Institute of Mary (as Mary Ward's Institute was
known in the seventeenth century) that had been
founded at Hammersmith in 1667 during the
early years of the reign of Charles II. As a nun
she followed lessons in Latin, Greek and Hebrew,
developing a considerable facility in these subjects.
In 1686, in her early thirties, she became the
second superior of the Hammersmith Institute.
After much tension in Europe over the authority
of the Institute and its legitimacy, she acquiesced
to political pressure and placed the house under the
authority of Bishop Gifford. She apparently deeply
regretted this move and in 1715 resigned her office
to retire to the Bar Convent in York. Her successor
at Hammersmith, who evidently never received
the promised Dial, was the 3rd superior, Mistress
Frances Barnard (1715– Nov. 7, 1753, the year of
Barnard's death).

Proclamation relating to the Popish Plot
Proclamation by the King: Commanding all
Papists, or Reputed Papists forthwith to depart
from the cities of London and Westminster, etc. ,
May 4, 1679
Printed in London, 14 ½ x 11 ½ in. (36.8 x 29.2 cm.)
College of the Holy Cross, Archives

The proclamation relates to a highly significant
event in English Catholic history, the so-called
Popish plot during the latter years of Charles

II. The Popish Plot was an alleged plot by
Catholics against the government whipped- up by
Titus Oates. Titus Oates was a failing Anglican
clergyman who converted to Catholicism, but was
twice expelled from his studies for the priesthood
and became an anti-Catholic informer. The
"Popish Plot" developed into national hysteria and
the worst persecution of Catholics since Elizabeth's
reign. The event caused the arrest of about a
hundred clergy, the execution of seventeen, and the
deaths of twenty-three in prison.

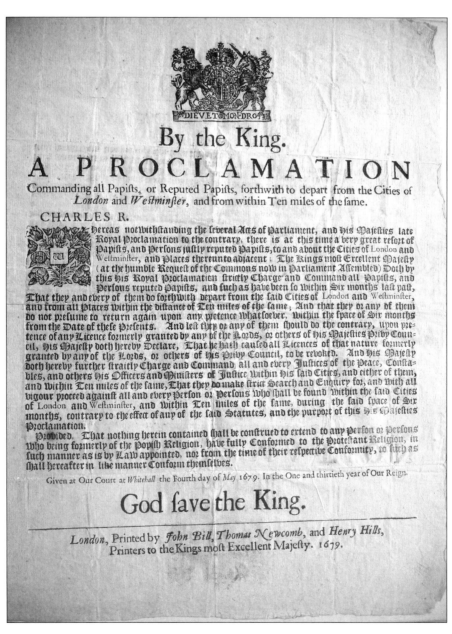

Proclamation relating to the Popish Plot, May 4, 1679, London, College of the Holy Cross, Archives

St. Omers to Stonyhurst: Jesuit Education of English Catholics 1593-1900

Janet Graffius

> *The aim of the youths being trained in this family is different from that of youths from other schools. The latter frequently have in view ecclesiastical or civil posts, such as may add to the honour of their parents' distinguished families or, if they are of lesser account, may win them renown. But the young men here, however noble be their families, look first and foremost to the conversion of England, each in his own degree. This indeed is why their friends have sent them there: in the first place that when they return home, where the Catholic religion and right living is so hotly persecuted by the heretics, that they may stand strong in faith and stedfast in virtue. And secondly, that amid so much false doctrine which they will have to face in England, they may see the right path themselves and lead the way for others. In a word, it is piety and learning that they set themselves to acquire.*

> (*Custom Book of St. Omers*, MS C II.19, p. 87, Stonyhurst College Archives)

Fr. Schondonch, Rector of St. Omers College, dictated these words shortly before his death in January 1617, recording for posterity the mission of the College founded in 1593 by the English Jesuit, Fr. Robert Persons.

Persons would have wholeheartedly agreed with his sentiments. He knew, from first hand experience, of the fines, restrictions and sanctions suffered by Catholics who refused to conform to Elizabeth I's state church. These penalties had increased greatly in severity following the advent of the Jesuit mission to England in 1581. By 1592, statutes had been passed declaring it to be treason to convert to Catholicism or to remain in England as a priest, banning Catholics from working as schoolmasters or private tutors, banning parents from sending their children to foreign seminaries, and even forbidding convicted recusants from travelling more than five miles from their homes. But it was a new threat, debated in the Commons in 1592-93 that spurred Persons into action. The debate centred on a proposal emanating from Cecil that children of convicted recusants should be removed from their parents at the age of seven, and placed with Protestant families. Their education was to be funded by the seizure of one third of the parents' assets. This project had long been in Cecil's mind- as early as 1583 a position paper entitled *Lord Burghley's Advice to the Queen in Matters of Religion* contained in the Somers Tracts advocated just such a plan, pointing out shrewdly that the children would, in effect, be hostages ensuring their parents' conformity in religion, and that ultimately, the Catholic faith would be eradicated.

St. Omers, photograph, early 20th century. Photo: Courtesy Stonyhurst College

Although the Commons ultimately rejected the proposal, the mere fact of its being seriously entertained as a possibility brought home to Persons the desperate need for a school for English Catholic boys. He approached Philip of Spain and obtained a substantial pension, promise of protection and the suggestion of St. Omers, then part of the Spanish Netherlands, as a home for the school. In September 1593 the College opened to a group of eighteen boys including Thomas Garnet (1575-1608) who was to be the protomartyr of the school, Ambrose Rookwood (1578?-1606) who gained notoriety as the last person to join Catesby's Gunpowder Plot, and Andrew White (1579-1656) who became known in later life as the Apostle of Maryland. (See in this catalogue "The Founding of Maryland and Catholics under British Colonial Policy.")

The school rapidly expanded to accommodate 120 boys by 1603, its reputation for learning and piety passing by word of mouth amongst the English Catholic community (naturally, it also came to the attention of the English authorities, who infiltrated the College with spies and frequently intercepted the correspondence between St. Omers and England.) The curriculum was based on the Jesuit system of education, the *Ratio Studiorum*, first published in 1599, which had its roots in the classical humanism of the day. Its aim was to educate in culture the whole man, the perfection of culture being expressed through the discerning use of reason, and of its expression in the spoken word - *ratio et oratio*.

The study regime included the ancient classical authors, particularly Aristotle, for the study of the faculty of reason, and Cicero, revered as the orator of orators. The pupil passed from the study of humanities, including rudimentary history and the geography of the classical world, languages such as Latin, Greek, Hebrew and French, to Philosophy, where Mathematics and Natural Philosophy, or Physics, was included, and on to the pinnacle of learning, the study of Theology, with particular reference to the works of St. Thomas Aquinas.

Great emphasis was laid on the importance of music - the College possessed four music "halls" where the pupils learned choral music, stringed instruments, psalmody and Gregorian chant, and provided a full orchestra. Plays, public declamations and dialogues formed a significant part of the curriculum. These were mostly written by Jesuit masters, or in some cases by boys, and tested the pupils' grasp of Latin and Greek rhetoric and their ability to perform in front of large, and often distinguished audiences. The fame of the boys' performances was widespread, and they regularly entertained important guests, such as the Papal Nuncio, Cardinal Guido Bentivoglio, who visited in 1609, and reported back to Cardinal Borghese: *I was again entertained with sacred music to my infinite delight...during the whole of my visit I truly seemed to be in Paradise and among angels.* Interestingly, he also commented, *I wore a cope that once belonged to King Henry VIII and which is preserved here as a rich and rare memorial.*

This is the first mention in the College history of a Catholic artefact that had been smuggled out of England and sent to St. Omers for safekeeping (see in this catalogue "Liturgical Vestments"). This practice became widespread in the seventeenth century as persecution waxed and waned, and items were shipped across to religious houses on the Continent, or given to the Jesuits in England, to await the day when they could once again be used as originally intended. It is obvious that English Catholics wished not only to perpetuate their faith through their sons, but also to preserve the physical remnants of their English Catholic heritage wherever possible.

The cope and matching chasuble and chalice veil survive, as do many other similar items such as a piece of the True Cross smuggled from the Crown Jewels in the Tower and given to Fr. Edward Lusher S. J. in 1647, the red Aragon vestments, supposedly the work of Henry VIII's first wife when incarcerated at Kimbolton, which were presented to St. Omers by James II, or the thorn from the Crown of Thorns in the Sainte-Chapelle belonging to the French Royal family, presented to Mary Queen of Scots, and given by her to Henry Percy, and by his daughter to Fr. John Gerard S. J., arriving at St. Omers in 1665, the year of the Great Plague. The presence of such artefacts provided an important and powerful symbol of the richness of the boys' Catholic past, and the severity of their present plight.

JESUIT EDUCATION
OF ENGLISH CATHOLICS

The Jesuits aimed to teach the boys self-control and self-discipline by keeping the example of the martyrs always before them. At supper a boy read in Latin from the Martyrology, and at the mention of an English saint or martyr, the boys removed their caps, while the passage was read over again for emphasis. According to the apostate James Wadsworth, who was educated at St. Omers and later turned priest-hunter, Sunday Vespers and the Saturday Litany of Our Lady were offered for the conversion of England, and, further that they had *written on their Church and Colledge doores in great golden letters, Iesu Iesu, converte Angliam, fiat fiat.* (James Wadsworth, *The English Spanish Pilgrime*, 1620, p. 16)

Later trials, such as the executions of six Jesuits - all old boys of St. Omers - during the Civil War (several at the hands of James Wadsworth (1604-1656?), their former classmate), and a further eight during the Popish Plot hysteria in London, tested the boys' courage and resolve, for while they were safe as long as they remained at the College, their families were often in danger, as Vice Rector Fr. Thomas Stapleton wrote in 1679,

> *For though they hear of their parents and relatives being thrown into prison, and are themselves in danger of losing their inheritances if further action is taken against them, yet they remain cheerful, speak of their parents as fortunate to be suffering for Christ, and hope that they themselves may some day suffer the same fate. For that they are already beginning to prepare.* (British Province Society of Jesus Archives, Anglia V, no. 90)

Mary Queen of Scots' Thorn, encased in reliquary dating from the 1590s. Photo: Courtesy Stonyhurst College

From 1593 to 1762, St. Omers flourished, but severe troubles were ahead. The territory surrounding St. Omers had moved from the control of the Spanish Netherlands to that of France. In the early 1760s, the plans of the French Parliament, led by Louis XV's minister the Duc de Choiseul and the King's mistress, Mme. de Pompadour, to expel the Jesuits from their soil also encompassed the College. In 1762 the government expelled the Jesuit order from France in its entirety, sequestrating their property. The authorities had no intention of sacrificing such a valuable asset as the school, with its roll of 170 boys, famous library, collections of rare artefacts, scientific laboratories, theatres, printing press and expansive buildings. They ordered that the Jesuits leave St. Omers College intact, and hand it - including the full complement of boys - over to secular clergy. The edict was made the more painful for the Jesuits as it became apparent that the clergy involved were English, who appeared only too willing to benefit from the misfortunes of their countrymen.

The Society had no intention of abandoning the school. The Rector, Fr. Lawson, secretly obtained a place of refuge in Bruges, and laid plans to transfer the boys there with as much of the contents of the school as possible. Over six weeks in August and September of 1762, all 140 boys and their masters, left in small groups, ostensibly on nature walks, and made their way on foot to Bruges. The content of much of the College was left behind, but important books, artefacts and relics were packaged up and carried by the boys and the priests. In Bruges the College was allowed to continue, under the protection of the Empress Maria Theresa of Austria.

The French, Spanish and Portuguese governments were motivated by a deep dislike of the order, suspecting it of intrigue and undue influence, and of interference in the Spanish and Portuguese use of slaves in South America. Having successfully expelled the order from all three countries, these Catholic monarchs kept up a relentless pressure on Pope Clement XIV for universal suppression. Clement procrastinated as long as he could, but ultimately was unable to resist and in August 1773 issued the Papal Brief *Dominus ac Redemptor* abolishing utterly and worldwide the Society of Jesus, and sequestrating its assets. The Empress withdrew her protection, the College's assets were seized, and the school was forced to make another hasty exit, this time to the Prince-Bishopric of Liege, where the Bishop, Monsignor Welbruck, offered them sanctuary. (A number of the items seized were eventually returned, such as Mary Queen of Scots' Thorn which was sought out years later, and restored to the College by Thomas Weld, and Thomas More's hat, delivered to Stonyhurst after a remorseful deathbed request by Mme. Therese Gaillard, who had inherited it from her parish priest who had "acquired" it from the College during the confusion of the Suppression. A further significant collection of artefacts was successfully hidden and transported to Liege.)

At Liege, the College moved into the English Jesuit Seminary, founded by Fr. Gerard in 1616 for the training of scholastics. Monsignor Welbruck proved to be a faithful friend to the College. He allowed the ex-Jesuits full rein in ordering their own affairs, and confirmed the appointment of Fr. Howard as the new Director (the Jesuit post of Rector no longer being valid) to the English Academy, as the College became known. He also petitioned the new Pope, Pius VI, for protection for the Academy, confirming its continuity with its Jesuit past, and providing it with authority for its continuing work with the English missions. The Pope obliged, with the Brief *Apostolici Praesules*, issued in 1778. This recognition not only protected the school from interference by diocesan authorities, but also confirmed to the Catholic world that the Academy still functioned as a recognised and approved College, and gave pontifical authority to the ex-Jesuits work in providing priests for the English mission.

In the light of the drastic fact of the Suppression, the Academy took stock if itself and issued its first prospectus in 1774, laying out, as it were, its manifesto for the future. It was the first major revision of the syllabus since the 1620s and makes interesting reading, *Boys are accepted from the age of six. They are taught to read, to write and every part of literature and philosophy; English, French, Latin, Greek and Hebrew; sacred and profane history; geography, arithmetic, algebra, geometry, astronomy, experimental physics and mathematics.* (Stonyhurst College Archives)

The curriculum laid a new emphasis on English literature and promotes the sciences to a greater extent than before, and certainly in a manner virtually unknown in England at the time. The Academy was no longer able to offer a Jesuit education by name- long its greatest selling point- and so perforce had to choose a new direction. It appears to have done this by playing to its strengths and concentrating on those scientific subjects for which many European Jesuits were justly famed. The change in the school uniform also reflects a subtle change in the tone of the school. At St. Omers, the boys had worn cassocks with white bands around the throat, emulating the Jesuits, perhaps in the hope that many of the boys would follow in their footsteps and be ordained. So similar to the priests were they that the Rectors occasionally had to deal with complaints from the townspeople, outraged that Jesuits appeared to be climbing trees, playing football or ice-skating. After the Suppression, the Jesuit gown was banned, and the uniform needed to be revised. The 1774 prospectus stated that *the dress of his Highness (the Prince-Bishop) and the lords of his court in the country is that of the pensioner (pupil). It consists of a cassock, maroon in colour, with steel buttons.* (Stonyhurst College Archives, ibid.). While undoubtedly wishing to pay a compliment to their generous benefactor and protector by dressing the boys in his court colours, the choice of this secular clerical dress was also a tactful response to the precarious position and uncertain future of the suppressed Jesuits.

This is not to assume that the former Jesuits had any intention of disappearing in an obliging manner. The Brief of Suppression had not been promulgated in Prussia or those parts of Russia under the jurisdiction of Empress Catherine the Great, and in 1782 Fr. Howard applied unsuccessfully for permission to affiliate the former English Province with that of White Russia. His successor as Director,

Fr. Strickland, worked tirelessly to this end for the next twenty years, finally achieving his goal in 1803 when the English Province was given verbal permission from the Pope to affiliate to the White Russian Jesuits.

Two hundred and one years of continental education came to an end in 1794 with the French and English at war and the French Revolutionary Army preparing to lay siege to Liege. The Prince-Bishop warned the Director that he could no longer guarantee the safety of the school or its pupils. It was clearly time to leave - but where could they now find sanctuary?

Stonyhurst College in 1794, anonymous engraving, Stonyhurst College Archive. Photo: Courtesy Stonyhurst College

In 1778 and 1791 the English Parliament had passed the First and Second Relief Acts, allowing individual Catholics the right to buy or inherit land, possess property and open schools provided they swore an oath declaring that no Pope or foreign temporal prince had any civil or temporal authority in England. For the first time since the Reformation it again became possible to teach English Catholics legally on English soil. Thomas Weld, a former pupil from Bruges days, visited the Academy in January 1793 to collect his sons, and obviously realised the precarious nature of the political situation. He offered his former schoolmasters the use of a large, empty Elizabethan mansion in a remote part of Lancashire in the north west of England, should the need arise. The Welds had inherited Stonyhurst Hall in 1754, but since they lived principally in Dorset, in the extreme south, the building had lain unoccupied for forty years.

A final migration, not without adventure, much of which has passed into Stonyhurst legend, began on July 14, 1794. The possessions of both the Seminary and the Academy had been rapidly packed into crates, which were loaded onto canal barges. It rapidly became apparent that there were far too many packing cases, and Fr. Wright, the Procurator, promptly held a quayside auction of the excess baggage. No records were kept of what was sold in the confusion, and he was strongly criticised later for the manner in which he had handled the evacuation: *I say nothing of his disposal of the library, the mathematical room, the church plate, and Fr. (Peter) Wright the Martyr's body, all of which at a moderate expense and with some care might have been brought to Stonyhurst* (Stonyhurst College Archives MS A.II. 29, No. 17).

They reached an ill-prepared house on August 29. The new Director, Fr. Marmaduke Stone, immediately began the process of putting it in order, rallying support from the wide circle of English Catholic sympathisers, former pupils and benefactors: *the house is indeed very much out of repair and will require very heavy expenses to make it proper for our purpose. But I rely upon Divine Providence and the assistance of our numerous friends. We have already fixed upon rooms for a refectory, study place and dormitories. We have twenty bedsteads nearly ready.* (Stonyhurst College Archives, Ms letter from Fr. Stone to Lord Arundell, Sept. 1794)

The newly named Stonyhurst College (attempts to Latinize it to Collegium Saxosylvanum were thankfully given short shrift) opened its doors again on October 21, 1794, some thirteen weeks after leaving Liege. Undoubtedly the first few years in their new home were uncomfortable for both pupils and priests. The local community, although much of rural Lancashire was Catholic, was suspicious of these "French" foreigners, hardly surprising since England was still at war with Napoleon. Money was in short supply and pupil numbers low. The future of the College and its former Jesuit teachers seemed uncertain. There were days when the priests went without food to ensure that the boys ate. But with the secret restoration of the Society in 1803, the situation slowly improved. Thomas Weld made over to the restored Jesuits the small estate of Hodder, a mile or so away from Stonyhurst, for a noviciate - a most welcome vote of confidence in the future. To deflect local worries of "Romish seminaries" in their midst, a small school of about 30 boys between the ages of five and ten years opened at Hodder on January 1, 1807, providing cover for the novices. Its descendant, the present day St. Mary's Hall, may well be the oldest Catholic preparatory school in England.

The predominance of science in the curriculum at Liege was carried on at Stonyhurst. A subscription of £2,239 was raised in 1808 to build a new Mathematical and Philosophical Room. In 1824 the equipment included a model steam engine, an 8-inch telescope, electrical machines, an air pump, an astronomical circle and several globes. A Chemistry Laboratory opened that year, unique among English schools at the time.

The unofficial nature of the affiliation of the Jesuits to the Russians in 1803 continued to hamper development at Stonyhurst. The mere presence of Jesuits in England caused problems, even with the secular Catholic clergy, who were largely opposed to formal recognition of the Society - even after it was restored worldwide in 1814 - fearing that the spectre of the Jesuit bogeyman would hinder the chances of Catholic emancipation in England. The College only really began to flourish after the passing of the Catholic Emancipation Act in 1829, which year also saw the final official recognition of the restored English Province by Pope Leo XII.

The *Ratio Studiorum* was revised in 1832, and Stonyhurst took note of its recommendations to promote the study of vernacular languages, history, geography and mathematics; scientifically, of course, it was already in advance of its time. A further academic boost came in 1840 when the College agreed on an external affiliation to the University of London, providing English Catholics with the opportunity of studying for their degrees at Stonyhurst, taking the degree certificate exams in London and graduating from the University of London, which uniquely among English universities, was open to Catholics. For the first time since the Reformation, Catholics could obtain a degree from an English university. Jesuit professors from all over Europe came to Stonyhurst to teach the undergraduates, and the number of Philosophers, as the students were called, peaked at 50 in 1880. The College's renown benefited greatly from the academic excellence of its teaching and, probably equally, from the influx of European nobility and minor royalty who became Philosophers. They were, to be honest, attracted perhaps as much by the excellent local fishing, hunting and shooting as by the chance of being taught Physics by Fr. William Kay, who had learnt at the feet of Faraday.

By 1879, Stonyhurst was advertising to potential students: *Lectures…in the subjects required for Examinations of the London University, for the Competitive Examinations for Woolwich, Sandhurst and the Indian Civil Service, as well as in the studies necessary for the Medical Profession…There are also Resident Professors of English, French, Italian, Spanish, German, Hindustani and Sanskrit, including compositions and literature* (Catholic Directory, 1879).

The inclusion of the Army Colleges of Sandhurst and Woolwich in this list, as well as the Civil Service and medical professions indicates how far Catholic integration had progressed in England. A large part of the College's hard-won place in public opinion was due to the notable prowess of former pupils in the Armed Services, and the enthusiasm with which they served. Underlying this enthusiasm was always

Stonyhurst College in 2005. Photo: Courtesy Stonyhurst College

the unspoken desire to prove their allegiance to a country that had long regarded their co-religionists with deep suspicion. This was expressed in the wording on the College Boer War (1899-1902) memorial dedicated *to a great company of old Stonyhurst boys who in the same campaign left for all time an example of Catholic loyalty and service worthy of the traditions of the College.*

The vast building programme at the College during the 1880s was a physical expression of its confidence in the future. The Jesuit and poet Gerard Manley Hopkins spent several years at Stonyhurst, first as a Seminarian, then as a teacher of Classics from 1882 to 1884. A letter he wrote to the poet Robert Bridges at the time encapsulates this confidence:

> *I wish I could show you this place. It is upon my word worth seeing. The new College, though there is no real beauty in the design, is nevertheless imposing and the furniture and fittings are a joy to see. There are acres of flat roof, which, when the air is not thick, as unhappily it mostly is, commands a noble view of this Lancashire landscape, Pendle Hill, Ribblesdale, the fells, and all around, bleakish but solemn and beautiful.*
>
> *There is a garden with a bowling green walled in by massive yew hedges, a bowered yew walk, two real Queen Anne summerhouses, observatories under government, orchards, vineries, greenhouses, workshops, a plungebath, fivescourts, a mill, a farm, a fine cricketfield besides a huge playground; then the old mansion, ponds, towers, quadrangles, fine ceilings, chapels, a church, a fine library, museums, MSS illuminated and otherwise, coins, works of art...*

One feels sure that Fr. Persons would have approved.

J. R. Hutchinson, Stonyhurst College, west front from the south, ca. 1890-1900
Etching, 11 ½ x 15 ⅝ in. (29.2 x 39.7 cm.)
Published by W. H. Benyon, Cheltenham, ca. 1890-1900
Stonyhurst College, Lancashire

The central gatehouse and range to east of 1592-5, parts of the original Shireburn mansion, embellished with the pair of cupolas and the gate piers 1712, are the key to development of this great west front. This range was continued to the west (L) of the gatehouse in 1843-56, probably by the Jesuit architect Fr. Richard Vaughan, and the infirmary 1842-3 stands in front of it. The sunken garden and forward wing (R) of 1799 for the Jesuits. The 'archaeologically' convincing church of St Peter 1832-5 by J.J. Scoles architect is sometimes credited with converting Pugin. [**Roderick O'Donnell**]

J. R. Hutchinson, Stonyhurst College, the Boys' Chapel, ca.1884-90
Etching, 15 ⅝ x 11 ½ x in. (39.7 x 29.2 cm.)
Published by W. H. Benyon, Cheltenham, ca. 1890-1900
Stonyhurst College, Lancashire

This dramatically-lit chapel is at the west end of the vast south-facing block (designed 1874, begun 1878) by the architects E.J.Dunn & A. M. Hansom of Newcastle. The interior with its Perpendicular style fan vaults and internal oriels (for the community to observe the boys at their prayers) is reminiscent of the Tudor royal chapels. The structural and decorative carved woodwork, especially the towering reredos of the life of St Aloysius, is characteristic of this practice. [**Roderick O'Donnell**]

J. R. Hutchinson, Stonyhurst College, west front from the south, etching, ca. 1890-1900, Stonyhurst College

J. R. Hutchinson, Stonyhurst College, the Boys' Chapel, etching, ca. 1890-1900, Stonyhurst College

THE FOUNDING OF MARYLAND AND CATHOLICS UNDER BRITISH COLONIAL POLICY

Virginia C. Raguin

MARYLAND AND CATHOLIC WORSHIP

The English colony of Maryland came into being through the agency of George Calvert (1580-1632), First Lord Baltimore. Calvert was an able statesman highly favored by King James I who entrusted him with many commissions, especially in Ireland where he was granted a large estate with the stipulation that the inhabitants would conform to the Protestant Episcopal Church of Ireland. In 1624, having become a Catholic, he surrendered these estates but the king restored them to him with the religious clause omitted. In 1625, James elevated him to the Irish Peerage as Baron Baltimore of Baltimore in County Longford. Calvert had already established a settlement in Newfoundland in 1620 with the provision of religious toleration. In 1628 he requested a new grant in a better climate and after some opposition from the Virginia Company, received a grant for land north and east of the Potomac. He died before the charter was granted and Maryland was founded by his son Cecilius Calvert (second Lord Baltimore), and named for Henrietta Maria, the Catholic queen of Charles I (1625-1649).

Maryland's history gives some indication of the considerable flux in tolerance levels for nonconforming religions in England throughout the Early Modern period. The colony was intended as a Catholic refuge and functioned as such during its initial years. In the popular view concerning settlement of the area that has now become the United States, religious freedom often appears as a founding principle. The position most commonly adopted, however, was one of a state regulated religion with little acknowledgment of dissenting creeds, and quite often, a high degree of intolerance to the public display of anything other than the dominant creed. The Massachusetts Bay Colony, for example, founded in 1620 by Puritans, was a veritable theocracy that expelled Quakers, Jews, and Catholics equally. Pennsylvania, founded by the Quaker William Penn, initially accepted Catholics. Rhode Island was unusual in that its founding charter granted religious liberty to all.

Maryland displays some of the social and economic characteristics of the areas in England that had retained a sizable Catholic population, predominantly the less developed areas of the north, the counties of Lancashire, Durham, Yorkshire, Northumberland, and also areas of Wales. The settlement in Maryland was established with the desire to reproduce a quasi-manorial system that had become largely obsolete in England. The colony was further a part of the relaxation of penalties against English Catholics under the reigns of James I and Charles I. The Catholic population had consolidated, as assessed notably by John Bossy, whose meticulous research records Catholic population, landholders, clergy, and customs. Catholic missionaries, in particular, increased from 300 in 1600 to about 750 in 1640 (Bossy 1975, 279). By the 1620s a general *modus vivendi* had developed between the Crown and the small segment of the landowning class which was Catholic. Catholic gentry were able to accept a lawful sovereign and distance themselves from earlier papal policies seeking to depose the ruler, even by force. Bossy reports that from the reign of Elizabeth to the later eighteenth century, "every attempt to count Catholics reveals them as coagulated in local groups at the centre of which a gentleman's household will usually be found" (Ibid., 175). Thus there developed a pattern of housing residence tutors who also functioned as the local priest. Since Elizabeth's Supremacy Act of 1559 required that all individuals standing for "any degree of learning" take an oath that the queen was "the only supreme governor . . . in all spiritual or ecclesiastical things or causes" (Gee and Hardy, 449, 451) Catholics were precluded from universities. Older children were therefore routinely sent to the continent for subsequent education, many to the Jesuit school of St. Omers, a process which resulted in a class of considerable sophistication and international connections. The gentry also became more prominent in clerical recruitment in the 1600s and their interest ensured a steady economic support for the missions. As Bossy states, "Without the gentry there would certainly have been Catholic recusants – for how long? – but I find it very difficult to believe that there would have been a Catholic community" (Bossy 1975, 181).

Maryland's government was controlled by Catholics for its first sixteen years except for the period of Ingle's Rebellion (1645-47). In 1649, the year of Charles I's beheading and the beginning of the Commonwealth, the governing Assembly passed the famous act of religious toleration. Church vessels date from this early era. A secular cup taken over for use as a chalice (CATALOGUE) was made in London in 1640-41 and used probably as early as the 1650s and 1660s in the mission of St. Francis Xavier at Newtown, St. Mary's County. It was provided with a paten that was most probably produced locally. Likewise, for expedience, base metals rather than the traditional silver and silver gilt were pressed into service. A pewter chalice and paten (CATALOGUE) of presumed Maryland manufacture long associated with the missions date to about 1650-1700.

Maryland's fortunes reflected its era and given the general pattern of immigration in colonies, far more Protestant than Catholic settlers arrived subsequently. Between 1658 and 1668 they took control of the government, barring Catholics from office and restricting public worship. These and later changes must be seen against equally shifting policies in the mother country, although a certain time lag is evident.

In England James I (1603-1625) had occasionally implemented a more tolerant attitude. His son, Charles I (1625-1649), however, married the Catholic Henrietta Maria, daughter of Catherine de Medici and Henri IV of France. His Catholic marriage and Charles's increasingly autocratic rule plunged the country into a civil war resulting in the king's execution in 1649. Henrietta Maria fled to France, returning briefly during the restoration of her son Charles II in 1660. England was governed by a Commonwealth from 1649 to 1660, headed by Oliver Cromwell. The Restoration of Charles II (1660-1685) brought some calm. However he was followed by his brother James II (1685-1689) who had become a Catholic convert in 1674. James's Declaration of Indulgence of 1687 suspended penal laws against Catholics and other non-conformists, giving them "free exercise of their religion . . . and the perfect enjoyment of their property" (Gee and Hardy, 641). Parliament deposed him and offered the crown to his daughter Mary and his son-in-law William of Orange, Stattholder of the United Provinces of Holland. A Bill Of Rights of 1689 by Parliament declared that it is "inconsistent with the safety and welfare of this Protestant kingdom, to be governed by a popish prince" (Ibid., 652). James fled to France to gain support from Louis XIV, then to Ireland where he was defeated by William (William III) at the Battle of the Boyne, July 1, 1690. All these conflicts ensured a distrust of Catholicism as a threat dominated by foreign influence and royal absolutism.

William revoked the grant to the second Lord Baltimore and made Maryland's government conform as a royal province in 1692. Vehement anti-Catholic legislation followed by which the Church of England became the official, tax-supported church and Catholic worship was proscribed. In 1693 similar restrictions were extended to Pennsylvania where Catholics were removed from public office by the administration of a Test oath that demanded the repudiation of the doctrine of Transubstantiation and the Sacrifice of the Mass. In 1702, Maryland granted toleration to all Christians except Catholics, a policy mitigated by intervention from Queen Anne. In 1704, she allowed private chapels in individual homes, a policy that reflected the unofficial condition of Catholics in England. Thus for most of the eighteenth century, manor chapels and the "Priests' Mass-Houses" in private buildings owned by the clergy were the locus of worship. As in England, Catholics were still officially forbidden to conduct religious instruction and equally forbidden to send children out of the colony for such instruction. Although the first three Lords Baltimore, George, Cecilius, and Charles, were Catholics, in 1713 Benedict Calvert, fourth Lord

Baltimore, converted to the Church of England in order to save his American property. His four sons who were then students at St. Omers (see previous essay), as would be Charles and John Carroll, were removed and educated as Protestants (Muir, 44). By 1718, Catholics were denied the right to vote and in 1754 there was a failed attempt to confiscate the property owned by clergy. Benedict's successors, the Lords Baltimore Charles and Frederick, continued in the Protestant faith.

Still, Catholics maintained worship. An account made in 1773 by John Mattingly (1745-1807), then teaching at the English College in Rome, described the experience of Sundays for Maryland priests:

> Travel to various chapels [from their central residences] which are called congregations, 10, 15, or even more than twenty miles away, to carry out their duties on Sundays and feast days; so that Mass is celebrated in each chapel at least once a month, the sacraments administered, and the word of God preached; in the principle places, however, twice or more frequently, according to the number and the needs of the faithful. Everything is done more or less in the following manner: from early morning until 11 o'clock they hear confessions; then they celebrate Mass & distribute holy communion; once Mass is finished they preach to the congregation, and Christian doctrine is explained. (Archives of the Sacred Congregation for the Propagation of the Faith, quoted in Curran 1988, 12)

It a difficult to say precisely how social groups respond when pressured to modify their traditional ways of life. Did Catholics intensify their cherished observances in the face of restrictions – or might commissions be mere coincidence? A silver gilt monstrance, dating about 1700 is presumably of local Maryland manufacture (CATALOGUE). The base bears an inscription exhorting the viewer/user, *Ora pro Georgio Tompsono* (pray for George Thompson). Thompson (fl. 1658-1663) was the first Clerk of Court in Charles County, and the monstrance was presumably commissioned by one of his descendants as a commemoration. Its inscription can be compared to the pocket shrine with the Instruments of the Passion (see in this catalogue "Veneration of the True Cross, the Holy Rood of Bromholm, and Passion of Christ," pp. 121, 124) which states, as does the 1684 Rookwood chalice (see "Liturgical Vessels," pp. 55-56), that it was a gift of the maker (*Ora pro Tho. Lusher qui fecit 1623*). The display and veneration of the host is a ritual unique to Catholicism, and it is significant that this rite was obviously cherished as restrictions on Catholic worship began to mount after 1690.

Veneration of the Eucharist was an explicit element of American Catholic preaching, in particular, the sermons delivered during Masses to celebrate the feast of Corpus Christi. The feast had been established in 1264 by Pope Urban IV who commissioned Thomas Aquinas to compose hymns. After the 1314 bull issued by Pope Clement VI, it gained great popularity and was

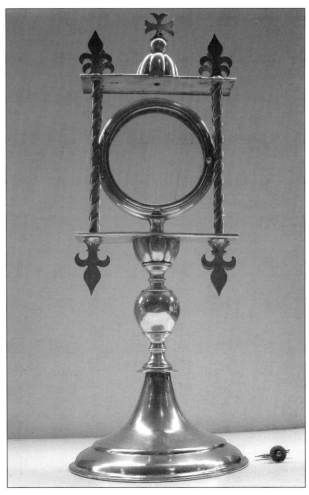

Silver gilt monstrance, Maryland? ca. 1700, Georgetown University Collections. Photo: Virginia Raguin

most often celebrated by processions, pageants, and declamations (Rubin 1991). Fr. James Frambach (1729-1795) was typical in using the moment to stress the Catholic doctrine of the Eucharist in a sermon in 1762: "Christ has given truly and realy his body and blood to his Apostles at the Last Supper, and that Christ gives us daily the same blood and body in the Blessed Sacrament" (Link, 31, 153). He continues by stressing the awe the worshipper should feel before the Sacrament: "Oh, what reverence we ought to bring with us when we draw near to so tremendous a Majesty. . . O, how would a Christian be affected, if he visibly and evidently saw his God before him in his approaching to this Blessed Sacrament!" (Ibid., 34, 165). The practice of processions apparently did take place, although documentation is imprecise. John Bolton (1742-1809) refers in a 1799 sermon to the "ceremonial usually practiced on this day in Catholic countries, in carrying our Saviour's body in procession and pomp" (Kupke, 207). At the Jesuit mission in Goshenhoppen Pennsylvania, discussed below, Protestant onlookers mistook a procession for a military drill. Report of the event led the Pennsylvania Assembly in 1757 to pass a law against Catholics bearing arms (Link, 37).

Catholics were tenacious and in the early eighteenth century Mass was celebrated in the Lancaster plantation in Rock Point, Charles County, with what is presumably the oldest recusant chalice in the United States. An Elizabethan chalice (CATALOGUE and "Liturgical Vessels," pp. 52-53) dating to about 1550-1600 is typical of recusant liturgical vessels of that time. Its two joints allow it to be disassembled into three parts, possibly to facilitate clandestine storage. On the foot is an image of Christ crucified. The cup was used with a paten bearing the IHS, the monogram of the name of Jesus with a cross resting on the crossbar of the H and a heart and supporting three oversize nails below. The IHS may be associated with Jesuits, who adopted the motto, but could also relate to the widespread veneration of the name of Jesus in the late Middle Ages and its continuity in recusant devotion (Block et al.). The altar stone used with the Elizabethan chalice allowed the celebrant mobility, an important element in time of persecution. Rather than having to locate a fixed altar for the service, the priest could place the stone with its marking of the cross at the compass points and its cavity with relics anywhere needed.

Catholics, however much a minority, were still influential, even under penal laws. In the year preceding the American Revolution the most prominent and influential citizen of Maryland was the Catholic Charles Carroll of Carrollton (1737-1832), one of the signers of the Declaration of Independence. His grandfather, also named Charles Carroll, had come to Maryland from England in 1688. Under the third Lord Baltimore, Carroll received large grants of land and important political positions in the colony. These were augmented by his son Charles Carroll of Annapolis (1703- 1783), the father of Charles Carroll of Carrollton.

Charles's education is an example of what the wealthy, able, and socially prominent Catholic would devise. At the age of ten, with his cousin, John Carroll, afterwards Archbishop of Baltimore, he spent a year at the Jesuit grammar school at Bohemia on Harmon's Manor in Maryland. In 1748, both boys entered the Jesuit college at St. Omers. Charles spent six years at St. Omers and then at the age of seventeen an additional year at the Jesuit college in Reims. Subsequently he entered the prestigious College of Louis-le-Grand in Paris, remaining in France between 1753 and 1757 studying law. The followed seven years were spent in London, where he continued to study law, returning to his estate of Carrollton in Frederick County in 1765.

He was immediately active in politics of the colony, holding many elected positions in the ten years before the Revolution. Carroll vigorously supported independence despite the largely conservative stance of the Maryland legislature. In doing so, he had the most to lose of all the signers as he was the wealthiest man in the colonies at that time. Four days before the Declaration of Independence was drafted, Maryland withdrew its objections, and Carroll represented Maryland with his signature. He was active as a framer of Maryland's constitution and served in both the senate of Maryland and that of the United States. The influence of the Carrolls, moreover, extended through church and education, as well as the state.

Charles was related to the family of Daniel Carroll (d. 1750) from Ireland who became an enterprising merchant in Maryland. The ties were augmented by their marriages; Daniel married Eleanor Darnall who was a relative of Mary Darnall (d. 1782) whom Charles had married in 1762. Daniel produced two distinguished sons, John Carroll, who was appointed the first Bishop of Baltimore in 1790, and Daniel (1733-1829) prominent statesman and benefactor of Georgetown College. By 1776, only a few states, Maryland, Pennsylvania, Virginia, and Delaware, had removed restrictions against Catholics. With the National Convention in Philadelphia of 1787, religious liberty was extended to all. In 1784, Pope Pius VI appointed the Rev. John Carroll as Superior of the missions of the United States, with power to administer confirmation. At this time there were 15,800 Catholics in Maryland out of a total population of 254,000.

The Jesuits in Maryland

In reflecting on the specific Jesuit contribution to English-speaking America, the small group of men laid an extraordinary foundation. The members of the Society, apart from a few Franciscans, were at one time the whole of the Catholic Church in British North America. The Jesuits were English themselves. A Jesuit Province for England having been approved by the Jesuit General Mutius Vitelleschi in 1623, they made it possible for the Irish and later Catholic immigrants to adopt an Anglo-American culture without leaving their faith. John Carroll, the first national leader of the Church in America, emerged from this group and helped shape its evolution in the early national period.

The Jesuits came to minister to the Catholic colonists, but also with an eye to the conversion of the native population. "Who then can have a doubt," Andrew White wrote before leaving England, "but that by this one work so glorious, many thousand souls may be led to Christ?" Fr. Andrew White (1579-1656) and his companions overcame the hostility of some of the tribes, the prejudice of Proprietor and English settlers, and the great barrier of language to convert several tribal chiefs. White's account of the voyage to Maryland that he sent to Mutius Vitelleschi describes the hostility of English settlers in Barbados and the reception by natives (Curran 1988, 47-55). At St. Mary's City, White made of an Indian house the colony's first chapel. Chapels were built to serve colonists and natives, including one on the Port Tobacco River which was succeeded in 1798 by St. Thomas's Manor church built by the Rev. Charles Sewell, S.J. But these efforts were not encouraged; Proprietor and settlers preferred to disperse the Indians. Determined to bring Christianity to them in their own tongue, White laboriously composed a catechism for the Piscataways. The fragment of prayers surviving at Georgetown was probably a draft prepared for another missioner.

The promising seedtime, however, was not to realize the harvest White had foreseen in England. Yellow fever took the lives of White's first companions, John Altham and Thomas Gervase; Ferdinand Poulton was killed in a shooting accident. In 1645 the Protestant revolt expelled White and Thomas Copley who were taken to England in chains. Returning some time later with a restored Lord Baltimore, Copley found that the Indians had been driven off, and thereafter the Jesuits' ministry was limited to the English settlers and their servants, among whom were already numbered African slaves.

From the first the Jesuits shared the culture of the new colony. Indeed, Maryland was unique; granting unprecedented religious toleration, it supported no established church. The Jesuits had to support themselves. Under the Conditions of Plantation of 1636, Thomas Copley obtained 24,500 acres, including St. Inigoes Manor near St. Mary's City. Later purchases and gifts led to the founding of other manors in southern Maryland and on the Eastern Shore. The plantations of the Jesuit "gentry" were worked at first by indentured servants, but by the end of the century that source of hands had run dry and slaves gradually filled up the vacancy. A French Jesuit visiting Maryland in 1674 found the lifestyle puzzling, remarking on "two of our Fathers and a Brother, . . . the Fathers being dressed like gentlemen, and the Brother like a farmer."

Petre chalice (paten probably not same origin), London, 1640-1660, Georgetown University Collections. Photo: Virginia Raguin

But the substantial manor houses at St. Inigoes, Newtown, and elsewhere were not for all; many Jesuits lived simply on isolated farms. Joseph Mosley, at St. Joseph's on the Eastern Shore, was proud that he could support himself and his missionary work, but deeply regretted his isolation from his fellow priests. From these farms, which served as mission centers, Jesuits went out as circuit riders to minister to Catholics spread throughout southern and eastern Maryland, frequently traveling on horseback 300 miles in a week. "This, you'll say, is hard," Mosley wrote his sister in London, "it's easy . . . to what it was."

A chalice imported from England to the Maryland Province (CATALOGUE) is part of the group Lord Petre commissioned for the Jesuit missioners in East Anglia. The chalices have been assigned a date of 1640-1660 which encompasses the last decade of the Restoration and the years of the Commonwealth, 1649-1660. The provenance of this chalice is not known but its presence in the New World gives an unmistakable aura of familiarity to missionary work in inhospitable territory.

After the "Glorious Revolution" of 1688-1689 Catholics in the colony found themselves under the same anti-Catholic laws which had caused them to flee England. Priests were virtually barred from the colony under the threat of life imprisonment. The harshest of these laws were not often applied: Jesuits, occasionally arrested, were never imprisoned. But Catholics, deprived of many of their rights, were subject to the arbitrary actions of a Protestant majority which used anti-Catholic feeling as a political tool. A crisis came during the French and Indian Wars (1755-60) when the loyalty of Catholics was suspect. A series of repressive measures, including a double tax on Catholics' property, prompted Charles Carroll (the father of Charles Carroll of Carrollton) to petition for the restoration of Catholic rights and to advise his son to seek his happiness elsewhere. Not surprisingly, the Jesuits looked toward Pennsylvania as a new field of endeavor.

Rev. Theodore Schneider, S.J., for example, founded a mission at Goshenhoppen (now Bally), Pennsylvania in 1741 for which he needed to provide the materials of saying Mass. He copied by hand two missals and altar cards about 1745 (CATALOGUE). The missals contain the changing Latin readings – such as the gospels and epistles for the year. The altar cards contain the unchanging prayers, such as the Gloria and the words of the Canon of the Mass that the celebrant needed to say orally. Such expedients reflect the situation of a minority religion, where from 1700 to 1805 about ninety Jesuits can be counted as members of Maryland's mission, of whom about sixty were English, sixteen born in the Colonies, and the others Irish, French, German, Welsh, and Belgian. The scarcity of Catholic devotional and liturgical books was a constant problem until well into the nineteenth century.

Catholics supported the Revolution in disproportionate numbers; they had long familiarity with "taxation without representation," and Charles Carroll of Carrollton played a prominent role. The war brought great changes for the better for

Page opened to the Canon of the Mass, hand copied Roman Missal, Goshenhoppen mission? ca. 1745, Georgetown University Library Special Collections

Catholics, but the Declaration compounded a crisis begun in 1773 with Clement XIV's suppression of the Society of Jesus. The twenty-three Jesuits in Maryland and Pennsylvania, no longer subject to Jesuit superiors in England and Rome, were, after the Revolution, cut off from the authority of the Apostolic Vicar of London.

Into this vacuum John Carroll returned from Europe, where he had been teaching at a Jesuit seminary in Liege. In 1753 at the age of eighteen Carroll had entered the Society of Jesus and was ordained a priest at the age of thirty-four. He was exposed to the volatile political fortunes of Jesuits. St. Omers, where he had studied between 1748 and 1753, was threatened with dissolution in 1762 by the French authorities. Secretly, with considerable hardship, the instructors and students escaped to Austrian-controlled Bruges (Muir, 60-63). Carroll himself then left Liege for Bruges in 1771 and was almost immediately directed to serve as tutor to Charles-Philippe, the son of Lord Stourton, a Catholic nobleman on an itinerary throughout France, Germany, Austria, and Italy. In 1773, back in Bruges, the news of the suppression of the Jesuits arrived. This catastrophic event, however, had an unintended consequence (Curran 1993, 7). This was the only way a "regular" priest of his unusual intellectual abilities and European culture would be allowed to relocate to America. The culture of Europe that Carroll represented is apparent in the Roman Missal, printed in Antwerp, 1574 (CATALOGUE) that was known to be in his possession. This is an edition of the Tridentine missal, the kind of possession that assured the uniformity of Catholic worship throughout the world since the Council of Trent. It was probably given by Carroll to another priest and later in 1825-1850 received a new binding. The gentry-based English recusant tradition was reflected in his consecration as a bishop in the private chapel of the Weld family at Lulworth Castle, Dorset, England in 1790.

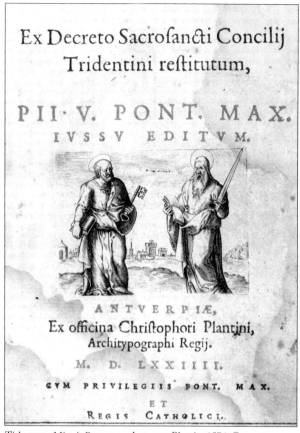

Title page, *Missale Romanum*, Antwerp, Plantin, 1574, Georgetown
University Library Special Collections

Carroll, more than anyone else, shaped the foundations of the American Church, leading the organization of the Select Body of the Clergy that wrote a constitution for the American Church and elected him its first bishop in 1789. The Revolution, which freed Catholics from the penal laws, made possible the re-organization of the clergy and the fulfillment of a hope for a Jesuit college that went back to 1640. Land for Georgetown College was acquired in 1787, and four years later it received its first student. John Carroll was its founder. The need for it, as he said, was great: "On this Academy is built all my hopes of permanency and success of our H. Religion in the United States," which shows him still thinking in European terms of the education of an elite. The ex-Jesuits still had a living to make, and so, under Carroll, they formed the Corporation of the Roman Catholic Clergy of Maryland to protect their estates, which continued to be the main support of their apostolic work.

This planning and activity was carried on with the hope that the Society of Jesus would be restored, and several times during this period former Jesuits considered attempting a liaison with the Jesuits who survived the suppression in Russia, whose Orthodox Tsar did not recognize papal authority. Finally, in 1802, a year after Pius VII recognized the Russian Province of the Society, seven American ex-Jesuits petitioned Carroll to use his influence so that they might be allowed to affiliate themselves with the Russian Jesuits. Although he himself held back from re-entering the Society on this basis, Carroll agreed to make the request, and permission was granted in 1804. The following year five former Jesuits renewed their vows, and Carroll turned over to them the college at Georgetown. As with the formation of John Carroll, St. Omers continued its influence as the first two presidents of Georgetown, Robert Plunkett (1773-1830) and Robert Molyneux (1738-1808) had attended the school (Muir, 59; Curran 1993, 32-46). Thus began the second era of the Maryland mission of the Society of Jesus; from Georgetown that mission would grow with the nation until it also spanned the continent.

Georgetown has a particularly close relationship with the College of the Holy Cross. When Boston's Bishop Benedict J. Fenwick founded the College in 1843, it took life as the eldest child of Georgetown. Fenwick himself had earlier been president of Georgetown, and the first three Holy Cross presidents also headed Georgetown College at various times. Jesuit priests, scholastics, and brothers traveled north to Worcester in the early years to work as administrators, teachers, and staff at Holy Cross. Georgetown supplied surplus books, pictures, and other teaching materials for the fledgling school. A further, unique link between the two schools was forged in 1849, the year of the first commencement at Holy Cross, when the Massachusetts General Court turned down the College's appeal for a charter. Because the academic programs at the two colleges were almost identical, and because Georgetown held a Congressional rather than a state charter, its directors were able to award Georgetown degrees to Holy Cross graduates. The practice continued until Holy Cross finally received a charter in 1865.

This essay incorporates the work of George M. Barringer, Hubert J. Cloke, Emmett Curran (in 1976, part of the Department of History, Georgetown University), Jon K. Reynolds and Anthony J. Kuzniewski, S.J.

CATALOGUE

Chalice and Paten with Altar Stone
Silver, 5 1/8 in. (13 cm.); paten, 3 3/8 in. (8.6 cm.);
altar stone 5 ¼ x 7 (13.3 x 17.8 cm.)
England, 1550-1600?
Provenance: Gift of Charles Calvert Lancaster and
Malinda Jenkins Lancaster
Georgetown University Collections

This chalice is typical of recusant liturgical vessels of the Elizabethan period which faithfully continued the forms of chalices from the reign of Henry VII. A sexfoil star-shaped foot ends in a hexagonal button. The hexagonal stem is interrupted by a circular knop decorated with square-shaped flowers canted between raised moldings. The bowl rests on a disk. The image on the foot showing Christ crucified is a standard element of recusant chalices. Here, however, the image is three dimensional and surrounded by four fronds on either side of the cross. Within a glory (a sunburst pattern), the paten displays the IHS, the monogram of the name of Jesus, with a cross resting on the crossbar of the H and a heart and supporting three oversize nails below.

A traveling chalice of about 1500 now in the Roman Catholic church of West Grinstead, Sussex (Oman, 44, pl. 14a) shows very similar structure, although the foot has a slightly straighter angle of rise. The crucifix is also raised. Compare for the paten, that associated with a chalice dated about 1630-50 showing a similar, although more crudely executed motif of the IHS within a glory (Victoria and Albert Museum, M1 and M1a-1986: Glanville 1990, 495-96, No. 143).

The moldings on the lowest edges of the foot, the segment of the foot bearing the crucifix, the knop, interior of the cup, and the center of the paten are gilt. Two joints allow the chalice to be disassembled into three parts. This method of construction apparently was first designed to facilitate transport since there were medieval chalices, such as that of West Grinstead that disassemble. During penal times such construction aided clandestine storage as well as transport. The cup's makers' marks have been deliberately disfigured and erased so that they are no longer legible (Pearce, 287-88, fig. 1).

According to Catholic practice, an altar stone containing relics was necessary for proper celebration of the Mass. Crosses at the four compass points and one in the center mark the stone, as they do large altars, one of the items of the church that were targets for iconoclasts.

In the early eighteenth century, this chalice was used to celebrate Mass in the Lancaster plantation in Rock Point, Charles County, Maryland. Descendents of the family, Charles Calvert Lancaster and Malinda Jenkins Lancaster gave the chalice, paten, and altar stone to the University.

Petre Chalice and Paten (paten probably from another provenance)
Silver, with gilt interior of cup, 5 ¼ in. (13.3 cm.);
paten 3 ¼ in. (8.3 cm.)
London, 1640-1660, associated with Silversmith
Albert Moore, City of London
Georgetown University Collections

Molded seraphim surrounded by wings decorate the knop and an incised image of Christ crucified is on the base (Pearce, 288, fig. 4). The paten shows the emblem of the Society of Jesus: within a glory the IHS, with a cross resting on the crossbar of the H and a heart and supporting three oversize nails below similar to the paten image on the Elizabethan chalice, discussed above. These details suggest that the chalice now at Georgetown formed part of the set commissioned by William, the fourth Lord Petre (1627-1683), for Jesuit missions in East Anglia. Like the other Petre chalices, it is produced without a maker's mark. Its interior and the underside of the paten are gilt. The Georgetown chalice increases the Petre chalice list (see "Liturgical Vessels," pp. 54-55). The itinerary of this chalice in the colonies is not known. It is most probable that it arrived in Maryland with a Jesuit missioner or Catholic family from East Anglia.

Secular cup taken over for use as a chalice
Silver, 4 ½ in. (11.4 cm.); paten 3 ¼ in. (8.3 cm.)
England, London, 1640-41, maker's mark IG with mullet below
Georgetown University Archives

This silver cup was made in London and exhibits similarities to London goblets of the same era. A circular foot adorned with a plain horizontal foot-ring leads to a baluster-shape stem. The cup is bell-shaped. On the rim are four London marks of 1640-41, including the maker's mark IG with mullet (star) below (Pearce, 288-90, fig. 2). Presumably, the same silversmith (an IG with mullet below enclosed in a heart-shaped shield) made church plate for the Church of England, attested to by a silver gilt cup and paten dated 1638, for Great Greenfield Church, Middlesex, and others of 1663 (Chaffers, 224, 228; Howard, 221). A similar bell-shaped goblet made in 1654, London, is two inches taller. A slighter earlier London goblet, 1634, is the same height but shows a more tapered cup (Wenham, 52-53, pl. XXXVI). Compare also to the mid-seventeenth century cup presented to First Church, Boston for use as a communion cup, engraved TBC [The Boston Church] The Gift of Friend T*C. It was made by Robert Sanderson and John Hull, two of Boston's most prominent silversmiths, its form inspired by English examples of the first half of the seventeenth century (Clarke, 221, pl. IV). The London cup was converted to a chalice and necessitated a paten; this plain, unmarked paten was probably produced in Maryland. Both were used probably as early as the 1650s and 1660s in the early mission of St. Francis Xavier at Newtown, St. Mary's County, Maryland.

Such conversions, as well as the use of base metal, as in the pewter chalice and paten (below) helped alleviate the scarcity of church vessels.

Chaffers, William. *Hall Marks on Gold and Silver Plate*, 10th ed., London: Reeves and Turner, 1922.
Howard, Montague, *Old London Silver: Its History, Its Makers, and Its Marks*, New York: Charles Scribner's Sons, 1903.
Clarke, Herman Frederick, *John Hull: A Builder of the Bay Colony*, Portland Maine: The Southworth-Anthoensen Press, 1940.
Wenham, Edward, *Domestic Silver of Great Britain and Ireland*, London and New York: Oxford University Press, 1935, 52-53, pl. XXXVI.

Secular cup taken over for use as a chalice, London, 1640-41; Paten, Maryland, 1650s? Georgetown University Archives. Photo: Virginia Raguin

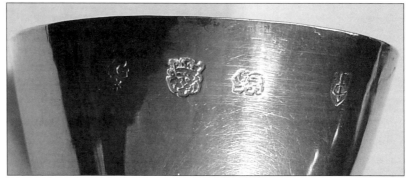

Secular cup, detail of maker's mark and hallmarks, Georgetown University Archives. Photo: Virginia Raguin

Chalice and Paten
Pewter, 5 ½ in. (8.9 cm.) paten 3 ½ in. (14 cm.)
Colonial, Maryland? ca. 1650-1700
Georgetown University Collections

Pewter, a mixture of generally seven parts tin to two
to three parts lead, but often with other metals such
as copper, was in use for ecclesiastical vessels even
during the Middle Ages. London's Worshipful
Company of Pewterers dates to 1348 (Bell, 10, pl.
21; Moore, 35-43; Cotterell, 2-6). Objects such
as this chalice would be cast in molds and then
hammered. Sepulchral chalices, made to be buried
with a priest, were quite often in pewter (Cotterell,
pls. XXVII a, d). In recusant practice, however,
the use of the metal is rare since it was a cherished
matter of pious practice to render special honor
to the Eucharist by the use of silver and gilt. The
choice of pewter for a chalice, like the secular cup
made into a chalice, was occasioned by the lack of
suitable vessels in the missions, with which this
chalice was associated. The maker is presumably
from Maryland, although unidentified (Pearce,
289-90, fig. 3). Although there were pewterers with
names beginning with R and I, none of the touches
resemble the unadorned letters "RI" in the published
records for England, Scotland, or Ireland. By
contrast, a constant number of communion cups in
pewter were made for the Church of England from
Elizabethan times through the nineteenth century.
Cotterell illustrates twenty examples (96-100).

Bell, Malcolm. *Old Pewter*. New York: Charles
Scribner's Sons, 1905.
Cotterell, Howard Hirshell. *Old Pewter, its Makers
and Marks in England, Scotland, and Ireland*.
London: Batsford, 1929.
Moore, N. Hudson. *Old Pewter*. Garden City, NY:
Garden City Publishing Company, 1933.
Shea I, 36.

Monstrance
Silver gilt, 14 in. (35.6 cm.)
Colonial, Maryland? ca. 1700
Georgetown University Collections

A monstrance is meant to receive the consecrated
host for public veneration (McLaughlin, 401-
403; Rubin 1991, 290-94). The ceremony of the
Benediction of the Blessed Sacrament included

Pewter chalice and paten, Colonial, Maryland?, ca. 1650-1700,
Georgetown University Collections. Photo: Virginia Raguin

special prayers and hymns stressing the Catholic
belief in the mystical Body of Christ present in
the host. Some hymns, such as the *Adoro Te*, are
attributed to the thirteenth-century theologian
Thomas Acquinas. The form of this monstrance
is simple, suggesting that is a Colonial production,
made by a silversmith unfamiliar with European
forms. It consists of a curved base rising from a
plain horizontal foot ring. A sloped transition
leads to a baluster-shaped stem. The horizontal
piece just under the circular holder for the host
is supported by a lobed cup. Two thin columns
wrapped with doubled wires at either side of the
circular container terminate in flat fleur-de-lis
finials top and bottom. The wire-wrapped columns
give the visual impression of gadrooning, a pattern
of alternating concave and convex molding as
exemplified in the Loving Cup of 1701 by John
Coney of Boston, given by Governor William
Stoughton to Harvard College (Buhler, 30, fig.
23), or in works by Coney's contemporary Edward
Winslow. At the top is another horizontal element

on which, in the center, a Maltese (equal-armed) cross surmounts a small dome similar to the lobed cup at the top of the stem. The underside of the base of this otherwise unmarked piece is engraved "Ora pro Georgio Tompsono." Thompson (fl. 1658-1663) was the first Clerk of Court in Charles County, Md., and the monstrance was probably executed as a memorial provided for in his will or at the expense of one of his near descendants.

Buhler, Kathryn C. *American Silver*. Cleveland: The World Publishing Company, 1950.

Emblem of Georgetown University
Etched copper plate, 3 x 2 ½ in. (7.6 x 6.3 cm.)
Colonial, Maryland, 1798
Georgetown University Archives

A ledger entry of May 11, 1798, records the payment of 15 shillings to a college employee named Justane, for "the Seal of the Corporation." Though not, properly speaking, a seal, this plate is linked with that entry, and later official seals have employed various modifications of this original design.

Missale Romanum
Paper, 6 ¼ x 4 in. (15.9 x 10 cm.)
Low Countries, Antwerp, Plantin, 1574
Binding American, ca. 1825-1850
Georgetown University Library Special Collections

The volume is an early octavo edition of the Tridentine missal. This is the approved missal issued after the long process of the Counter Reformation Council of Trent (1543-63) when Catholic policies and practices were reviewed to strengthen the Church's position against Protestant challenges. According to Bishop James Van de Velde and others, this missal was used by John Carroll while attending the missions at Rock Creek. The pages, however, do not show the kind of wear that would be associated with daily use. This well-illustrated missal with images characteristic of Antwerp Mannerists may have been a gift from Carroll to a fellow priest.

Emblem of Georgetown University, Maryland, 1798, Georgetown University Archives

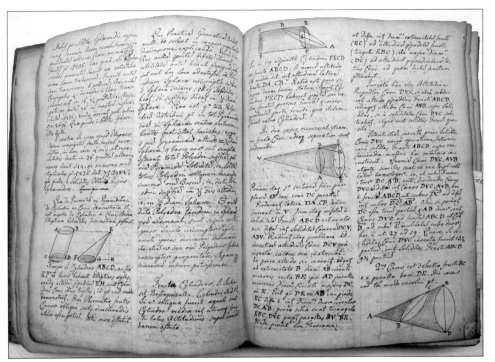

Collection of mathematical treatises and notes in Latin and English, presumably copied in Europe, ca. 1720, Georgetown University Library Special Collections

Collection of Mathematical Treatises and Notes in Latin and English
Paper, with ink, bound in leather, 8 x 6 3/8 in. (20.3 x 16.2 cm.), not paginated
Presumably copied in Europe, ca. 1720
Georgetown University Library Special Collections

This manuscript is associated by tradition with Rev. Henry Neale, S.J., recognized as a talented mathematician, who died in Philadelphia in 1748. Such hand-copied manuscripts, derived from lectures in the European Jesuit colleges, often served in place of printed books both for teaching and for reference. Neale also had a printed copy of Newton's *Principia Mathematica*, making it one of the first volumes of Newton's seminal work to reach the English Colonies.

Missale Romanum
Paper, bound in leather, 7 3/8 x 5 7/8 in. (18.7 x 15 cm.)
Goshenhoppen mission? ca. 1745
Georgetown University Library Special Collections

This is one of two missals copied out by Rev. Theodore Schneider, S.J., founder of the mission at Goshenhoppen (now Bally), Pennsylvania, in 1741. The missal contained the essential texts for the performance of Mass during the liturgical year where portions of the ceremony stayed the same and other sections, such as reading of the Gospel and Epistles, changed. The scarcity of Catholic devotional and liturgical works was a constant problem until well into the 19th century.

Resurrection, *Missale Romanum*, Antwerp, 1574, Georgetown University Library Special Collections

Three Handwritten Altar Cards
Cardboard and ink, 7 5/8 x 4 7/8 in. (19.3 x 12.4 cm.)
and 4 7/8 x 4 7/8 (12.4 x 10.2 cm.)
Goshenhoppen mission? ca. 1745
Georgetown University Library Special Collections

These materials were used for the celebration of the
Mass in the mission at Goshenhoppen (now Bally)
Pennsylvania. Printed material was scarce and
home-made devotional and liturgical aids were thus
produced. The three cards contained the essential
texts that the priest was to recite out loud for the
congregation. The cards were hand copied by Rev.
Theodore Schneider, S.J.

Handwritten Altar Card with Printed Image
Paper backed with wood and ink, 7 3/8 x 5 7/8 in.
(18.7 x 15 cm.)
Goshenhoppen mission? ca. 1745
Georgetown University Library Special Collections

This altar card contained the text of the
consecration of the Mass when the bread and
wine is transformed into the Sacramental body
and blood of Christ. The hand-written text is
surmounted by a printed image of the crucifixion.
The altar card is associated with the Rev. Theodore
Schneider, S.J. around 1745.

Handwritten altar card with printed image, Goshenhoppen mission?
ca. 1745, Georgetown University Library Special Collections

Costessey Hall Chapel in Its Context: Nineteenth-Century Private Catholic Church Building in The County Of Norfolk.

Roderick O'Donnell, FSA

The careful title of John Bossy's *The English Catholic Community 1570-1850* makes three points: his choice of dates distances the study from the high politics of kings or parliaments; the use of *Community* underlines discontinuity with the medieval Church, and his almost three-hundred year time span identifies with the *longe durée* of the French *Annals* historical school. This "Community" was maintained by landed proprietors (seigneur, French, i.e. feudal lord, hence 'seigneurial' means aristocratic or gentry or landlord-based) whose rural aristocratic leadership gave way from 1770 to an urban oligarchic one, which was replaced by a proletarianised church ruled by the clergy with the restoration of the Hierarchy in 1850. The county of Norfolk shows examples of all his three phases. On the second phase, Bossy's views on private Catholic chapel building about 1770-1850 are quite clear: "chiefly medieval play-acting [which] far from reversing the decline of seigneurial Catholicism, showed how inescapable the process was," citing the career of the Leicestershire convert squire Ambrose Phillipps de Lisle – much concerned with architectural projects- as the "classic example" (Bossy 1975, 329; O'Donnell 2002, 15, 87-92, 99-101). Does the history of post-Reformation Catholic church building in the county of Norfolk, which began with the opening of the chapel of Costessey (hereafter "Cossey") Hall in 1809 bear this out?

Apart from its few Catholic landed estates, Norfolk was one of the least Catholic counties in England by 1780 with only eight places of worship and perhaps only 0.4 % of the population (Trappes-Lomax, 27-46). There were no more than seven churches by 1829 and eight by 1850: these were in four towns- King's Lynn, Norwich (with two churches), Thetford and Yarmouth and two estate villages, with the private chapels at Oxburgh Hall and Cossey Hall, in addition to the village church in Cossey. To 1914, the modest rise in church buildings keeps roughly the same balance, with three new private chapels built at Lynford Hall (1878) and Gillingham Hall (1898), Stoke Holy Cross Hall (1910) and two modest churches for the coastal resorts of Cromer (1905) and Sheringham (1908-36). In King's Lynn the church had been rebuilt for the third time, and the two Norwich churches closed and replaced by a single church of cathedral proportions given by the Duke of Norfolk- one of the most extravagant "seigneurial" gestures of the nineteenth century. By 1910, though, the chapel at Cossey Hall had closed, and, passing out of the Jerningham family, its contents were dispersed and the chapel and house demolished in 1919. Had a landlord–based Catholicism been such medieval play-acting?

The classical development that Bossy cites is of a priest or congregation distancing themselves from the patronage of the landlord and his private chapel: this in fact happened at Cossey where the priest Fr. Husenbeth built a church in the village specifically citing the need of the congregation to be independent of the patron: "the time has surely arrived when we ought not to expect to be supported by our nobility [but] to erect public chapels" (*Orthodox Journal* V (1837): 145-47). So at least he phrased his appeal, but the move was also partly at the suggestion of the mistress of Cossey Hall, Lady Stafford, who was perhaps tired of the farmers, tenantry and all comers crowding into her chapel; the smell must have been an issue too. That Thorndon Hall chapel was so "full of the poor of his Lordship's estate" was cited as the reason for building a church (1836-7) in the town of Brentwood at the gates of Lord Petre's park (*Orthodox Journal* IV (1836): 319-20). In Cossey village a substantial church 110 ft. long by 25 ft. wide and 40 ft. high of brick with stone dressings and slate roofs in the Lancet Gothic style was built, with a presbytery and walled burial ground (*Orthodox Journal* vii-xii (1835): 109). And the independence of

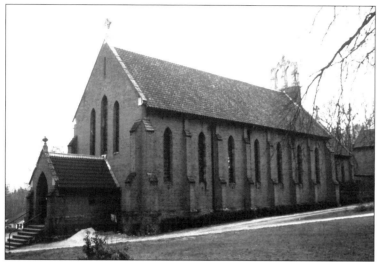

1 Exterior, Church of St. Wulstan, Norfolk, 1836-41. Photo: Roderick O'Donnell

2 Interior, Church of St. Wulstan, Norfolk, 1836-41. Photo: Roderick O'Donnell.

the congregation was perhaps not all it seemed; the site and the largest donation of £200 was given by Lord Stafford. The church of St. Wulstan (1836-41) (figs. 1 and 2) took seven years to complete (*Tablet* (1841): 360) and after Fr. Husenbeth's death it was often closed for lack of a priest or the means to support him; its continuous staffing and use dates not from 1841 but 1910 when the Hall chapel closed.

Cossey was only a few miles from the large city of Norwich, with its economic pull. Elsewhere however the overwhelmingly agricultural county was in relative economic and demographic decline. Oxburgh (pronounced "Oxborough," as the village name was spelt) was deep in the heart of the county, on the edge of even more cut-off Fens. Here the Catholics never distanced themselves from their patrons the Bedingfelds (pronounced "Bedingfield"); Mass was long maintained in house and later in two cottages in the village. It was surely these which are referred to by the newly married 6th baronet, "Sir Henry Bedingfeld [who] on his return from the Continent, where he had been accustomed to the splendours . . . of all the offices of religion, was struck by the contrast which was presented to him at Oxburgh. . . The Rev. Mr. Gascoyne was informed, the materials for a new chapel of good dimensions and elegant architecture were placed at his disposal, with a sum of money sufficient to defray the expenses of the workmanship. . . in the following morning, the labourers were at work digging the foundations" (*Orthodox Journal* I (1835): 109; V (1837): 40- 41). The local brick rubble and slated church of Our Lady and St. Margaret of Scotland (1835-6/7) (fig. 3), with its apsed east end, is also lancet Gothic, but in a less assured mood than at Cossey Hall or St. Wulstan's church. The church survived the sale of the house, collection and estate in 1951 when Sybil, the Dowager Lady Bedingfeld (1883-1985) bought them back from her son and in 1952 gave them to the National Trust; the chapel however continued in family ownership; she continued to live here and provide for priests (Bedingfeld). This writer had his First Holy Communion day there in May 1959, but Mass is now reduced to once a quarter. Oxburgh Hall is owned by the National Trust and open to the public (Garnet).

3 Interior, Chapel of Our Lady and St. Margaret of Scotland, Oxburgh Hall, Norfolk, 1835-37. Photo: Roderick O'Donnell

4 Chapel of Our Lady of Consolation, Lynford, Norfolk, 1878. Photo: Roderick O'Donnell

Like the chapel at Oxburgh, Lynford (1879) was another "seigneurial" whim; Mrs. Lyne-Stephens, the widowed proprietress of Lynford Hall was embarrassed by a guest, Lord Lovat, who complained of the eight-mile drive by carriage to Mass at Thetford. She therefore built the church of Our Lady of Consolation (1878) (figs. 4 and 5) in the grounds by the architect Henry Clutton. It is a knapped flint and stone dressed church in an Early English style, internally lined-out to imitate ashlar, and certain French furniture, as befits her roots in Paris (Roberts). The diocese closed this chapel overnight in the autumn of 2004. But she was also the *grande dame* of gifts to the poverty-stricken Northampton diocese established in 1850, paying for the complete church and presbytery of Our Lady and the English Martyrs, Cambridge (1884-93) (fig. 6: O'Donnell 2003). The Duke of Norfolk paid for the site which moved the Catholics from their back street to one of the most prominent sites in nineteenth-century Cambridge. Were Sir Henry Paston-Bedingfeld, the 15th Duke of Norfolk and Mrs. Lynne Stephens all play-acting?

The last nineteenth-century Norfolk private church, Our Lady of Perpetual Succour (1898-1903), Gillingham, was built by the convert John G. Kenyon, who also had a private chapel in Gillingham Hall itself

5 Chapel of Our Lady of Consolation, Interior. Photo: Roderick O'Donnell

NORFOLK: 19TH CENTURY
PRIVATE CATHOLIC CHURCHES

6 Church of Our Lady and the English Martyrs, Cambridge, 1884-93. Photo: Roderick O'Donnell

(*Kelly's Directory: Norfolk*, 1916, 161). The church was not in the Gothic but the classical style, a small scale model in brick of an Italianate basilica; it is still open for Mass. In the twentieth century a domestic chapel was fitted out by 1910 at Stoke Holy Cross Hall, a Tudor Revival style house of 1852, for Geoffrey Birkbeck, a convert of 1901, but services were never advertised (Ibid. 457; Anon., 150). Miss Charlotte Boyd bought the fourteenth-century Slipper chapel at Houghton St. Giles, a few miles from Walsingham. She then became a Catholic, had it restored by the architect Thomas Garner, as part of the attempt to restore the pilgrimage to the famous shrine, but it was not to be furnished or opened until 1934. A final gesture of this culture can be seen in the chapel of the Holy Family and St. Michael at Kesgrave, Suffolk (1931; additions 1993), built as a memorial by the widow to Capt. Michael Roper RN who was killed in the R101 disaster in 1930.

Bossy's "play- acting" therefore provided half the Catholic churches in Norfolk up to about 1914, and a wider view of the role of lay patrons saw them providing what are still the two most prominent Catholic churches - Norwich and Cambridge - in East Anglia. The Cambridge church was so much to the astonishment of the University town in which Catholics had been literally invisible since the Reformation that it was dubbed "the Cathedral" shortened colloquially to "the Cath." while the church of St. John the Baptist, Norwich (1893-1910) actually became the cathedral of the new diocese of East Anglia in 1975 (Rossi; Stamp, 123-136). In fact, lay church building was the product of a culture which emphasised the learning and piety of the individual donor or their families, as well as their taste and scholarship, even if not perpetuating the political control of the "Community" in Bossy's sense. But art-historically they are of great importance.

The building of the chapel at Cossey Hall in 1809 to the design of the amateur architect Edward Jerningham, a younger son of Sir William Jerningham, 6th baronet, gave Norfolk its first free-standing Catholic church since the Reformation. It was in the Gothic style, heavily buttressed and battlemented,

8 Bedingfeld chantry (right), church of St. Mary, Oxborough , Norfolk, 1513. Photo: Roderick O'Donnell

plaster vaulted internally with an apsed east end. The scale was large: ninety-feet long by thirty-five feet wide and forty-feet high. Invariably its model was said to be that of King's College Chapel, Cambridge; it was consecrated by Bishop Milner, the local Vicar Apostolic and noted partisan of the Gothic style, who described it as "built according to the useful as well as the sublime and beautiful manner of our wise and religious ancestors" (Husenbeth, 167-68). Its pious antiquarianism was in the same mood as the revival of the Stafford title in 1824 (Cockayne, vol. 12, Pt. 1 [1953], 188-92, 195-97) descended from the Earl of Stafford martyred in 1680 in the hysteria of the "Popish Plot." It was filled with a collection of over 84 subjects in stained glass, including the east window of the nearby Ringland church, given by their neighbour. The complete collection, including woodwork, which had been bought by the Norwich dealer Knapp was integrated into the design of the chapel, rather than being, like much antiquarian collecting, an afterthought as at Oxburgh. Indeed Mary B. Shepherd has argued strongly that the impact of its complete cycle of stained glass, its iconography carefully arranged to underline Catholic Eucharistic themes, perhaps explains the comparison with King's College Chapel that contemporaries made (Shepherd; see in this catalogue "Stained Glass: Medieval Context and Modern Catholic Retrieval,"pp. 201-203). The new chapel allowed the chapel in the attics of the house to revert to its status as a family oratory; as recorded in 1910 it looks largely eighteenth-century in format, but reputedly its function went back to the first building of the house in 1565 on the estate granted them by Queen Mary. The room is now reassembled at Swynnerton Hall, Staffs (Anon., 192-213).

Oxburgh Hall (fig. 7) was built by Sir Edmund Bedingfeld in 1478-

7 Oxburgh Hall, Norfolk, the gate house, 1478-82. Photo: Roderick O'Donnell

82, so that the family's historic roots in Norfolk were even deeper than those of the Jerninghams; both families were leading actors in Catholic restoration under Queen Mary (1553-58) and they frequently intermarried. Margaret Bedingfeld founded in 1513 a chantry (fig. 8) in a side chapel attached to Oxborough church in which she was buried and masses said for her repose. The "Bedingfeld Chalice and Paten", now a prize possession of the Victoria and Albert Museum, was produced in London about 1518-19 in silver-gilt work with the vernicle (the face of Christ). It is a rare example of the pre-Reformation liturgical vessels kept in Catholic hands after the confiscation of the chantries was decreed beginning in 1547 (see in this catalogue "Liturgical Vessels"). No doubt it was used in the Hall when the Mass was once again banned in 1559; the family sold it in 1905 (Victoria and Albert Museum, M.76&a-1947: Marks and Williamson, 341, No. 218; Oman, 45, 67, pls. 19, 30). The Bedingfield chantry continued to be used for family burials and memorials, but with no public Catholic rites.

These functions therefore transferred to the new chapel in the grounds of the hall, reflecting, as the *Orthodox Journal* put it in 1838, "the correct taste and antiquarian skill displayed by Sir Henry Bedingfeld in the interior fittings and furniture of [this] modern edifice" a comment remarkably Puginian in tone (*Orthodox Journal* VII (1838): 339). The interior of about 1855, as recorded in a watercolour by a Bedingfeld daughter, shows two aspects which do not survive: the lining out of the walls to imitate ashlar and, on the altar, a Benediction "throne" rearranged shortly afterwards (Wainwright 1993). The current altar and reredos is certainly a highly antiquarian confection: the mensa frontal made up of wooden carvings from disparate sources and tabernacle are still here, but the superimposed Benediction "throne" was sold off in 1951. It was spotted at a local sale in 2004 and bought back by the National Trust, for display in the house. Its place in the church had already been superseded by the large five compartment reredos and wings painted on both sides (fig. 9), and its arrival on the quay of the local port, King's Lynn was greeted with "there's another crate of idols for Oxburgh" (Wainwright 1993, 43). It shows in the outer panels the Four Latin Doctors of the Church, with inner scenes from the Passion (left) and Entombment (right) narratives, and incidental details from the life of St. James (McClure and Woudhuysen, 20-23). It was sold by the family to the National Trust in 1982 and the painted doors were conserved in 1987. These are attributed to the Lowlands artist Pieter Coeke van Aelst (1502-1550: Grossinger, 171-78). The carved oak reredos within has now been identified from guild stamp marks as an Antwerp piece dating from after 1470, with figure carving in a local Mannerist style of between 1515 and 1535. The reredos sits on a two panel predella each with a female saint, framing a three-sided tabernacle. The reredos proper is of two registers, the lower with carved scenes, possibly the judgements of Pilate and of Ciaphas either side of a recessed niche, and the upper has panels with the Carrying of the Cross, the Crucifixion in a tree of Jesse setting and the Entombment. It is one of six Antwerp carved altarpieces in England, of which two others were imported by Catholic collectors, Charles Townley and Charles Scarisbrick (Woods, 148-50). Two sets of carved and polished wooden communion rails are found in the church; those in front of the altar are early eighteenth-century Flemish and those at the rear of the chapel are Flemish late seventeenth century; they divide off the raised family tribune with its two sets of stalls of four seats each, which are early seventeenth-century Flemish (Tracy, 120-21, 259). Both are very like the altar rails Pugin installed at Oscott where his role both as designer and as middleman to the suppliers of the antiques at the opening of the chapel in May 1838 was well known (O'Donnell 1988). Perhaps the appearance of Sir Henry Bedingfeld's name and address in Pugin's diary 22 December 1838 refers to contacts over such antiques (Wedgwood, 41)? The stained glass includes Continental late Gothic and Renaissance fragments set in clear fields, with some notable English medieval fragments, and heraldic glass by Thomas Willement in 1838 (Willement, 55).

Tudor and Gothic Revival style country house building was all the rage in Norfolk after 1815, notably by the Norfolk architect W. J. Donthorn at the nearby Hillington Hall and elsewhere (O'Donnell, 1978). Cossey Hall was not only carefully romanticised and re-Tudorised (but also so massively extended that it was said to have bankrupted the Jerninghams) from 1826 to the 1860s by two generations of the

9 High altar, chapel of Our Lady and St. Margaret of Scotland, Oxburgh, ca. 1837 and rerados, ca. 1470-1535 added 1862. Photo: copyright, the National Trust, 2005.

Bucklers of Oxford. The great brick gatehouse of the moated Oxburgh Hall was drawn by A. C. Pugin in 1828-29. He published his drawings firstly in romantic reworkings by Joseph Nash (Leeds). and secondly with the letter-press of the Catholic antiquary and architect Edward J. Willson (Pugin and Willson, vol. 1, 45-49) where its Catholic traditions and priest-hole are explained (Pugin and Willson, 47). Although visited by J. C. Buckler in 1830, the restoration of Oxburgh does not seem to have much involved architects. The Bucklers regularly showed watercolours of Cossey in the Architecture Room at the Royal Academy, but never Oxburgh (for an alternative reading see Garnet). And whereas the Bucklers designed and published Fr. Husenbeth's church in the village, the chapel at Oxburgh also lacks an identifiable architectural hand; certainly the traditional attribution "to a design by Pugin" (*Catholic Record Society* VII, *Miscellanea* VI, the Bedingfeld papers (1909): 244-45) is highly suspect, and has been challenged by this writer (O'Donnell, 1994). The plan of the church echoes that of Cossey Hall (see the following essay, "Stained Glass"), and its vernacular materials - the black and white marble flagged floor in the Bedingfeld watercolour is in fact made of terracotta pammet tiles and bricks - suggest the work of builders or estate staff implementing a plan by a professional hand. Perhaps "the correct taste and antiquarian skill" of Sir Henry Bedingfeld was sufficient to be his own architect for the chapel if not the house? However the chantry-like transept, housing in a marble altar-tomb the 6th Baronet (died 1862) can be attributed to Charles Alban Buckler (1825-1905), the third generation of the scholarly architectural practice. He became a Catholic in 1844, and a decorated member of the Order of Malta, who did much work for Catholic landowners from the Duke of Norfolk downwards, who made him Surrey Herald in 1880 (Buckler).

Country house building and collecting in the century 1815-1914 was an expression of aristocratic and gentry "politics"; for Catholics, historically marginalised in this process, an architectural and collecting culture found special expression in church building, liturgical and devotional display. But this aspect has been ignored even by the leading historian of the English country house in the period (Girourard) as well as by economic historians Wilson and Mackley (Wilson and Mackley, 32-40, 204-21). Thus the reaction of Sir Henry Bedingfeld "on his return from the Continent" provides the key to the physical expression of the nineteenth-century Catholic Revival in an area where every economic, demographic and political force went against it. Far from being "chiefly medieval play-acting", the lay-piety behind the building of churches ranges far beyond Bossy's politico-economic models: "quantitative judgements don't apply. . . If only one soul was saved. . . that is full compensation," as Captain Guy Crouchback's father explained (Waugh, 546-47).

BIBLIOGRAPHY: See also general Bibliography

[Anon.] *A Great Gothic Fane, the Catholic Church of St. John the Baptist, Norwich.* Brighton: Pike, 1913.

Bedingfeld, Henry. *Oxburgh, the First Four Hundred Years,* Norwich: Jarrolds, 1987.

Buckler, Charles A. *Bucleriana, Notices of the Family of Buckler.* London: Mitchell and Hughes, 1886.

Cokayne, George E. ed. *The Complete Peerage or a History of the House of Lords and All Its Members from the Earliest Times.* 14 vols., London: St. Catherine Press, 1910-1998, vol. 12, Pt. 1 (1953).

Garnet, Oliver. *Oxburgh Hall, Norfolk,* London: The National Trust, 2000.

Grossinger, Christa. *North European Panel Painting: A Catalogue of Netherlandish and German painting before 1600 in English Churches and Colleges.* London: Harvey Miller, 1992.

Husenbeth, Frederick C. *Life of Milner.* Dublin: J. Duffy, 1862.

McClure, Ian and Renate Woudhuysen, "The Oxburgh Chapel Altarpiece: Examination and Conservation," *Apollo,* No. 139 (May 1994): 20-23.

Girourard, Mark. *The Victorian Country House.* New Haven: Yale University Press, 1979.

Leeds, William. H. *A Series of Views Illustrative of Pugin's Examples of Gothic Architecture.* London: 1830.

O'Donnell, Roderick. "Pugin's Church in Cambridge: Architectural Sources and Influences," and "Dunn and Hansom 's Church Cambridge" in Nicholas Rogers, ed. *Catholics in Cambridge.* Leominster: Gracewing, 2003: pp. 239-45 and 246-55.

O'Donnell, Roderick. *The Pugins in the Catholic Midlands.* Leominster, U.K.: Gracewing, 2002.

O'Donnell, Roderick. "A Pugin Puzzle," *Country Life,* 128, No. 2, (13 January 1994): 73.

O'Donnell, Roderick. "Pugin at Oscott," in 150th anniversary issue, *The Oscottian* (Oscott College Birmingham) ed. Judith Champ, 1988: pp. 45-66.

O'Donnell, Roderick. "W. J. Donthorn (1799-1859): Architecture 'with Great Hardness and Decision in the Edges,'" *Architectural History* (JSAH, GB) 21 (1978): 83-92.

Pawley, Margaret. *Family and Faith.* Norwich: Canterbury Press, 1998.

Pugin, Augustus. C. and Edward J. Willson. *Examples of Gothic Architecture,* 3 vols. London: H. G. Bohn, 1830.

Roberts, Jennifer. *The Strange History of the Lyne-Stephens Fortune.* Chippenham: Templeton Press, 2005.

Rossi, Anthony. *Norwich Roman Catholic Cathedral, A Building History* in The Chapels Society *Miscellany,* I, London, 1998.

Stamp, Gavin. *An Architect of Promise: George Gilbert Scott Junior (1839-1897) and the Late Gothic Revival.* Donington: S. Tyas, 2002.

Tracy, Charles. *Continental Church Furniture in England, A Traffic in Piety,* Woodbridge, Suffolk: Antique Collectors' Club, 2002.

Trappes-Lomax, T. B. "Roman Catholicism in Norfolk, 1559-1780," *Norfolk Archaeology* 32 (1958-61): 27-46.

Wainwright, Clive. "Oxburgh Hall Norfolk I," *Country Life,* 127 No. 49 (1993): 40-43'… II', No. 50 (1993): 48-51.

Waugh, Evelyn. *The Sword of Honour.* 1952. London: Penguin, 1987.

Wedgwood, Alexandra. *A.W.N. Pugin and the Pugin Family.* London: Victoria and Albert Museum, 1985.

[Willement, Thomas]. *Concise Account of the Principal Works in Stained Glass That Have Been Executed by Thomas Willement.* London: Printed for Private Distribution, 1840.

Wilson, Richard and Alan Mackley. *Creating Paradise: The Building of the English Country- house 1660-1860.* London: Hambledon and London, 2000.

Woods, K. W. "Some Sixteenth-Century Antwerp Carved Wooden Altarpieces in England," *Burlington Magazine* 141, No. 1152 (March, 1999): 144-55.

Stained Glass: Medieval Context and Modern Catholic Retrieval

Virginia C. Raguin

> A Chirche and A Chapaile [chapter house] · with chambers a-lofte,
> With wide windowes y-wrought · & walles wel heye,
> That mote bene portreid and paynt · & pulched ful clene,
> With gay glitering glas · glowyng as the sunne
> (*Pierce the Ploughmans Crede*, Skeat, lines 119-22)

Stained glass, considered a precious object, was linked in the twelfth and thirteenth centuries to the aesthetics of precious stones and metalwork; it thus received a place of honor in the building. In the Middle Ages and the Renaissance, buildings carried great narrative themes - on the exterior of buildings by sculpture, and on the interior by glass and wall painting. Durandus, bishop of Mende (ca. 1220–96) wrote that "the windows of the church which are made of transparent glass are the Sacred Scriptures which keep away the wind and the rain, . . . but allow the light of the True Sun, that is God, into the hearts of the faithful" (Neale and Webb, 28). The emotional and intellectual effect of stained glass programs was therefore of extraordinary importance. Indeed, the majority of buildings in this era were inconceivable without their glazing. Architects designed their elevations to house these great tapestries of colored light, which integrated the architectural space and served as planes for story telling.

As expressed in the fourteenth-century poem, *Pierce the Plowmans Crede*, stained glass was an expected element of medieval building. Whether parish church, monastic foundation, or even secular palace, embellishment was achieved with painted walls and glazed windows – "glowing as the sun." It was a costly medium, although brilliant and highly permanent, demanding expenditure for the production of the glass, its design and execution in paint, and then its setting in lead, solder, and iron frameworks. The hue of the glass was not the result of stain, with the exception of a silver-stain yellow, but colored with

St. Katherine of Alexandria, detail, Private collection, Memphis, Tennessee. Photo: Virginia Raguin

Reverse of Katherine panel showing typical weathering pattern in medieval glass. At the top and at the far left, three segments present a solid matt appearance marking them as modern replacements.

Saints Katherine of Alexandria and Agnes, England, East Anglia, 1450-60, Private collection, Memphis, Tennessee. Photo: Virginia Raguin

Annunciation, church of Sts. Peter and Paul, 1463-1480, East Harling (Norfolk). Photo: Virginia Raguin

metallic oxides while still in the molten state, and thus called pot metal. The molten glass was then blown or rolled, and shaped into sheets that were later cut into segments conforming to a subject pattern laid out by the designer (Clerkin Higgins, 32-45).

The selection of this all-important subject matter, the "superstitious images" that were the target of Reformers, was highly controlled, as reflected in a commission for the windows of Beauchamp chapel at Warwick of 1447 (Marks 1993, 14, 188-89, pls. IIc, IIId). The contract between the executors of the Earl of Warwick and John Prudde of Westminster, "glasier" demanded that he execute:

> all the windows of the new chappell in Warwick . . . with the best, cleanest, and strongest glasse of beyond the seas that may be had in England, and of the finest colours: of blew, red, purpure, sanguine, and violet, and of all other colours that shall be most necessary to make rich and embellish the matters, images, and stories, that shall be delivered and appoynted by the said executors by patterns in paper, afterwards to be newly traced and pictured by another painter in rich color at the charges of the said glasier. All the proportions the said John Prudde must make perfectly to fine, glase, eneylin it and finely and strongly set it in lead and solder it as well as any glass in England (Winston, 347-48).

The executors for the funerary chapel were clearly delivering plans on paper, very probably the "good and true patrons called a vidimus" discussed in the contract of 1526 for King's College chapel, Cambridge (Winston, 348). The glazier John Prudde would have workmen who would then make full-scale drawings used as the basis to cut the pieces of glass and most probably as a guide to the painting.

Segments of glass, for example, a face or sections of a robe, were executed with vitreous paint consisting of a mixture of finely ground glass, iron or copper oxide, and flux, applied to the glass with a brush. The painted glass was then fired ("eneylin it" in the contract) so that the ground glass in the paint fuses with the surface of the glass, producing an image of great permanence. Painting was often applied to the back of the glass as well. Such painting can be an extremely simple application of trace-line to indicate features, or the creation of three-dimensional effects using back-painting, matting, stippling, and removal of matt with a brush, stick or even needle. Details of the head of Abbot Blommeveen (CATALOGUE) show great sensitivity in this kind of application and removal. A technique called silver stain is seen in his crosier and morse (clasp) of the cope and the architectural framing. This technique uses a transparent yellow stain produced from the early fourteenth century on, containing a compound of silver. It is applied to the glass surface and fired, producing varying shades of yellow from lemon to gold (Clerkin Higgins, 46-50).

Philipp von Daun, Deacon of the Cathedral (later Bishop), detail, Passion Window, Cologne Cathedral, north nave, nXXI, 1508. Photo: Virginia Raguin

Once the window receives its fired-on paint, the many segments of glass

STAINED GLASS

Donor Portrait of Prior Peter Blommeveen, Germany, Carthusian Monastery, Cologne, 1510-20, formerly Costessy Chapel (Norfolk). Worcester Massachusetts, Worcester Art Museum, 1920.105. Photo: Worcester Art Museum

are then joined together by narrow lead strips called cames that are fitted around the glass segments. The cames are then soldered at their joints ("strongly set it in lead and solder" in the contract). In the modern practice, the windows are puttied to make them watertight. Medieval leads were molded, not extruded, and were often not puttied. The sections of the leaded window must then be placed into a metal, stone, or wood window frame. Additional strength is provided by saddle-bars on the interior to which the panels of glass are attached.

Over time, windows invariably needed some repair, especially those taken from their original settings. These two medieval panels of Katherine and Agnes provide a vivid example of mixture of original glass, unrelated old glass called "stop gap" reset in the window, and modern glass painted to approximate the original. This is typical of almost all historic panels. An evaluation of such interventions over time demands the sensitivity to period styles that is required in all connoisseurship and in addition, the examination of the production techniques of painting and abrasion applications, evidence of cutting tools, and of the type and condition of the lead cames that form its matrix. The glass must be examined from the front and back by touch and under both transmitted and raking light. From a review of the exterior, particularly well represented in St. Katherine (CATALOGUE), the integrity of the panel can be seen by the uniform weathering pattern of the original segments. More disruption appears in St. Agnes (CATALOGUE), where replacements can been seen in the saint's feet and the head of her lamb, for example. New glass appears in the background around her head.

Saints Katherine and Agnes

The panels representing Katherine and Agnes can be attributed to East Anglia and dated to about the mid-fifteenth century. It is assumed that most glass painters from this region were influenced by painters in Norwich, which during the fifteenth century was the second most prosperous city in England, and for some aspects of life actually excelled London. East Anglia's economic preeminence was a result of the wool trade and commerce in English cloth from the region. Buoyed by the wealth, a large number of churches was built or enlarged during the fifteenth century (Platt, 91-98; Cautley; Wilson, 112). After London and Westminster, East Anglia had the largest concentration of image makers (Marks 2004, 249). The paucity of what remains is one of the tragedies of English history.

One of the touchstones of this region for the extent of is preservation, is the east window of St. Peter Mancroft, Norwich, which shows a range of subjects: narrative scenes, single figures of saints, and smaller figures in the tracery lights (Woodforde 1950, 18-42, pls. I-VII). The window is closely related to another impressive and almost intact window: the "Joys and Sorrows of Blessed Virgin Mary" from the parish church of Sts. Peter and Paul in East Harling (Ibid., 42-55, pls. IX-XV). Woodforde's statement that the "most marked general characteristic of Norwich glass painting at this time is the excellence of the drawing and colouring coupled with the vigour and liveliness of the presentation of the subject-matter" (Ibid., 161) can be seen in these two panels and the glass in Norwich and East Harling.

The hair is distinctive, seeming to consist of ropes undulating to frame the ear and to cascade around the shoulders. The heads are rounded, and especially in the female, a softness of features avoids any musculature of the cheek or forehead. The eyes are the most striking element, delineated through concentric circles with prominent upper and lower lids. Below a straight nose and distinctive nostril, the small mouth is shadowed to define the distinction between upper and lower lips. A delicate, circular chin anchors the lower part of the face. Hands, as well, are drawn with great skill, allowing effective gesture and distinction in the slenderness of the fingers. The technique of silver-stain appears tinting the halos and hair for both saints and Katherine's crown and wheel. Throughout, contours are modeled by a pale matt over which a linear hatch or cross hatch is preferred to heavy modeling with tonal values. The resultant linear "drawing" over color creates a visual dynamic highly pleasing to the eye.

The standing figures of saints from St. Peter Mancroft, in their three-quarter pose and simplicity of form, evoke the silhouettes of Katherine and Agnes. Katherine's pale tunic edged with silver-stain yellow, especially as it folds over itself on reaching the ground, evokes the pattern for St. Edward the Confessor and a companion royal saint at St. Peter Mancroft (Ibid., pl. I). The boldness of the figures, however, and their simple contours suggest a date earlier than the Peter Mancroft or East Harling windows. It is unfortunate that no border framing remains attached to the figures. Often the Norwich glass painters employed a distinctive motif of leaves wreathed around a rod or a simple architectural setting, both choices found at East Harling and at Peter Mancroft. The two saints can also be compared to a female saint, possibly Mary Magdalene, in the Burrell Collection, Glasgow (Marks and Williamson, 401, No. 288). The Burrell saint dates to about 1445-55 and is similar to tracery-lights panels in Norfolk churches.

The subject matter, as seen above, was important. The representation of saints was one of the most common types of imagery for glass at this time. Indeed, the great rows of English saints under arcades in the glass of the fourteenth and fifteenth centuries parallel the English love of the sculpted façade filled with statues in sculpted niches, exemplified by the great program of the cathedral of Wells. England was particularly important in developing systems that integrated both grisaille and figural glass where colored panels float upon the shimmer of grisaille-filtered light. The extraordinary disposition of the reworked choir of the cathedral of Gloucester, dated about 1351 to 1367, serves as an example.

The choice of saints is equally typical of the time. Katherine, in particular, was one part of the great virgin "trinity" comprising Barbara, Margaret, and Katherine. The demonstrative, but entirely common, Margery Kempe evoked St. Katherine continually, imagining her own place in heaven with Christ's "blyssed modyr and . . . holy awngelys and twelve apostelys, Seynt Kateryne, Seynt Margarete, Seynt Mary Mawdelyn" (ch. 22, Windeatt, lines 1630-31). Stories of Katherine and Agnes appear in Osbern Bokenham's *Legends of Hooly Wummen* written between 1443 and 1447. Bokenham was an Austin friar born in Suffolk, one of the counties comprising East Anglia, and he finished his life at Clare Priory, Suffolk. Thus his accounts of Agnes and Katherine were being written in the same area and at the same time that the two panels were being produced.

These panels could very well have been in a window with other saints, in a series that might have included other Christian heroines such as Margaret, Anne, Christine, Faith, Dorothy, Mary Magdalene, Cecelia, Agatha, Lucy, or Elizabeth who were also subjects of Bokenham's compilation. He based his work on a number of sources, chief among them the late thirteenth-century *Golden Legend* of Jacobus de Voragine and John Capgrave, whom he calls his spiritual father (Delaney, 126). For Katherine, he addresses the saint, saying that he made of "your legend a short translation into English" for the spiritual comfort and consolation of two Katherines, Howard and Denston (Delaney, 140). For St. Agnes he also cites St. Ambrose's history of the saint, mentioning that her name "agna" means lamb, a very meek and simple animal, whose qualities are also found in Agnes's meek and simple innocence.

Given their small size of 15 3/4 x 6 inches, the panels may have been originally set in tracery lights, the openings in the ornamental stone patterns at the top of windows. The Perpendicular era, a style dominant from the middle of the fourteenth century to the end of the Middle Ages in England, emphasized a "consistency of treatment and [a] maximum of fenestration" (Wilson, 98). St. Mary's church in Nottingham, for example, was described by John Leland in the 1540s as having "so many fair wyndowes yn it that no artificer can imagine to set mo[re] in ther" (Ibid. 98). Glass was obligatory, in such vast programs a mixture of grisaille and figural panels, which may also have been the original setting for the two saints.

DONOR PORTRAIT OF PRIOR PETER BLOMMEVEEN

The panel portraying Prior Blommeveen has been identified with the cloister of the Carthusian monastery of St. Barbara in Cologne, and represents the qualities of the Northern Renaissance (Raguin 1987, 73, No. 31) Despite its reputation as a medieval art form, stained glass is actually even more prevalent in the larger window openings of the early Renaissance. As in England just before the Reformation, the German cities of Cologne and Nuremberg supported great programs of stained glass both as installations in new churches and as embellishment to the old. Cloister glazing, in particular, opened a rich new field. Each of the four sides of a cloister could have numerous multi-light windows, and the panels were most often arranged in registers, as many as three to a light. Narrative systems, placing one scene after another sequentially, were exploited to great effect for the extensive and often thematically complex glazed cloisters at the monasteries of Altenberg, Mariawald, Steinfeld, the Carthusian monastery of Louvain, and in Cologne, St. Cecilia and St. Barbara.

Unlike the communal workshop tradition of earlier centuries, production became more specialized. Many artists' studios functioned as design centers, delineating commissions and then transferring designs to glazing workshops for fabrication. The glass painters developed highly sophisticated painting techniques to render the three-dimensionality of panel paintings then in vogue. Techniques varied, but often stipple washes were applied in layers to give smooth transitions from light to dark. Dark line was used sparingly, often simply as an accent to strengthen the outline of the nose or ear. Sanguine, a russet color, was introduced to produce a reddish tone to lips or a cheek. Often near life-size figures in volumetric rendering took on a sculptural presence in the lancets of a window.

The relationship between glass designing and painting was complex. In some cases, panel painters – such as Hans Baldung Grien and Bernard van Orley – supplied models or cartoons to workshops that specialized in making windows (Scholz, 83-120). Some shops, such as that of Jan Swart van Groningen, specialized in producing stained glass designs, a situation that is clear evidence of the increase in stained glass commissions in the Lowlands (Husband, 166-74). The Hirsvogel shop in Nuremberg, or the Brussels glass painters who carried out the designs of Bernard van Orley, were trained specialists who could produce windows on the basis of a designer's model (Helbig and Vanden Bemden, 77, 85–6, 88, 106, 124–5). The Hirsvogel glass painters evidently selected colors (Scholz in Butts and Hendrix, 79-80). Workshops associated with two panel painters, known as the Master of the Holy Kinship and the Master of St. Severin, glazed the north nave aisle of Cologne cathedral. These panel painters appear to have exerted considerable control over the ultimate result, including color. Infra-red photographs of underdrawings of panels in an altarpiece designed by the Master of the Holy Kinship reveal color notations, directions that tell the painters which colors to use, and thus explain that draftsmen and colorists were different individuals. None of the cartoons – technically the equivalent of underdrawings – for the windows in the north aisle of Cologne Cathedral are extant. It is likely that if color notations were given to panel painters, they would have been given to glass cutters as well (Raguin and Zakin, I, 27).

The glass painter Hermann Pentelinck, who fabricated the cathedral's windows of the Passion (nXXI) 1508, and the Coronation of the Virgin (nXXV) 1509, designed by the Master of St. Severin probably also produced the glass of Cologne's Carthusian monastery (Rode, 186-207). Details of the painting are similar. The building of a volumetric illusion is achieved primarily through granular washes, downplaying line, with an extraordinary detail reminiscent of contemporaneous engravings. The panels are not only superbly designed and painted, but demonstrate a high level of firing skill. The vitreous paint has been applied with so even a layer and the firing so controlled that the paint is integrated with the glass surface. The glass itself is of a high quality, showing an attractive smooth surface, quite silken to the touch, and a high resistance to corrosion. Despite the general uniformity of surface that provides such a fine receptacle for painted detail, subtle imperfections in the mouth-blown glass create additional variations for the transmission of light.

This examination allows us to posit the existence of highly proficient artists and designers, working reciprocally. In some ways, one might argue that delight in craftsmanship has a certain independent reward for the viewer. Painting of glass, certainly in Renaissance aesthetic, combines the ability to use color and at the same time exploit graphic techniques that had become so much a part of the growing appreciation for the art of drawing and print. The substrata has color but it is modulated through paint overlay, applied as wash and also as hatch, allowing the viewer the delight in the play of linear pattern that is far different from the blending brushwork of oil painting.

Donor portraits were common in churches and cloisters. The sites mentioned above, Altenberg, Mariawald, Steinfeld, and the Charterhouse of Louvain as well as that of St. Cecilia and St. Barbara in Cologne presented donor and/or heraldic shields in the lowest levels. In the north nave of the cathedral similar representations are made and the format for both Pentelinck windows, the Passion and the Coronation of the Virgin, place the kneeling donor, three-quarter turn, kneeling, framed in an architectural niche in a pose similar to Worcester's Prior Blommeveen. The donor panel of Philipp von Daun in the Passion window is particularly close. The treatment of Blommeveen's elaborate crosier with its jewels and richly worked cope compares well with those of the garments of God the Father from the scene of the Coronation of the Virgin. The prior's shield, a crosier over two budding stems on a grassy field, is a play on his name "flower-fen" in Dutch (Wayment, Correspondence).

SURVIVAL AND A NEW SETTING

As discussed in the earlier essay in this catalogue "Picture and Policy: Contested Control of the Image," a staggering amount of stained glass was either actively destroyed by iconoclasts or allowed to deteriorate, to be replaced with panels devoid of the "superstitious imagery" (Davidson, 101; Marks 1993). On the continent, with the changing taste of the seventeenth and eighteenth centuries, medieval and Renaissance figural windows were often removed and replaced with clear glass. Simple neglect, as in England, took the greatest toll. This practice was widespread; in an oft-quoted letter dated 1788, John Berry, glazier at Salisbury, offered to sell stained glass panels to a Mr. Lloyd of London, since, as Berry frankly states, it was less trouble to sell the glass intact than to break it in order to get at the [valuable] lead (LeCouteur, 164; Wainwright, 66).

The phenomenon of collecting disparate objects that were once a part of an architectural environment developed as antiquaries began to prize the ancient art of Italy, Greece, and also the Middle East. An international elite, English, French, and German connoisseurs,

J. C. Buckler, interior of the Chapel of Costessy Hall, pen and ink drawing, dated 23 September 1820. Norwich County Council Library, Gunton Collection, C/Cos 25.

Window of the Chapel of Costessy Hall. The panels show, from the top: Solomon and Sheba, Pentecost, Mocking of Christ, Adoration of the Magi, a female saint with angels playing music, and kneeling female donors with ecclesiastic patron saint. The three women each hold large sets of rosary beads. Photo © Dennis King Norwich

scholars, and fashionable dilettantes, frequented sites of discovery. Lord Nelson, accompanied by the fascinating Emma Hamilton, visited excavations in Pompeii. Lord Elgin brought the fragmentary sculptures from the Parthenon to England and Charles Towneley acquired objects that still hold pivotal positions in the British Museum (Scott, 193-208). With the secularization of churches in France, Belgium, and the Rhineland in the wake of the French Revolution, religious objects of the Middle Ages and the Renaissance became available. In Germany, Sulpiz and Melchior Boisserée began a collection that would form the core of Munich's Alte Pinakotek.

Stained glass had become of some interest to English antiquarians, such as Sir Horace Walpole who installed antique panels at Strawberry Hill. By the 1750s London dealers offered stained glass "in fancy Frames of Colour'd windows" suggesting that the panels were mostly small, as were Walpole's, and destined to be suspended in front of existing windows (Wainwright, 65-69). The importation of large-scale panels for architectural construction was facilitated by the Napoleonic Wars that liberated many works of architectural decoration. Much of the glass from the Rhineland arrived through the agency of John Christopher Hampp and his Norwich colleague William Stevenson (Lafond; Woodforde 1938). Hampp was a German emigré living in Norwich, who bought glass on the Continent and took it to England. A Norfolk neighbor, Sir William Jerningham (1736-1809), the first Earl Brownlow of Ashridge, was one of the earliest purchasers from this stream of expatriated works of art. The Jerninghams were a recusant Norfolk family whose country seat was Costessy Hall just south of Norwich. Around 1800 Sir William built a new Gothic Revival chapel which remained in use for the family and a good portion of the village of Costessy until 1841. The chapel was furnished with more than eighty medieval glass panels (Shepard; Haward, 205-207, 229-30), among them, the Worcester Art Museum's Prior Blommeveen (Drake 1920, cat. p. 7, No. 26).

The majority of panels made available by Hampp were from the later fifteenth and early sixteenth centuries, the era frequently referred to as the "Northern Renaissance" in modern scholarship. This was the time that three-dimensional ocular perspective became widespread, as pioneered, for example, in the art of the Lowlands painter Jan Van Eyck in the mid-fifteenth century. Such representation of the figure in believable space and modeling of the body that approximated the detail and volume of real life was of particular attraction for a world that had become imbued with the principles of art as articulated by the Academies. The attraction of classical realism, exemplified by the Towneley collection, was associated with prevailing taste for aesthetic canons that prioritized verisimilitude. The stained glass eagerly acquired by Sir William Jerningham was not only religious in theme, but exerted a great attraction for an early modern audience, schooled in three-dimensional realism.

For Sir William, the impetus to acquire stained glass was deeply associated with a recusant faith. Consecrated in 1809, and dedicated to St. Augustine of Canterbury, the chapel was a precocious harbinger of style as well as a clear statement of Catholic legitimacy. Sir William's youngest son William was the architect. In 1791, the Catholic Relief Act allowed the celebration of the liturgy in registered chapels whose exteriors were devoid of steeples, bells, or other overt indications of worship space. Costessy's chapel conformed to these regulations although it had lofty proportions, ninety foot in length, thirty five in width and forty foot in height, possibly in the emulation of King's College, also in East Anglia, which was arguably the single most impressive glazing program to survive. The Gothic style was also identified by Sir William with Catholic faith, a belief he shared with a close friend and colleague working for Catholic emancipation, Rev. John Milner (1752-1826). Milner had written on ecclesiastical architecture, especially the antiquities of Winchester, praising Gothic for its suitability (Shepard, 191-95, 203). The chapel was indeed remarkable, and praised by Eastlake "one of the best and earliest designs in modern Gothic" (Eastlake, 58).

Eighty panels of glass were acquired for the most part by 1802. Of different provenances, primarily from sites in the Rhineland but also from Rouen, Paris, and England, they date from the thirteenth through the sixteenth centuries. Carefully arranged to balance formally and thematically, the panels filled double-lancet side windows and single lancet chancel windows. In the chancel the theme of Catholic veneration of the Eucharist was most apparent. The central window showed a scene of St. Maximinus, vested in bishop's robes, giving communion to St. Mary Magdalene just before her death (now Marion Koogler McNay Art Museum, San Antonio, Texas). Below, just above the altar, was the image of the elevation of the host, the priest with his back toward the worshipper, before an altar, lifting up the consecrated wafer, an image that would be repeated by the actual celebrant during the Mass. On either side were windows grouping three scenes each of Christ's teaching and his Passion. The two final windows flanking the ensemble emphasized the veneration of the Virgin Mary, including panels of the Coronation of the Virgin and the Virgin clothed with the Sun (Shepard, 200-203, figs. 19-24). The ensemble could not have been more focused doctrinally or experientially.

The other windows in the chapel were equally rich with vivid imagery. Narrative scenes in a square format primarily from Rhineland cloisters filled some windows, for example a window containing six panels: King Solomon and the Queen of Sheba, Pentecost, Mocking of Christ (now Memphis Brooks Museum of Art, Memphis, Tennessee), Adoration of the Magi (now Harvard University Art Museums), a saint, possibly Cecilia, surrounded by angels, and three female donors with rosary beads presented by a sainted bishop. A highly specific theme appears in two tracery lights from Saint-Herbland, Rouen dating 1520-30 and showing Emblems of the Church and Laity (now Victoria and Albert Museum, London: Williamson, No. 97). The mitre, crosier, cardinal's hat, and papal tiara in one panel complement the secular accoutrements from all levels of society in the other, including spade, halberd, sword, scepter, and several crowns. The hierarchical nature of Catholic worship, with its emphasis on ceremonials, is here evoked. The selection from Hampp's stockpile was clearly deliberate. There were many donor panels to be had, for example, but few examples show with such clarity kneeling women and their "beads," the kind of ritual prayers condemned by the established church.

The chapel ceased its function as a "parish" church when a town chapel was built in 1844 in the village of Costessy. After the death in 1913 of Sir Fitzherbert Stafford-Jerningham, eleventh Baron Stafford, Costessy Hall was dismantled and the glass was sold in its entirety to Gosvenor Thomas (1858–1923) a dealer who furnished numerous panels to American Collectors (Beaven). By the late nineteenth century the ownership of medieval objects was again in flux and Thomas played an important role in the transfer of many works in glass from England's manor homes to collections in the United States. Thomas presented medieval glass in an "exhibition" at the Charles Gallery, New York in 1913 which included over two hundred and fifty heraldic panels (Drake 1913). The financial success of this venture encouraged future acquisitions such as the Costessey/Jerningham collection in late 1917 a purchased so extensive that he brought in "Durlacher Bros." as a silent partner. Thomas apparently first showed the collection in Glasgow and by 1922 he had sold about two thirds of the original lot. The Jerningham panels are represented in the collections of the Metropolitan Museum of Art, the Portsmouth Abbey, Portsmouth, Rhode Island; Trinity Cathedral, Cleveland Ohio; Toledo Museum of Art; The Walters Art Gallery; the Pitcairn Museum, Bryn Athyn, Pennsylvania; and the Philadelphia Museum of Art, as well as prominent European collections, especially the Victoria and Albert Museum and the Burrell Collection of Glasgow.

CATALOGUE

St. Katherine of Alexandria and *St. Agnes*
Pot metal glass and white glass with silver stain,
15 ¾ x 6 in. (38.7 x 15.2 cm.) each
England, East Anglia, 1450-60
prov. Ashridge Park, Hertfordshire?
Private collection, Memphis, Tennessee

Donor Portrait of Prior Peter Blommeveen
Pot metal glass and white glass with silver stain and saguine, 26 ¾ x 22 ¼ in. (68 x 56.5 cm.)
Germany, Carthusian Abbey, Cologne, 1510-20
prov. Costessy Chapel, Norfolk, collection of Sir William Jerningham, the first Earl Brownlow of Ashridge; Roy Grosvenor Thomas, London Worcester Massachusetts, Worcester Art Museum, 1920.105

Bibliography

Aston, Margaret 1988. *England's Iconoclasts: vol. 1, Laws Against Images.* Oxford: Clarendon Press, 1988.

Aston, Margaret 1989. "Iconoclasm in England: Official and Clandestine," in Davidson and Nichols: 47-91.

Aston, Margaret 1993. *Faith and Fire: Popular and Unpopular Religion, 1350-1600.* London; Rio Grande, Ohio: Hambledon Press, 1993.

Barnwell, P. S., Claire Cross and Anne Rycraft. *Mass and Parish in Late Medieval England: The Use of York.* Reading: Spire Books, 2005.

Barrett, Dom Illtud. "The Relics of St. Thomas Cantilupe," in Jancey: 181-85.

Beaven, Marilyn. Grosvenor Thomas typescript.

Bennett, J. A. W. *Poetry of the Passion.* Oxford: Oxford University Press, 1982.

Binski, Paul. *Medieval Death: Ritual and Representation.* Ithaca: Cornell University Press, 1996.

Block, Hugo, Geoff Egan, John Hurst, and Elizabeth New. "From Popular Devotion to Resistance and Revival in England: The Cult of the Holy Name of Jesus and the Reformation," in *The Archaeology of Reformation 1480-1580,* ed. David Gaimster and Robert Gilchrist [Papers Given at the Archaeology of Reformation Conference, February 2001] Leeds: Maney, 2003: 175-203.

Blundell, Rev. F. O., O.S.B. "Old Time Lancashire Chalices," *Historical Society of Lancashire and Cheshire: Transactions* New Series, xl (1924): 114-24.

Borenius, Tancred. *St. Thomas Becket in Art.* London: Methuen & Co., 1932.

Bossy, John. *The English Catholic Community 1570-1850.* London: Darton, Longman and Todd, 1975.

Brown, Andrew D. *Popular Piety in Late Medieval England: The Diocese of Salisbury 1250-1550.* Oxford: Clarendon Press, 1995.

Brown, Peter. *The Cult of the Saints in the Early Church.* Princeton: Princeton University Press, 1985.

Buckley, J. J. *Some Irish Altar Plate.* Dublin: John Falconer for the Royal Society of Antiquaries of Ireland, 1943.

Butterworth, Charles H. *The English Primers, 1529-1545: Their Publication and Connection with the English Bible and the Reformation in England.* Philadelphia: University of Pennsylvania Press, 1953.

Butts, Barbara, Lee Hendrix, et al. *Painting on Light: Drawings and Stained Glass in the Age of Dürer and Holbein* [exh. cat., The J. Paul Getty Museum] Los Angeles, 2000.

Camm, Dom Bede, O.S.B. *Forgotten Shrines: An Account of Some Old Catholic Halls and Families in England and of Relics and Memorials of the English Martyrs.* London: MacDonald, 1910.

Cassidy, Brendan, ed. *The Ruthwell Cross.* Princeton: Princeton University Press, 1992.

Cautley, H. Munro. *Suffolk Churches.* Suffolk Historic Churches Trust, (1937) 1982.

Caviness, Madeline Harrison. *The Early Stained Glass of Canterbury Cathedral: circa 1175-1220.* Princeton: Princeton University Press, 1977.

Caviness, Madeline Harrison. *The Windows of Christ Church Cathedral, Canterbury* (Corpus Vitrearum Medii Aevi Great Britain, 2) London, 1981.

Chambers, Mary C., I.B.V.M. *The Life of Mary Ward 1585-1645.* ed. James Coleridge, S.J., 2 vols. London: Burns & Oats, 1 1882, II 1885.

Cheetham, Francis. *Alabaster Images of Medieval England.* Woodbridge, Suffolk: Boydell Press, 2003.

Church of England. *The Book of Common Prayer;* 1662 Version (includes appendices from the 1549 version and other commemorations, with an introduction by Diarmaid MacCulloch, London: Everyman's Library, 1999.

Cooper, Trevor, ed. *The Journal of William Dowsing: Iconoclasm in East Anglia during the English Civil War.* Woodbridge Ecclesiological Society, Woodbridge, Suffolk: Boydell Press, 2001.

Costley, Claire L. "David, Bathsheba, and the Penitential Psalms," *Renaissance Quarterly* 57 (2004): 1235-77.

Cripps, Wilfred Joseph. *Old English Plate.* New York: Charles Scribner's Sons, 1901.

Cross, Claire. "Monastic Learning and Libraries in Sixteenth-Century Yorkshire," in *Humanism and Reform: The Church of Europe, England and Scotland, 1400-1643, Essays in Honour of James K. Cameron,* James Kirk, ed. [Studies in Church History: Subsidia 8] Blackwell Publishers, Oxford, 1991.

Curran, Robert Emmett. *The Bicentennial History of Georgetown University;* foreword by Leo J. O'Donovan. Washington, D.C.: Georgetown University Press, 1993.

Curran, Robert Emmett, ed. *American Jesuit Spirituality: The Maryland Tradition, 1634-1900* [Sources of American Spirituality series] New York; Mahwah, N.J.: Paulist Press, 1988.

Davidson, Clifford. "'The Devil's Guts': Allegations of Superstition and Fraud in Religious Drama and Art during the Reformation," in Davidson and Nichols, 92-144.

Davidson, Clifford and Ann Eljenholm Nichols, eds. *Iconoclasm vs. Art and Drama.* Kalamazoo Michigan: Western Michigan University, 1989.

Dillon, Anne. *The Construction of Martyrdom in the English Catholic Community, 1535-1603.* Aldershot, Hants: Ashgate, 2002.

Downside Guide; An Introduction and Guide to Downside Abbey. Stratton on the Fosse, Somerset: Downside Abbey, 1994.

Doerksen, Daniel. *Conforming to the Word: Herbert, Donne, and the English Church before Laud.* Lewisburg: Bucknell University Press, 1997.

Drake, Maurice 1913. *The Grosvenor Thomas Collection of Ancient Stained Glass.* pts. I and II [exh. cat. Charles Gallery] New York, 1913.

Drake, Maurice 1920. *The Costessey Collection of Stained Glass, Formerly in the Possession of George William Jerningham, 8th Baron Stafford of Costessey in the County of Norfolk.* intro. Aymer Vallance, Exeter, 1920.

Duffy, Eamon 2001. *The Voices of Morebath: Reformation and Rebellion in an English Village.* New Haven: Yale University Press, 2001.

Duffy, Eamon 1992. *The Stripping of the Altars: Traditional Religion in England c. 1400-1580.* New Haven: Yale University Press, 1992.

Duggan, Anne 1982. "The Cult of St Thomas Becket in the Thirteenth Century," in Jancey: 21-43.

Duggan, Anne 2005. *Thomas Becket.* Oxford: Oxford University Press, 2005.

Durandus, Bishop of Mende. *Manuel pour comprendre la signification symbolique des cathédrales et des églises.* Château-Gontier: La Maison de Vie, 1966.

Eastlake, Charles L. *A History of the Gothic Revival.* intr. by J. Mordaunt Crook, Leicester: Leicester University Press, 1978.

Erasmus, Desiderius. *Ye pylgremage of pure deuotyon* http://www.gutenberg.org/files/14746/14746-8.txt. Release Date: January 20, 2005 [EBook #14746] David Starner, Louise Hope, David King, eds.

Finucane, Roland C. *Miracles and Pilgrims.* London: J. M. Dent & Sons, 1977.

Fleming, John V. "Chaucer and Erasmus on the Pilgrimage to Canterbury: An Iconographic Speculation," in Heffernan: 148-66.

Gee, Henry, and William John Hardy. *Documents Illustrative of English Church History, Compiled from Original Sources.* London and New York: Macmillan, 1896.

Gerard, John, S. J. *Stonyhurst College Centenary Record.* Belfast: Marcus Ward & Co, 1894.

Gibson, Gail McMurray. *The Theater of Devotion: East Anglian Drama and Society in the Late Middle Ages.* Chicago: University of Chicago Press, 1989.

Glanville, Philippa 1987. *Silver in England.* London: Allen & Unwin, 1987.

Glanville, Philippa 1990. *Silver in Tudor and Early Stuart England.* London: Victoria and Albert Museum, 1990.

Goldberg, P. J. P., trans. and ed. *Women in England, c. 1275-1525.* Manchester and New York: Manchester University Press, 1995.

Haigh, Christopher. *Reformation and Resistance in Tudor Lancashire.* London and New York: Cambridge University Press, 1975.

Harris, Barbara J. *English Aristocratic Women, 1450-1550.* New York: Oxford University Press, 2002.

Haward, Birkin. *Nineteenth-Century Norfolk Stained Glass.* Norwich: Geo Books, 1984.

Heal, Felicity. *Reformation in Britain and Ireland.* Oxford: Oxford University Press, 2003.

Heffernan, Thomas J. ed. *The Popular Literature of Medieval England.* Knoxville: University of Tennessee Press, 1985.

Heffernan, Thomas J. and E. Ann Matter, eds. *The Liturgy of the Medieval Church.* Kalamazoo, Mich.: Western Michigan University, 2001.

Helbig Jean, and Yvette Vanden Bemden. *Les Vitraux de la première moitié du XVIe siècle conservés en Belgique: Brabant et Limbourg* (Corpus Vitrearum Belgique, 3), Ledeberg-Ghent, 1974.

Hillgarth, J. N. ed. *Christianity and Paganism, 350-750.* Philadelphia: University of Pennsylvania Press, 1986.

Clerkin Higgins, Mary, "Origins, Materials, and the Glazier's Art," in Raguin, Virginia. *Stained Glass from its Origins to the Present.* New York: Abrams, 2003: pp. 32-55.

Husband, Timothy. *The Luminous Image: Painted Glass Roundels in the Lowlands, 1480-1560* [exh. cat., MMA] New York, 1995.

Inglis, Eric. *The Hours of Mary of Burgundy.* London: Harvey Miller Publishers, 1995.

Jancey, Meryl, ed. *St. Thomas Cantilupe Bishop, of Hereford: Essays in his Honour.* Hereford: Published by the Friends of Hereford Cathedral, Publications Committee for the Dean and Chapter, 1982.

Jerningham, Frances Dillon, Lady. *The Jerningham Letters (1780-1843) Being excerpts from the correspondence and diaries of the Honourable Lady Jerningham and of her daughter Lady Bedingfeld.* 2 v. Edited with notes by Egerton Castle, London: R. Bentley and Son, 1896.

Johnstone, Pauline. *High Fashion in the Church: The Place of Church Vestments in the History of Art, from the Ninth to the Nineteenth Centuries.* Leeds: Maney, 2002.

Keiser, George R. "The Middle English 'Planctus Mariae' and the Rhetoric of Pathos," in Heffernan: 167-93.

King, Donald, *Opus Anglicanum; English Medieval Embroidery* [exh. cat. Vicoria and Albert Museum] London: Arts Council, 1963.

Kirkus, M. Gregory I.B.V.M. 2001. "The Presence of the Mary Ward Institute in Yorkshire, 1642-1686," *Recusant History (The Catholic Record Society)* 25 No. 3 (May 2001): 434-48.

Kirkus, M. Gregory, I.B.V.M. "Cecily Cornwallis c. 1653-1723," typescript: Bar Convent Archive Reference G1/2/c5(v).

Kline, Naomi Reed. *Maps of Medieval Thought.* Woodbridge, Suffolk: Boydell Press, 2001.

Knowles, David. *The Religious Orders in England.* vol. III, *The Tudor Age* Cambridge: Cambridge University Press, 1959, paperback 1970.

Krautheimer, Richard. *Early Christian and Byzantine Architecture.* Harmondsworth and New York: Penguin Books, 1979 (1965).

Kupke, Raymond J., ed. *American Catholic Preaching and Piety in the Time of John Carroll.* Lanham, Maryland: The Catholic University of America Press, 1991.

Lafond, Jean. "Le commerce des vitraux étrangers anciens en Angleterre au XVIIe et au XIX siècles," *Revue des Sociétés Savantes de Haute-Normandie* 20 (1960): 5-16.

Linck, Joseph C. 2002. *Fully Instructed and Vehemently Influenced: Catholic Preaching in Anglo-Colonial America.* Philadelphia: Saint Joseph's University Press, 2002.

Linck, Joseph C. 1991. "The Eucharist as Presented in Corpus Christi Sermons of Colonial Anglo-America," in *American Catholic Preaching and Piety in the Time of John Carroll*, Raymond J. Kupke, ed., Lanham, MD: The Catholic University of America Press, 1991: 27-53.

LeCouteur, J. D. *English Mediaeval Painted Glass.* London, 1978, 2nd ed.

Littlehales, Henry, ed. *The Prymer; or, Prayer-book of the Lay People in the Middle Ages in English Dating about 1400 A.D. from the Manuscript (G 24) in St. John's College, Cambridge.* London: Longmans, Green, 1891.

Littlehales, Margaret Mary. *Mary Ward, Pilgrim and Mystic. 1585-1645.* Tunbridge Wells, Kent: Burns & Oates, 1998.

Loades, David M. 1989. *Mary Tudor: A Life.* Oxford, UK ; Cambridge, Mass.: Basil Blackwell, 1989.

Loades, David M. 1991. "The Piety of the Catholic Restoration in England, 1553-1558," in *Humanism and Reform: The Church of Europe, England and Scotland, 1400-1643, Essays in Honour of James K. Cameron*, James Kirk, ed. [Studies in Church History: Subsidia 8] Blackwell Publishers: Oxford, 1991: 289-304.

Love, Nicholas. *The Mirror of the Blessed Life of Christ, A Reading Text.* Michael G. Sargent, ed., Exeter: University of Exeter Press, 2004.

MacCulloch, Diarmaid. 1996. *Thomas Cranmer: A Life.* New Haven, Conn.: Yale University Press, 1996.

MacCulloch, Diarmaid. 2005. *The Reformation: A History.* New York: Penguin Books, 2005.

Marks, Richard 1993. *Stained Glass in England during the Middle Ages.* Toronto: Toronto University Press, 1993.

Marks, Richard 2004. *Image and Devotion in Late Medieval England.* Thrupp, Gloucestershire: Sutton Publishing, 2004.

Marks, Richard, and Paul Williamson, eds. *Gothic: Art for England 1400-1547* [exh. cat. Victoria and Albert Museum] New York: Harry N. Abrams, Inc., 2003.

Mayer-Thurman, Christa C. *Raiment for the Lord's Service: A Thousand Years of Western Vestments.* foreword by John Maxon; essays by Aidan Kavanagh, Donald L. Garfield, Horace T. Allen. Chicago: Art Institute, 1975.

Martz, Louis L. *Thomas More: The Search for the Inner Man.* New Haven and London: Yale University Press, 1990.

McLachlan, Elizabeth Parker. "Liturgical Vessels and Implements," in Heffernan and Matter: 369-429.

Monnas, Lisa and Hero Granger-Taylor, eds. *Ancient and Medieval Textiles: Studies in Honour of Donald King.* London: Pasold Research Fund, 1989.

Monnas, Lisa 1989. "New Documents for the Vestments of Henry VII at Stonyhurst College," *The Burlington Magazine* CXXXI (1989): 345-49.

Monnas, Lisa 1994. "Opus Anglicanum and Renaissance Velvet: The Whalley Abbey Vestments," *Textile History* XXV/1 (1994): 3-27.

Morey, Adrian. *The Catholic Subjects of Elizabeth I.* Totowa, N.J. : Rowman and Littlefield, 1978 (1975).

Morgan, Penelope E. "The Effect of the Pilgrim Cult of St. Thomas Cantilupe on Hereford," in Jancey.

Morris, John, S. J. "English Relics I: St. Thomas of Hereford," *The Month* 44 (Jan.-Apr., 1882): 112-26.

Muir, T. E. *Stonyhurst College 1593-1993.* London: James & James, 1992.

Neale, John Mason and Benjamin Webb, eds. *Durandus's Rationale Divinorum Officiorum,* trans., *The Symbolism of Churches and Church Ornaments.* Leeds: T.W. Green, 1843.

Netzer, Nancy and Virginia Reinburg, eds. *Fragmented Devotion: Medieval Objects from the Schnütgen Museum, Cologne* [exh.cat., McMullen Museum of Art, Boston College], Chestnut Hill, Mass., distributed by the University of Chicago Press, 2000.

Nichols, Ann Eljenholm. "Broken Up or Restored Away: Iconoclasm in a Suffolk Parish," in Davidson and Nichols: 164-96.

Nichols, John Gough. *Pilgrimages to Saint Mary of Walsingham and Saint Thomas of Canterbury by Desiderius Erasmus.* London: Westminster, 1849.

Norman, Edward. *Roman Catholicism in England, from the Elizabethan Settlement to the Second Vatican Council.* Oxford: Oxford University Press, 1986.

O'Donnell, Roderick. "The Architectural Setting of Challoner's Episcopate," in *Challoner and his Church: a Catholic Bishop in Georgian England,* ed. Edmund Duffy, Darton: Longman and Todd, 1981: 55-70.

Oman, Charles C. 1957. *English Church Plate, 1597-1803.* London: Oxford University Press, 1957.

Oman, Charles C. 1962. "English Medieval Base Metal Church Plate," *The Archaeological Journal* CXIX (1962): 194-207.

Orchard, M. Emmanuel, I.B.V.M., ed., *Till God Will: Mary Ward through her Writings.* London: Darton: Longman and Todd, 1985.

Panofsky, Erwin, ed. *Abbot Suger on the Abbey Church of St.-Denis and its Art Treasures.* 1946, second ed., Gerda Panofsky-Soergel, Princeton: Princeton University Press, 1979.

Peacock, Edward, ed. *Instructions for Parish Priests by John Myrc; edited from Cotton MS. Claudius A. II.* London: Pub. for the Early English text society, by K. Paul, Trench, Trübner & co., ltd., 1868 [1902].

Pearce, John. "Roman Catholic Church Plate in the Maryland Area 1634-1800, Part I," *The Connoisseur* 173/ No. 698 (April 1970): 287-291.

Peters, Henriette. *Mary Ward: A World in Contemplation.* trans. Helen Butterworth. London: Gracewing, 1991.

Pfaff, Richard W. *Liturgical Feasts in Later Medieval England.* Oxford: Oxford University Press, 1970.

Pfaff, Richard W. *Liturgical Calendars, Saints, and Services in Medieval England.* Aldershot Hampshire: Valorium, 1998.

Platt, Colin. *The Parish Churches of Medieval England.* London: Chancellor Press, 1995.

Raguin, Virginia. *Northern Renaissance Stained Glass: Continuity and Transformations* [exh. cat. Cantor Gallery, College of the Holy Cross] Worcester, 1987.

Raguin Virginia and Helen Zakin. *Stained Glass before 1700 in Midwest Collections, Illinois, Indiana, Michigan, Ohio* (Corpus Vitrearum United States of America, VIII) London: Harvey Miller Publishers, 2002.

Ragusa, Isa, trans. *Meditations on the Life of Christ.* Princeton: Princeton University Press, 1961.

Rode, Herbert. "Die Namen des Meister der Hl. Sippe und von St. Severin," *Wallraf-Richartz Jahrbuch* 31 (1969): 249-54.

Rode, Herbert. *Die mittelalterichen Glasmalereien des kölner Domes* (Corpus Vitrearum Medii Aevi: Deutschland, 4/1) Berlin, 1974.

Rogers, D. M. *The Primer . . . in English 1615* (English Recusant Literature 1558-1640, vol. 390), London: The Scholar Press, 1978.

Rowe, Donald F. *The First Ten Years. Notable Acquisitions of Medieval, Renaissance, and Baroque Art. The Martin D'Arcy Gallery of Art: The Loyola University Museum of Medieval and Renaissance Art.* Chicago: Loyola University of Chicago, 1979.

Rubin, Miri 1991. *Corpus Christi: The Eucharist in Late-Medieval Culture.* Cambridge: Cambridge University Press, 1991.

Rubin, Miri 1993. "Choosing Death? Experiences of Martyrdom in Late Medieval Europe," *Martyrs and Martyrologies* [Papers Read at the 1992 Summer Meeting and 1993 Winter Meeting of the Ecclesiastical History Society] Diana Wood, ed., Oxford: Blackwell Publishers, 1993: 153-83.

Scholz, Hartmut. *Entwurf und Ausführung: Werkstattpraxis in der Nürnberger Glasmalerei der Dürerzeit* (Corpus Vitrearum Medii Aevi Deutschland Studien Series, 1) Berlin, 1991.

Scott, Jonathan. *The Pleasures of Antiquity.* New Haven: Yale University Press, 2003.

Shea, John Gilmary *A history of the Catholic Church within the limits of the United States, from the first attempted colonization to the present time.* New York, 1886-92. [I] *The Catholic church in colonial days. The thirteen colonies, the Ottawa and Illinois country, Louisiana, Florida, Texas, New Mexico and Arizona. 1521-1763.* [II] *Life and times of the Most Rev. John Carroll ... Embracing the history of the Catholic Church in the United States. 1763-1815.*

Shepard, Mary B. "'Our Fine Gothic Magnificence': The Nineteenth-Century Chapel at Costessy Hall (Norfolk) and its Medieval Glazing," *Journal of the Society of Architectural Historians* 54 No. 2 (1995): 186-207.

Simmonds, Gemma. "Recognition at Last," *The Tablet* (7 February, 2004): 11.

Skeat, Walter W., ed. *Pierce the Ploughmans Crede.* EETS 1867, New York: Greenwood Press, reprint, 1969.

Smith, Elizabeth Bradford, Kathryn McClintock, R. Aaron Rottner, et al. *Medieval Art in America: Patterns of Collecting 1800-1940* [exh. cat., Palmer Museum of Art, The Pennsylvania State University] University Park, Pa., 1996.

Spencer, Brian. *Pilgrim Souvenirs and Secular Badges* (*Medieval Finds from Excavations in London:* 7) London: The Stationary Office, 1998.

Stapleton, Thomas, ed. *The Plumpton Correspondence.* Gloucester: Allan Sutton, 1990. reprint of J. B. Nichols, ed., Camden Society, 1839.

Stanbury, Sarah, ed. *Pearl.* Kalamazoo, Mich.: Western Michigan University, 2001.

Strange, Richard, S. J. *The life and gests of S. Thomas Cantilupe, Bishop of Hereford, and some time before L. Chancellor of England. Extracted out of the authentique records of his canonization as to the maine part, Anonymus, Matt. Paris, Capgrave, Harpsfeld, and others.* Collected by R.S.,S.J. at Gant, Printed by Robert Walker, 1674.

Stuckeley, William. *Itinerarium curiosum, or, an Account of the Antiquiries, and remarkable Curiosities in nature or art, observed in travels thro' Great Britain.* London, Printed by the author, 1724.

Sweeney, Tony. *Irish Stuart Silver: A Short Descriptive Catalogue of Surviving Church Plate 1603-1715.* Dublin: Éamonn de Búrca for Edmund Burke Publisher, 1995

Todd, Henry John. *The History of the College of Bonhommes at Ashridge in the County of Buckinghamshire founded in the year 1276 by Edmund, Earl of Cornwall . . . to which is added a Description of the Present Mansion Erected on the Site of the Ancient College.* second ed. London: R. Gilbert, 1823 (1812).

Trollope, Rev. A. *An Inventory of the Church Plate of Leicestershire.* Leicester: Clark and Hodgson, 1890.

Trowell, Brian L. "John Benet's 'Lux Fluget ex Anglia, O Pater Pietatis – Salve Thoma,'" in Jancey: 159-80.

Vauchez, André. "Liturgy and Folk Culture in the *Golden Legend,*" in *The Laity in the Middle Ages: Religious Beliefs and Devotional Practices.* ed. Daniel E. Bornstein, trans. Margery J. Schneider. University of Notre Dame Press: South Bend, Indiana. 1993.

Vauchez, André. *Sainthood in the Later Middle Ages.* trans. Jean Birrell, Cambridge and New York: Cambridge University Press, 1997.

Voragine, Jacobus de. *The Golden Legend.* trans. Ganger Ryan and Helmut Ripperger, New York: Arno Press, 1969.

Wainwright, Clive. *The Romantic Interior: The British Collector at Home 1750-1850.* New Haven: Yale University Press, 1989.

Wayment, Hillary, formerly King's College, Cambridge. Correspondence with Virginia Raguin and the Worcester Art Museum.

Wayment, Hillary. *King's College Chapel, Cambridge: The Side-Chapel Glass.* Cambridge: Cambridge Antiquarian Society and the Provost and Scholars of King's College, 1988.

Westlake, Herbert Francis. *The Parish Gilds of Mediæval England.* London: Society for Promoting Christian Knowledge; New York: Macmillan, 1919.

Wettner, Immolata, I.B.V.M. *Mary Ward* (pamphlet). Regensburg: Schnell & Steiner, 1996.

Whinney, Margaret 1964. *Sculpture in Britain 1530-1830.* Baltimore: Penguin Books, 1964.

Wieck, Roger S. *Time Sanctified: The Book of Hours in Medieval Art and Life.* New York: George Braziller, 1988.

Wieck, Roger S. *Painted Prayers: The Book of Hours in Medieval and Renaissance Art.* New York: George Braziller, 1998.

White, Helen Constance. *Tudor Books of Private Devotion.* Madison: University of Wisconsin Press, 1951.

Williamson, Paul. *Medieval and Renaissance Stained Glass in the Victoria and Albert Museum.* London: Victoria and Albert Museum, 2003.

Wilson, Christopher. "'Excellent, New and Uniforme': Perpendicular Architecture c.1400-1547," in Marks and Williamson: 98-119.

Windeatt, Bary 2000. *The Book of Margery Kempe.* Harlow: Longman, 2000.

Winston, Charles. *An Inquiry into the Difference of Style Observable in Ancient Glass Paintings, especially in England: with Hints on Glass Painting, by an Amateur.* Oxford: J. H. J. Parker, 1847.

Winston-Allen, Anne. *Stories of the Rose: The Making of the Rosary in the Middle Ages.* University Park, Pennsylvania, Pennsylvania State University Press, 1998 (1997).

White, C. H. Evelyn, ed. *The Journal of William Dowsing, of Stratford, Parliamentary Visitor, Appointed under a Warrant from the Earl of Manchester for Demolishing the Superstitious Pictures and Ornaments, etc. within the County of Suffolk, in the Years 1643-1644.* Ipswich: Pawsey and Hayes, 1885.

White, Helen Constance. Tudor Books of Private Devotion. Madison: University of Wisconsin Press, 1951.

Woolley, Linda. "Two panels from an Orphry Showing Scenes from the Life of St. Thomas of Canterbury," in Monnas and Granger-Taylor: 265-73.

Woodforde, Christopher 1954. *English Stained and Painted Glass.* Oxford: Clarendon Press, 1954.

Woodforde, Christopher 1950. *The Norwich School of Glass-Painting in the Fifteenth Century.* London, New York: Oxford University Press, 1950.

Woodforde, Christopher 1938. "Foreign Stained and Painted Glass in Norfolk," *Norfolk Archeology* 26 (1938): 73-84.

Wormald, Francis. "The Rood of Bromholm," *Journal of the Warburg Institute* 1 (1937-8): 31-45, Reprinted in J. J. G. Alexander, T. J. Brown, and J. Gibbs, eds., *Francis Wormald: Collected Writings: II Studies in English and Continental Art of the Later Middle Ages.* Harvey Miller, London, 1988, 123-38.

Index of Objects Exhibited Keyed to Essays

OBJECTS

Paintings and Prints

Printed Books